GUITAR MAN

GUITAR MAN

WILL HODGKINSON

DA CAPO PRESS
A Member of the Perseus Books Group

Typeset by Hewer Text UK Ltd, Edinburgh

First published in Great Britain in 2006 by Bloomsbury Publishing.

Cataloging-in-Publication data for this book is available from the Library of Congress.

ISBN-13: 978-0-306-81514-0
ISBN-10: 0-306-81514-1

First Published by Da Capo Press edition 2007
A Member of the Perseus Books Group
http://www.dacapopress.com

Da Capo Press books are available at special discounts for bulk purchases in the U.S. by corporations, institutions, and other organizations. For more information, please contact the Special Markets Department at the Perseus Books Group, 11 Cambridge Center, Cambridge, MA 02142, or call (800) 255-1514 or (617) 252-5298, or e-mail special.markets@perseusbooks.com.

1 2 3 4 5 6 7 8 9

To NJ

CONTENTS

Chapter One

You Can't Always Get What You Want

The golden light of creation was shining. Harmony filled the world. I closed my eyes and let the guitar resonate with the sweet vibrations of eternity.

'STOP IT! I can't stand that guitar. It's driving me crazy!'

I was getting used to this kind of reaction from my wife. It seemed that my every rendition of the chorus of 'You Can't Always Get What You Want' by The Rolling Stones was like a needle piercing the nerve-endings of her brain. But it wasn't NJ who was complaining. It was our three-year-old son Otto.

'I don't want you to play your guitar any more,' he cried, sticking his fingers in his ears. 'I don't like it. It's horrible.'

I had only had the guitar for two weeks – a cheap acoustic of dubious pedigree but reasonable quality called a Walden – and my family were rebelling against any attempts to bring a bit of musical provenance into their lives. But I had set myself a task which, having been foolish enough to boast about, there was no getting out of: to perform before an audience in six months' time. This was before I had picked up a guitar, when the idea still sounded fun; a way of forcing myself into doing something I had only talked of for the last two decades. The possibilities of life are infinite, limitless and exciting before you start attempting to do something. But as soon as you apply yourself to learning a new skill, you are confronted with the severity of your limitations. I tried once again to make the guitar sound good, imagining how Keith Richards would be languidly strumming the simple but elegant sequence of chords that make up 'You Can't Always Get What You Want' while some beautiful girl, Anita Pallenberg perhaps, lolled about at the other end of the sofa as the ash from her joint burnt a hole in her peasant tunic. At the other end of the sofa Pearl, our one-and-a-half-year-old daughter, started crying.

'It just sounds *so* awful,' said NJ, not looking up from her book. 'Brian Jones must be turning in his grave.'

'But I'm playing the right chords,' I protested. There are only three of them – C, F and D minor. They represented my entire mastery of the guitar. After a week or so of practising I had managed to make the changes relatively smooth, but despite that brief moment of transcendence, NJ was right: the sounds coming out of my guitar were weedy, parochial and niggling. 'You Can't Always Get What You Want' is a song of tender glamour, evocative of broken dreams and hopeful acceptance. My version was evocative of being harassed by a careers officer.

'It's so jumpy. Why don't you try playing it a little gentler?' suggested NJ as Otto bashed the head of Pearl's doll against a wall.

It was the summer of 2004. Having reached the age of thirty-four and succeeded in avoiding any musical knowledge whatsoever, despite a lifetime of staring at album covers for hidden messages, it occurred to me that it might be a good thing to actually pick up the guitar rather than pick over the achievements of those who had. I had always retained a puerile admiration for anyone who could play something – anything – and had remained happy to spend hours listening to people make a sound resembling music on the thing while having absolutely no idea what they were doing. Then one evening, in the basement of our flat in London, I put on a record I had picked up by a guitarist called Davey Graham. I had heard the name before but knew nothing about the man beyond that he had been something of a cult figure in the early sixties, a hero to a generation of guitarists including Jimmy Page, Bert Jansch and Eric Clapton, and that he had dissolved into obscurity and rumoured narcotic oblivion as their stars had risen. I assumed he was dead.

On the album was an instrumental called 'Anji' that was captivating. It was played on an unaccompanied acoustic guitar, but it sounded like an orchestra: a blues bass and a folk melody merged to suggest an eastern raga. It had an ancient quality. Apparently, Davey Graham had written 'Anji' in 1961 at the age of twenty, a gift to his girlfriend of the time. When it came to an end I put it on again – and again. For the first time, I had heard a song I felt compelled to learn how to play. I picked up the guitar as a direct result of 'Anji'.

'Listen to that!' I said to NJ, who seemed more interested in the *Vogue* she was reading than the mystical weavings of this mysterious shaman. 'What is he doing?'

'Er . . . playing guitar?' she replied.

'Can you imagine knowing how to do that?'

'No. I went to piano lessons under severe duress until I was eleven and haven't been near a musical instrument since. Nor do I have any wish to.'

'That's what I have to do. I have to get a guitar and work out how to play "Anji".'

'Is that a good idea?' said NJ with a yawn.

'Give me one good reason why I shouldn't.'

'You're tone deaf, you can't sing, and although I love the way you dance because it's you, it does tend to prove that you have no sense of rhythm whatsoever.'

'Apart from that.'

I would ignore my wife, just as so many brave men had ignored theirs before me. Now that I was too old and set in my ways to be a rock star, it could be a good time to learn guitar for the sake of it. It would also be a way of addressing an issue I had not managed to shake off since adolescence. More than once I had been on the beach, or in the countryside, with a few beers and thoughts of romance spinning through my mind. I would be chatting to a pretty girl, and before long the possibility of a long and happy night was on the horizon. Then some chiselled, longhaired idiot would turn up with his guitar and start singing 'Hotel California' by The Eagles and all of a sudden the girl was by his side and not mine, and once again the evening's entertainment would consist of a Scrabble marathon with our school's volunteer library monitor. And his mother. I had missed out on so much simply because I never bothered to learn how to play the guitar. My wasted youth was long gone, but 'Hotel California' would be there for ever to torment me with this fact.

The first step was to buy a guitar. This is not as easy as it sounds. Denmark Street is a narrow, inauspicious little road in the West End of London that is one of the world's greatest guitar centres. Generations of musicians have salivated at the sunbursts and proud wood finishes of the guitars in the windows of the shops down this street, and on any day you'll see crowds of young men and a few women ambling up and down it with guitar cases in their hands, wondering how they will ever afford to get that 1965 Gretsch in the window of Andy's Guitar Centre. You have a good chance of hearing the opening riff to 'Smoke On The Water' by Deep Purple cranking out of one shop window and 'Smells Like Teen Spirit' by Nirvana from another. (Led Zeppelin's 'Stairway To Heaven' has received an unofficial ban due to overuse. 'Sweet Child O' Mine' by Guns N' Roses and 'Wonderwall' by Oasis are heading that way.) Guitars are sold on their association with a famous player. Underneath one shop is a little basement bar occupying the former site of Regent Sound, the tiny studio where The Rolling Stones cut their early discs. Opposite is the 12 Bar Club, an acoustic dive that Davey Graham came out of hiding to make an appearance at a few years back, only to play a set so chaotic and awkward that the audience were said to have winced in polite agony as they sat at the feet of a broken man.

As a complete beginner it would be pointless and uncool to spend huge amounts of money on a guitar that I couldn't play, so I went to Andy's, one of the oldest and most established shops on Denmark Street, in the hope of finding something suitable for the young(ish) neophyte. In the corner, on a little wooden stool, sat a teenage boy with long hair who was playing a virtuoso style of heavy blues on an electric guitar through a small amplifier, and behind the counter was an older man with a moustache who was staring at a magazine. It was a bright day, but the mass of guitars in the shop had pretty much cut out all natural light. There was a beautiful guitar on every surface: classic rockers like Fender Stratocasters and Gibson Les Pauls; big, ornate country twangers like the Gretsch Country Gentleman and folk-rock works of art like the Rickenbacker 12-string. But I couldn't find a price tag that didn't have at least four figures on it and I hadn't planned on spending more than a hundred pounds. High up on one wall was a guitar called a Gibson ES-335 that had a handwritten sign on it stating: 'Don't even think about asking to try out this one!!!' Even looking at it felt impertinent.

The man behind the counter asked me what I was looking for. I was about to tell him when three young men walked in and started asking about vibrola arms and truss rod adjustments. I couldn't bring myself to tell him that I wanted a guitar that, like, sounded good and didn't cost much. I mumbled something about coming back later and made to leave, but in my haste managed to knock over a 12-string acoustic guitar propped up near the doorway, sending a vehemently accusatory jingle-jangle crash out into the street outside. I have not set foot in Andy's since.

The next day I mustered the courage to enter The London Resonator Centre in North London, a shop that deals exclusively in acoustic guitars. The middle-aged man running the place seemed happy when I told him I wanted to learn the guitar. 'A wise move!' he said. 'You'll never be bored again. Do you want steel strings or nylon?'

'What's the difference?'

'Classical and flamenco guitars have nylon strings because they give a softer sound. Folk guitars have steel strings, which are louder with a greater resonation. It depends on what kind of music you want to play, but you don't look like someone who's planning to master classical guitar. Or are you?'

I thought of 'Anji', and then remembered the level of my natural abilities. 'It would be good to be able to do "Louie Louie" by The Kingsmen.'

'So you want something like this.' He brought out four guitars that ranged from £49 to £250. I started at the one for £49; it sounded awful and the strings were so far from the neck that pushing them down felt like an Olympic event. 'You can learn the basics on that, but I guarantee that within a few months you'll be wanting to get rid of it.' That was hopeful; it suggested that I would know what I was doing in a few months.

He gave me one that cost £170 and it was much, much better. 'There's a huge difference to the way this one sounds, partly because it has a solid body. This will keep you going for a good few years.'

Since I couldn't play anything on any of the guitars he gave me, it was hard to tell which would be right. But this one, a Walden, sounded good when I plucked the strings and that was a start. Like many of the low-end guitars it was made in China, where production techniques have become so sophisticated that even the lowest-priced guitars retain their quality. Elsewhere there was a Martin D45, one of the best acoustic guitars around, selling for around £5,000. For this part of the journey the Walden would be OK.

My friend Doyle came over the same afternoon I tormented NJ with 'You Can't Always Get What You Want'. Doyle looks like a roadie for Led Zeppelin circa 1970. A week before, what started out as a few drinks had ended up with Doyle on the floor of the bar, sinking his teeth into the ankles of a girl in a final and desperate attempt to seduce her. Doyle is often compared to Animal, the drummer from *The Muppets*. He works as a safety inspector on the railways.

'How's old Jeff Beck getting on, then?' he asked, picking up the guitar. Doyle is the kind of person who looks like he should be in a band, but he's always been too busy living a dissolute life to get around to it. I told him about my progress. After a couple of strums he launched into an exquisite version of 'Wild Horses' by The Rolling Stones. Otto stopped bashing the doll. Pearl stopped screaming. NJ looked up from her book. The saliva at the corners of Doyle's mouth stopped foaming. Using the back of his thumb to create a soft tone, Doyle captured the soul of the song perfectly. He wasn't doing anything difficult, but he was making music.

'When the hell did you learn how to play like that?'

'You just pick up guitars when they're around, don't you,' he croaked, segueing into the intricate intro of another of my favourite songs, 'Alone Again Or' by the Los Angeles sixties group Love. 'I learnt in the old days, when it was five in the morning and I would be speeding out of my head, and wanted to obsess over the minutiae of hitting the notes properly.'

It turned out that Doyle didn't know too much about the technicalities of playing guitar, and there was no chance of his ever learning to read music. But there had been plenty of evenings where there was a guitar within leaning distance and someone to show him where to start with it. Doyle had that madly elusive quality – feeling – that is at the heart of all music, however simple or complex, and defines the point of it. Just as there isn't much value in having a great voice unless it is used to express individuality, so the merit of having a technical knowl-edge of the guitar is limited unless it can be used to express something that is inside; unless the strings resonate with the character of their player.

The guitar is perfect for a man of Doyle's rough charm because, with a little bit of perseverance, anyone can let something of themselves soak into the instrument. When Doyle played guitar he found a way to express a delicate side of his character that his wild deeds did well to conceal. I found a way of making my children cry.

'But how do you play it the way you do?' I asked, hopelessly. 'Do you need to count in your head to get the timing right? How hard do you press on the strings? Is my right hand positioned correctly?'

Doyle was hunched over my guitar, open-mouthed in casual absorption. 'You just have to feel it,' he replied.

'But what if you have no feeling?'
'It will come.'

The first discovery the absolute beginner makes is that the tips of the fingers on your left hand will hurt like hell as you try and press down on the strings hard enough to stop them from either sounding dead or making an ugly buzz. Developing calluses is the first hurdle, and a spur to keep on playing is the thought of having to go through that agony all over again. The second discovery is that everyone in the world is a better player than you. Doyle's hidden talents were the biggest revelation, but so many people who came by the flat in those early weeks of learning could also do something on it. My own band experience had never developed past lugging amplifiers from the music room to the gym for the school band's end-of-term gig, but everyone else, it seemed, spent at least part of their teenage years learning their favourite rock songs when they should have been revising for their exams. Someone who came over played the Jimi Hendrix version of 'Hey Joe'; another displayed a great knowledge of the minor chords used by alternative bands in the mid-nineties. The guitar, so economical and transportable, is the instrument of the people like no other.

It is also tinted with the glamour of rebellion. This has always been the case, ever since the guitar made its first hazy steps into existence. Even in Ancient Greece its earliest ancestor failed to get any respect from the establishment: back in 400 BC Aristotle proclaimed the lyre-like 'kithara' an instrument 'not suitable to the education of youth'.

Centuries later it was the lute that made it into high society. Derived from the Arabic oud, the lute was played to kings and queens in the courts of Renaissance Europe and its high status was unquestioned. It was said that if the six to ten courses of strings on a lute are played in accordance with the divine symmetry of the spheres, all elements harmonize and the instrument produces an emotion that allows the human soul to return to its original state. The lute and the oud were bridges between the material and celestial worlds.

The English guitar's predecessor, meanwhile, was enjoying rather less salubrious company. The pear-shaped cittern, later known as the slattern or the slut, was getting a reputation for being easy to pick up in bars, especially after a few drinks. Consisting of four, and later five, courses (pairs) of strings made of wire and played with a plectrum, the cittern was very loud, making it suitable for rowdy conditions, and its relative simplicity meant that it was ideal for bawdy bards wishing to entertain drunken company. It was hugely popular from the fifteenth to the nineteenth centuries in England. Barbershops, which in the Renaissance era were an enclave of rough masculine behaviour, often had a cittern lying around for anyone who came in to pick up and pluck. 'Is she a whore?' asked Thomas Dekker in *The Honest Whore*, 'A barber's cittern for every man to play on?'

Then there was the four-course gittern, which had a bad reputation from the start. A tract from 1393 reports the growing problem of unruly, drunken abbots playing gitterns on holy days 'to geter the stynkyng love of damyselis'. In 'The Pardoner's Tale' Chaucer writes of young Flemish hoodlums occupying their time with vice, ribaldry and gittern-playing, while 'The Miller's Tale' recounts the rivalry between a good Oxford student of high birth who plays a psaltery privately at night, and a low-class tradesman who plays his gittern in taverns. The gittern was a disgrace.

With the guitar's current ubiquity in all forms of music, from high classical to rock'n'roll, it is hard to imagine how the cittern and the early guitar must have been viewed when many of its players were the kind of people who considered standing up in the bath before relieving themselves a sign of their good breeding. I wanted to understand the early guitar, not so much in terms of its history, but more the philosophy of its players and the place that it had in society. Early music societies always seemed to take such a reverential approach to their subject that I didn't believe I could really learn about the sickly soul of the cittern through them. Then I heard Circulus.

A friend had told me about a band that combined the music of 1972 with the music of 1272. Their leader, a man with a bowl hairstyle and a scrape-over called Michael Tyack, believed in the wisdom of the medieval fool; the outsider who, untainted by success or the corruption of being lied to by subordinates, is in a unique position to see things as they really are. This sounded closer to the reality of the cittern player, a tavern musician without sophistication who, like the pilgrims of Chaucer's *Canterbury Tales*, expresses an earthy, realistic vision of the world.

I went to see Circulus bring their medieval vision to an ornate chapel in North London on the night of the Summer Solstice. The main part of the chapel, with its high spires and solemn stained-glass windows, has played host to many illustrious musicians of worldwide fame. Circulus were relegated to a backroom in the building that is used to house the cleaning utensils. They were certainly untainted by success. All eight members were excellent musicians, with Tyack's cittern accompanying a crumhorn played by a medieval outdoor wind instrument enthusiast called Will Summers, and they looked dramatic in their flowing robes and wide-brimmed hats. A Guinevere-like lady hummed soft falsetto notes while holding a candle and swaying gently with her eyes closed as the band rocked in a medieval fashion. But their sophistication might well have been lost on the two boys, one adult (myself) and dog that made up the audience. As Tyack sang a tragic tale about a scarecrow who, running through the night to make it to the wheat fields by dawn, stops for a cigarette and sets himself on fire, the boys played a pocket computer game and the dog curled up in front of the stage and went to sleep.

I got chatting to Tyack after the concert and discovered that he really does embody the spirit of the early guitar players of the Renaissance. He has avoided all forms of conventional employment, having taken a vow of poverty in order to keep a free kind of life (or, according to NJ, being too bone idle to get a job), and despite living in a suburb of London he adheres to a pre-Christian nature-based philosophy in which elemental and cosmic forces decree our fate. Having respected, if not necessarily understood, Doyle's argument that all you need to play guitar is the right feeling, I was interested in Tyack's take on the instrument.

'The guitar was never designed as a high instrument,' said Tyack. 'If you look at its origins in sixteenth-century Spain you can see that the vilhuela, which was an equivalent to the lute, was played in the courts, and that the guitar was one for the commoners. For that reason there really are no rules about how it should be played, since there weren't any when it came into existence.'

I told him about my own problems with playing, and how the initial reaction to my attempts to be musical had been overwhelmingly negative. 'It really doesn't matter,' he said, 'because it is the act of playing, and of slowly getting better, that is the whole point of doing it. Just playing a guitar can be enough to completely blow your mind.'

By 1700 the Spanish guitar had become associated with the

majo and *maja*, bohemian men and women who lived outside polite society in a romantic kind of poverty and played music in the streets at night. Guitars accompanied drinking sessions for the lower classes and slumming intellectuals and artists such as the young Francisco Goya. In a letter to a friend sent in 1784, the painter wrote: 'I do not require much in the way of furniture for my house, for I think that with a print of *Our Lady Of Pilar*, a table, five chairs, a frying pan, a cask of wine, and a tiple guitar, a roasting spit and a lamp, all else is superfluous.'

I came across a little bit of guitar history that had particular relevance for my own situation. A luthier from Dresden named August Otto is among those credited with adding an extra string to the five-string predecessors of the modern guitar in the late eighteenth century, thereby moving one step closer to the instrument we all know today. I told Otto about his illustrious namesake's achievements. He said that he would be pleased to meet this man and discuss the development of the guitar with him, but only after he had drawn a picture of a boy falling down a toilet.

The French Revolution induced nationalist fervour in Spain and helped eradicate the old snobberies against the guitar: serious composers adopted dances like the fandango and the bolero and the guitar was accepted as an instrument of national articulation. A Cistercian monk in Madrid called Father Basilio helped make the guitar fashionable by demonstrating its potential as a solo instrument through playing with his nails, making the sound louder and more intricate; while an Italian player named Federico Moretti moved to Madrid to write musical notation for the guitar in 1799, thereby giving each note played its full value. The guitar came of age with Moretti. As the great Spanish guitarist Fernando Sor stated: 'I regarded him as the torch that serves to light up the lost path for guitarists.'

Fernando Sor was the modern guitar's first master and one of its most effective advocates. Having already learned piano, violin, singing and composition, Sor came to the instrument with enough rigorous training to take it seriously and with enough knowledge to be able to apply full musical notation to it. When he moved to England in 1815 Sor brought the six-string guitar to a new audience; on his London debut of the same year one critic wrote that the audience suppressed laughter at the sight of Sor emerging from behind the curtains of The Argyll Rooms clutching such a trifling object, and for the next hour and a half were spellbound by his magical playing. At least partially due to Sor's touring, the guitar became ubiquitous in Germany, Austria and even Russia.

Sor's fellow countryman Antonio Torres Jurado designed the modern classical guitar at some point in the 1850s. Born near Almeria and working in Seville, Jurado increased the size of the guitar's body, gave it a fuller figure with deeper sides and developed new patterns of strutting that are still used today. The result was a stronger, richer sound with a clear, balanced tone, and when nylon strings helped improve consistency of sound after the Second World War the template for the modern guitar was complete. Then along came Andres Segovia, the greatest classical guitarist the world has ever known, to show what the instrument, in the right hands, is capable of. Its popularity has been assured ever since.

The intricate tonalities of the classical guitar are lost on the beginner, though. A cittern would have been more suitable. And, as inspiring as it was to watch Doyle bend his taut and narrow fingers around the frets and bring out the lustre of various hippy rock classics from the sixties and seventies, he didn't appear to have much ability in telling anyone else how to do it. He ran through a quick rendition of 'Angie' – no relation to Davey Graham's 'Anji' – by The Rolling Stones in the pretence of showing me how it was done, but it was obvious that he wanted to show off the riffs that had lain dormant in him for so long. Having gone through God knows how many chord changes, he handed the guitar over to me and said: 'Now you try.'

I got it wrong from the off, and Doyle revealed an irascible side to his character that the louche exterior does well to cover up. 'No!' he barked. 'Who told you to put your fingers there?' He pulled the guitar off me. 'You start on A minor and then move to E, not the other way round. Why don't you concentrate?'

Once again he played the entire song, and he expected me to remember exactly what his fingers had done. But the beginner is faced with the fact that their fingers simply will not fall into place as they should, even if you know where they are meant to go. Playing a guitar is rather like patting your head while rubbing your tummy: you have to teach your hands to do two things at once. The left one makes the chord shapes that will create the different tones, while the right, either through strumming, picking or a combination of the two, creates the rhythm. I could get a strumming pattern going, but each time I tried to change chord I lost it. The two actions were not going together. They were not compatible.

'Your brain is stopping every time you try and do something with your left hand,' said Doyle.

'Maybe it's not wired in a way that can cope with the information going into it,' I offered, glumly. 'Some people have a natural ability at this sort of thing. Others don't.'

'Your problem is that you're not watching, listening and learning. I'm not doing anything difficult. I'm just moving my fingers around a little bit. Stop worrying about it so much and try to relax into the sound.'

This is something that people always say when they have got
the hang of swimming, riding a bicycle, or walking in a straight
line. There are certain skills that, when mastered, it is impossible to imagine not being able to do because they require no
special concentration. It's a necessary part of being a human – it
would be irritating to have to remember how walking goes
every time you got out of bed, for example. But what is
constantly forgotten is that the brain and the body have to
learn these mechanical skills in order for them to come
naturally. Nobody can ever ride a bicycle or swim the first
time they are balanced on top of two wheels or thrown into a
river. It is the same with playing a guitar. Doyle failed to
realize, when he sighed at my umpteenth strangulation of 'Hey
Joe', that learning the guitar is about learning a new physical
coordination.

Doyle was never going to be able to show me how to play like
he could. He was even elusive in telling me how he learned –
and his talking about minor sevenths and hammer-ons and
pull-offs, even if he hadn't had any formal education in the field,
suggested that he wasn't as much of an artistic primitive as he
liked to appear. The Mississippi blues legend Robert Johnson
may have been able to learn guitar by sitting at the feet of Son
House as he slid a broken bottle up and down the frets, but I
couldn't see how I would penetrate the core of the instrument
by watching Doyle live out his Jimmy Page fantasies. Just as the
guitar was developed and refined over centuries and continents,
so I needed to find someone who was prepared to let me start my
quest at the beginning.

Pete Millson is a photographer who lives in one of North
London's more distant suburbs. His parents had run a pub in
rural Berkshire, and the sight of his father dealing with so many
drunken locals put him off alcohol for life. So, while the local

kids spent after-school sessions getting wrecked on cheap cider and homegrown weed, Pete was in his bedroom, hunched over a guitar and learning the opening riff to 'Money For Nothing' by Dire Straits. This meant that he got good on the guitar pretty quickly. After an adolescence spent working in chicken farms and luggage factories in the Thames Valley district, he came to London, found a flat and a girlfriend that suited him and never left either. He joined a band too, but was dismayed to find that his new colleagues had no intention of doing anything other than signing on and sitting around all day, drinking tea and learning chord sequences. Pete's work ethic could never allow for such a life so he reconciled himself to the fact that playing guitar would always be a hobby. In doing so he joined the mass ranks of guitarists all over the world who will remain entirely anonymous and who play their instrument for no other reason than the fact that they love it.

I also had an inkling that Pete would be a good teacher because he was such a patient and measured person. I remembered a story he had told me about a family car journey from his childhood that helped explain where he got his temperament. His father hit a verge at the side of the road and realized that the car was going to turn over.

'Right then, everyone into crash positions,' said Pete's dad. The Millson family held steady as the car rolled on to its roof and back on to its wheels before coming to a halt.

'Nobody hurt?' said Dad. The family confirmed that they were all fine. 'Come on then. We'd better call the AA.'

Then Pete's mother said to him: 'Oh, and grab those sandwiches, would you dear. You never know how long the AA are going to take and we might get peckish.'

Although I didn't share his abiding passion for earnest singer-songwriters from the 1980s, I knew that Pete would be a much better bet than Doyle when it came to explaining the early stages of the guitarist's craft. He gave me strict instructions to arrive at his flat at 7.30pm, when his one-year-old baby would be asleep, and leave at 9pm so that he could get to bed at his usual time half an hour later. 'I've splashed out and bought some chocolate digestives,' he said as I arrived. 'I might even go crazy and order a pizza. Rachel's gone out and I think we should really let our hair down.' (Pete's hair had never been let down in his life: at the age of fifteen it went into a Morrissey-like quiff and remained that way, defiant of fashion's fickle follies, ever since.)

'It's a great way of getting some sense of achievement,' said Pete, on being asked why he played guitar. 'It's a very peaceful thing to do as well. Whatever's been happening in your life, you can switch off by playing guitar and enter into a much nicer world.'

Pete asked me what I could already do. That was easy: the chorus to 'You Can't Always Get What You Want'. I played him my three-chord strum and, amazingly, he was encouraging. 'For someone who has only been playing for two weeks, that's great. You've got a good sense of rhythm and timing and the fact that your fingers aren't quite hitting the strings in the right place doesn't really matter at this stage. If you keep practising that will come in time. It's more important to keep the rhythm than it is to get the chords perfect.'

'But I've always been told that I've got no natural sense of rhythm, timing, or melody,' I replied.

'Nobody's got *no* natural sense of rhythm and it's irresponsible of people to tell you that,' said Pete. (Note to self: relay this information to NJ at an opportune moment.) 'All that most people suffer from is a lack of confidence. The point about the guitar is that it's versatile enough for anyone to bring something of themselves to it. Even if you're a very simple person, that's fine – you can make simple music.'

'I am also tone deaf. My singing voice is proof of this.'

'OK. How does this sound to you?'

Pete hit one of the strings on the guitar and it sounded horrible; a toneless noise with a grating buzz.

'It sounds awful.'

'And how about this?' He hit the same note, but this time a pure and clean sound rang out, harmonious and true.

'It sounds good.'

'Then you're not tone deaf.'

I cannot tell you what a revelation this was. My music teacher at school was a man called Mr Stuckey, who knew someone who knew someone who knew the musical impresario Andrew Lloyd-Webber quite well. As a result of this fortuitous connection most of the boys in our year formed the choir for the London production of the musical *Evita*, and music lessons were given over to practising for evening performances in the show. When they weren't stretching their dulcet tones over 'Don't Cry For Me Argentina' (their big moment), the boys in the choir were talking about their adventures in the big city, of seeing the sex shops of Soho and being backstage in a real theatre. In our class there were five boys whose voices were too awful to contribute to the choir and I was one of them. For each music lesson we had to sit in an empty backroom of a prefabricated hut and keep quiet while Mr Stuckey, with his aviator shades and David Essex hairstyle, sat by the piano and led the chosen ones on a journey to Argentina via the West End. Their heavenly voices were interspersed with humorous anecdotes about 'Andrew' from Mr Stuckey followed by conspiratorial laughter from his wards. The message was clear: losers shouldn't try. The best thing they can do is not open their mouths. This led to a lack of musical confidence that is shared by a good proportion of people on this planet.

What Pete revealed to me, over chocolate digestives but sadly no pizza after he realized he still had half a loaf of sliced white bread in the cupboard, was that just as anyone can learn to speak a language, so anyone could learn to play music. There has been a huge conspiracy, chiefly orchestrated by musicians, but also aided by record companies, the media and self-serving music teachers, that you are either gifted or you aren't, and if the magic wand of talent has not struck you on the shoulder then you might as well not bother at all. It isn't true. Of course there is such a thing as talent, but there is also satisfaction to be gained from the positive art of learning an instrument. Your music may never bring light into other people's lives or provide a soundtrack to great romances and tragedies, but it won't harm the world either. Pete understood that learning how to play the guitar is something that should always be encouraged. Age, natural ability, and musical tastes are no boundary to this noble pursuit.

Something else worth revealing to the first-timer is that, as part of an interest-protecting policy, musicians have made what they do seem far more difficult than it really is. I grew up believing that musicians were magicians, mysterious beings with elemental forces within their grip and a deeper conscious-ness at their fingertips. In fact a lot of them, the rock and pop ones at least, are playing things that can be learned fairly quickly. The entire output of The Velvet Underground can be boiled down to a few chords. I still couldn't do anything on the guitar, but Pete was showing me how I almost certainly would be able to in the not-too-distant future. The first chords that most people learn are A and E. Playing the sixties Los Angeles band The Buffalo Springfield's most famous song, 'For What

It's Worth', involves moving from E to A and back again before ending up at D. Pete showed me how to do it, and although it didn't sound half as good as it did on the record, it was recognisable. From there it was possible to build up a rhythm by keeping a constant strum, and as far as strumming is concerned most men who have passed adolescence will already, in their solitary moments, have mastered this repetitive hand movement that, while rudimentary, can bring so much pleasure in so many ways.

It occurred to me that I still didn't really understand the rudiments of music. I knew that there are twelve notes in an octave and that the guitar is usually tuned in the Spanish tradition, with the strings in the order of E, A, D, G, B and E again in a higher octave. But I didn't understand the difference between major and minor chords, or which notes were to be found on different frets. 'It doesn't matter,' said Pete. 'You'll learn all of that in time. The only way to actually enjoy playing the guitar is to just do it and start off with something basic. All of the technical knowledge will come when you're ready to use it.'

Thinking that in rock guitar less is frequently more, I asked Pete to show me the basics of 'Get It On' by T-Rex, which contains one of the greatest riffs of all time. It is so basic that it would lack finesse on, say, the piano, but on the guitar it is magical. After the opening riff Marc Bolan alternates between two chords, and, although simple, the song is quite hard to play because it requires absolute precision to sound good – there are so few elements to it that they all count and there is nothing to cover up mistakes with.

There are certain songs that are entirely written with the guitar in mind and 'Get It On' is one of them. It doesn't matter that Marc Bolan has electric distortion to give it flavour; even on an acoustic the riff still has a fantastic rock power. 'Paperback Writer' by The Beatles has the same quality: a basic series of notes that could only ever have been created on the guitar. David Bowie's 'The Jean Genie' has it, too. So does 'Jumping Jack Flash' by The Rolling Stones. In fact pretty much every great rock song ever written is a product of the guitar.

By the end of the evening – well, by Pete's bedtime of 9pm – the seed of learning had been planted. Pete had shown me the rudiments of a power chord: he had intended on teaching me the kind of riff Pete Townshend does so well, but somehow we had ended up with the introduction to 'More Than A Feeling' by the American soft-rock seventies stadium band Boston. It illustrated the fact that once you start trying to do anything on the guitar you begin to see how uncomplicated so many famous songs are. But what marks out the good music from the bad is the inventiveness of the guitarist and the feeling that they put into their playing. It really is another form of language and it can be used crassly or delicately, with passion or with a mechanical lack of any real understanding. Discovering the guitar is like finding a new continent that exists within your fingertips.

The possibilities of the modern guitar as a simple instrument were realized in America. The German luthier C. F. Martin set up shop on New York's Hudson Street in 1833 after an industrial dispute with the guild of violinmakers in his home-town of Mark Neukirchin, and went on to change the guitar from being a relatively low-key instrument to the world's greatest tool of rebellion. In the 1850s Martin moved from making delicate, small-bodied instruments suitable for quiet drawing rooms to large-bodied flat-tops with a much higher built-in volume. By 1900, the company he founded was building steel-string models in response to a demand for guitars that could be heard in public places. In the decades that followed the popularity of vaudeville, country, blues and jazz grew enormously and so did the need for a loud, jumbo-sized instrument that could do the music justice under not always genteel circumstances.

Martin had competition from a Michigan shoe-store clerk called Orville Gibson who made instruments in his spare time until he went professional in 1894, and the demand for Gibson's large, loud arch-top guitars soon outweighed supply. In the first half of the twentieth century more and more brands emerged – Stella, Harmony, Guild, Ovation – and by the 1960s Japanese companies were knocking out cheap copies of Martins and Gibsons that were quickly rivalling their American counterparts for craftsmanship if not kudos. At the same time, the electric guitar began a cultural boom that has never really waned, despite the arrival of digital technology that should have made it redundant. Now we live in a world where almost anyone can have a guitar if they want to – a third of all homes in Britain do – and where the level of quality goes from Roger McGuinn of The Byrds commissioning Martin to custom-build a unique seven-string acoustic guitar that would, for anyone else, be priceless, to someone like, well, me buying a Chinese knock-off made by cheap labour that sounds perfectly good and offers all the versatility you need to get going.

There is little point in being overly precious about a guitar. The small, delicate instruments of the 1940s have been replaced by the big, robust products of today, which are built to cope with being thrown into the backs of tour buses and molested by musical philistines. Independent luthiers still handcraft nylon-stringed classical guitars, but even the finest steel-stringed folk guitars are usually factory-built, Martins included. Like in any

field there will always be a fetish for the object, but I don't
think the real magic of the guitar is to be found in its
craftsmanship or its quality of finish or its perceived value,
but in the fact that such a relatively cheap instrument can be
used for the expression of so many facets of mankind's situation.
One of the great soul cuts is 'Stand By Me' by Ben E. King. It
was written on a cheap guitar in King's bedroom one night after
he heard a gospel song by Sam Cooke called 'Stand By Me
Father'. In his casual way King picked out of the air a universal
sentiment of love that could be understood by anyone in the
world. The guitar was all it took to give that sentiment a body.

I returned from Pete's house that evening to find the kids
asleep and NJ in the basement, reading a book and wearing a
blue caftan. It felt like a scene from a film: steam curling from a
cup of cinnamon tea, the woman with a catlike smile and the
man leaning back in a wicker rocking chair, a guitar on his
belly, the notes cutting through the dank subterranean air and
filling the narrow space. This was the life I should have been
living all those years ago. Why did I wait until I was in my
thirties before discovering this wonderful instrument and everything that went with it?

'So how was your first lesson?' asked NJ.

'Pretty good,' I told her. 'Pete's a fantastic teacher and I'm
beginning to understand the possibilities of what this thing can
do. Plus I think I'm really coming on in leaps and bounds.'

'Let's hear it, then.'

I leaned over my Walden, taking care to place the tips of my
still-stinging fingers on the right strings. Then I let the chord of
C ring out before singing, in that word's widest definition: '*You
can't always get what you wa-hont . . .*'

NJ dug herself deeper into her book and declined to
comment.

Chapter Two

Django Reinhardt and Other Bohemians

About a month into my guitar-learning odyssey I got chatting to two French brothers, both guitarists, who played in a band called Phoenix. Christian and Laurent 'Branco' Brancowitz grew up in the Parisian suburb of Versailles where there was little to do except find a way to make life more interesting. Salvation came in the form of their parents' record collection. There was the Brazilian bossa nova guitarist João Gilberto next to the gypsy jazz legend Django Reinhardt and a smattering of seventies glam rockers like T-Rex and Roxy Music. The brothers started playing guitar at around the age of twelve, and in a typically French fashion they applied philosophy to their craft in a way that would never occur to American or English musicians. 'I have just been reading the work of the third-century missionary St Augustine,' announced Branco at a book-filled Left Bank café. 'And he talks about religious life consisting of three things: knowledge, style, and grace. Knowledge is learning the guitar and the work of other musicians. Style comes from understanding what to do with that knowledge. Grace is what you bring to the instrument through your own soul. And grace is the only thing that really matters.'

It would be a while before my own grace, what there was of it, would be adding anything to the great body of work that has been created on the guitar over the last two hundred years. But it was good to hear these laconic Frenchmen, who somehow looked so much more stylish in the standard uniform of frayed jeans, battered cowboy boots, leather jackets and stubble than most rock bands, reflect on what the purpose of the guitar, or music itself for that matter, really is. I told them about how much I liked T-Rex and how Marc Bolan's style was so inspiring for someone starting out and trying to understand how it might be possible to make music when you have little experience. 'Marc Bolan is a great guitarist because he is a bad guitarist,' said Christian. 'The only reason he is playing those chords on the chorus of "Get It On", which are G, A minor and E, is because it is easy to move from one to another. So his knowledge was poor but his grace was wonderful.'

I was reminded of seeing Marc Bolan on an English television show from the 1970s in which T-Rex played a few numbers in front of an auditorium of earnest schoolchildren before being quizzed by an upright man with a clipboard on how they made their music. It was an educational programme mostly devoted to classical musicians and composers, but in the spirit of modernity the producers had thrown a pop star into the mix. The clipboard-wielding presenter was patronizing to Bolan, especially when it was revealed that he could not read music and had only the most scant understanding of how it was structured. The presenter clearly thought that the little pop performer, with his feather boa, pouting lips and three-chord repertoire, was but a mere bauble of a thing. Maybe he was. But who cares when he wrote such cool songs? And Bolan used the older man's prejudices to his advantage. When asked how long it took him to learn how to play the guitar, he said: 'It took me a day. When I was fourteen I bought Bert Weedon's book *Play*

Guitar in a Day, did what he said, and never bothered to learn anything more since then.'

He was probably lying – at least I hope he was, now that I had been playing guitar for a month and had not progressed in any noticeable way – but what he said was philosophically true, if not empirically so. The guitar is made for people to imprint their own approach on to it rather than be dictated by its intricacies. All the great guitarists have invented their own way of playing which other people have then given names to, from classical masters like Andres Segovia and Julian Bream to low pop strummers like Marc Bolan. It is an instrument that rewards a reliance on instinct.

Those French brothers had mentioned the name of someone who I felt could provide some important lessons on how to approach the guitar. The gypsy jazz guitarist Django Reinhardt was a real free spirit; a cosmic improviser who made music yield to his intuition. Almost illiterate, Reinhardt never learned how to read music. But he combined the traditional styles of the Manouche gypsies to whom he belonged with the American jazz of Louis Armstrong and Duke Ellington to create delicate and sophisticated melodies rich with elegance and passion. He could tell if one musician was out of tune in the mass of a symphony orchestra. After a trip to Saint Marie de la Mare in the South of France to pay homage to St Sara, the black patron saint of gypsies, he started work on a mass in the style of Bach, dictating the music to his friend and fellow musician Gerard Levecque. 'It could have been a whole completed work,' remembered Levecque, 'but he was too lazy. He was always in bed.'

Django Reinhardt was born in Belgium on 23 January 1910. He spent his childhood in a horse-drawn caravan that travelled through Europe and North Africa, and, like most gypsies of the

time, he had no formal education. He didn't live in a house
until he was twenty. When he was eight his family joined the
gypsies that filled the rough outer edges of Paris, where
wrought-iron gates marked the city limits and entire commu-
nities lived in cardboard villages surviving on the endless
circulation of mostly stolen objects. Django ran with a gang
called The Red Neckerchiefs until his mother bought him a
guitar when he was twelve. By the time he was fourteen he had
made a name for himself in the dance halls of the Paris
underworld. He would perform at cafés and nightclubs for a
week at a time and soon became a legend within the city's gypsy
community.

A disaster in the autumn of 1928 led to the birth of Django
Reinhardt's unique playing style. He came in from a concert at
one in the morning to find that his wife had filled their caravan
with celluloid flowers. Bending down with a candle to in-
vestigate what he thought was the sound of a mouse he dropped
the wick of the candle on to a flower, which blazed up in an
instant. His wife escaped, but Django collapsed after grabbing a
blanket to shield himself. By the time he got out of the caravan
he was severely burned, with the hand that had grabbed the
blanket so inflamed and twisted that two of his fingers were
deformed and useless. His leg was so burned that a surgeon at
the hospital wished to amputate it. Django refused and spent
the next eighteen months bedridden in a nursing home,
learning how to play guitar with the two working fingers
on his left hand.

By the time Django returned to his caravan near the Porte de
Clignancourt he was poverty-stricken. But he began to play
around the cafés of Montmartre, later travelling south to Toulon
with his second wife Naguine and his brother Joseph, where he
was mistaken for a down-at-heel aristocrat. There he met an old-

fashioned bohemian called Emile Savitry who played him records by Duke Ellington and Louis Armstrong. Django, Naguine and Joseph moved on to Cannes, where they booked themselves into the most expensive hotel they could find (The Georges V on Rue Antibes) and played for tips in the waterfront bistros, sneaking out of the hotel after a few nights and, after landing a job with the bandleader Louis Prima at the Palm Beach casino, renting a bungalow that became a meeting place for local gypsies. Prima claimed that within days of Django landing the big band gig you could go to any gypsy caravan in Cannes and find a full set of Palm Beach Hotel cutlery inside it.

Django Reinhardt epitomized a certain attitude that has followed the guitar throughout its entire history: the pride of the outsider. For everyone, from gypsy musicians to itinerant blues guitarists to travelling rock bands, the guitar has been a vehicle to take its player beyond and above society. I could hear it in every strain of 'Anji' by Davey Graham, which I could not begin to understand how to play. From what I learned about Davey Graham, he had found a higher calling in the guitar that absolved him from the responsibilities of normal life. While still in his teens he was travelling through North Africa in search of musical adventure and discovery; a few years later he was proud to be a heroin addict like his heroes Miles Davis and Charlie Parker. Django Reinhardt, meanwhile, considered himself to be something of a prince, not just among his own community but also with the bourgeoisie who paid for a little piece of his artistic soul.

Django became a big star. His innate nobility stood him in good stead to move in high-society circles, although he would return to the caravans of his fellow gypsies in-between dinner dates with aristocrats. Not wishing to show his illiteracy, he pointed to clauses in contracts that he objected to before being told that he was holding the piece of paper upside down. He felt that it was beneath him to carry his own instrument and usually got his brother Joseph to do it for him. He had affairs with famous hostesses, leaving Naguine and their pet monkey in a one-room Montmartre flat for days on end. At the same time he held on to a freewheeling lack of professionalism, eschewing recording sessions and missing live appearances so that he could go fishing or visit a caravan to gamble away however much money he had made that week.

The spirit of Django seemed a long way away one rain-soaked July morning when I woke up at five in the morning, unable to sleep. I padded downstairs to the kitchen, picked up Ralph Denyer's *The Guitar Handbook*, and tried to get to grips with scales. Within two plucks of the C scale my wife had appeared, glowering in half-conscious fury, demanding that I put a stop to my antisocial fretwork at once. Did Django suffer from such affronts to his artistic dignity? Probably not, but then he started at an age when he had nothing to do but practise, not at thirty-four, when he had a wife and two screaming kids to love and provide for.

The other thing that was getting to me, and presumably gets to a lot of beginners, is the wall of theory that apparently has to be climbed before the instrument can really be understood. As Django Reinhardt was illiterate, it is doubtful whether he would have learned the rudiments of pentatonic scales, inverted triads and substituted sevenths. But how, then, did he understand how harmony, melody and rhythm – the three components of music – worked? It seems that until these are understood it is impossible to make any real progress on the guitar. A language needs to be learned before one can use it as a framework for creative thought, but at this stage, the language of music was all Greek to me.

Banned by my angry wife from actually playing the thing, I tried to come to terms with a bit of theory. A few pages into the practical section of Ralph Denyer's impeccably constructed guitar manual there are statements like: 'By now it should be obvious to you that all the tonic (root) notes are three frets apart.' Not only was it not obvious to me, I didn't even know what a tonic (root) note was. I began to relive a sensation that I had not experienced since revising for my chemistry and maths exams when I was sixteen: the awareness of being in possession of a blank mind unable to process and digest logical information. As an adult you can avoid confronting such academic weaknesses most of the time. The niggling pain of the accountant's bill is preferable to the all-enveloping horror of filling in a tax return. As a teenager you simply cannot escape from the classes you hate.

Now that awful feeling of empty panic returned as I zoned out at charts of inverted scales and chord substitutions. The words and diagrams sat uselessly on the paper. Unable to play guitar, baffled by the basic laws of music that are taught to schoolchildren from the age of eight upwards, I was like a eunuch in a whorehouse, staring at a world of colour and excitement I could never be a part of. Denyer wrote of the importance of understanding how to read music. What hope could there be for that when I couldn't even understand tablature, the system of guitar notation that was created specifically for idiots too stupid to learn how to read music?

I put the kettle on and stared at the rain coursing down the dirty windowpanes of the kitchen before facing up to *The Guitar Handbook* again. In five months' time I was meant to be getting up on some little stage and revealing my guitar-playing skills, like an end-of-term presentation, to I imagine about ten people without anything better to do that night. On all the album covers that I had stared at so intently while the records were playing, of Jimi Hendrix screaming in ecstasy as his enormous fingers twisted around the frets, of James Brown's band looking impeccably cool in matching suits and raised guitars, or of Emmylou Harris singing country-soul with a jumbo acoustic slung around her narrow shoulders, I never imagined that all these hip cats had to sit and study time signatures and circles of fifths before being granted permission to groove. The whole thing seemed like too much hard work. I put the guitar back in its case and crawled into bed.

That evening, after a disheartening day wondering how I was ever going to get to grips with this instrument, a visit from two young men from Akron, Ohio brought a bit of hope. Dan Auerbach and Patrick Carney are the sole members of a band called The Black Keys, and they were passing through London as part of a tour when a mutual friend brought them round to our place for their evening off. Friends since high school, Dan and Patrick make dense, blues-based rock music that sounds like it was recorded at the bottom of a well. Dan plays guitar and sings and Patrick plays drums, and with these simple elements they create a huge sound that is embedded in the blues tradition. They recorded their second album in a day. Their third, 2004's *Rubber Factory*, was made, aptly enough, in a rubber factory. Ohio used to be the rubber capital of the USA, and since the trade moved elsewhere at the end of the 1970s the outskirts of the small city are filled with cavernous, empty factories and warehouses falling into dereliction. It is the atmosphere of these vast, decaying industrial spaces that is reflected in The Black Keys's ominous music.

I had been listening to the wailing guitar on *Rubber Factory* and loved the way it was so brutal but also possessed such a great mood: pleading and emotional, yet defiant. Of course I had no idea how Dan made these sounds, and assumed that he would have an intimate knowledge of the rules contained in Ralph Denyer's *The Guitar Handbook*. NJ made The Black Keys a glass of Pimm's, which they thought was like the sangria served in their local Tex-Mex restaurant in Akron, and Dan and Patrick revealed themselves to be a well brought-up, affable and slightly awkward pair. They explained how they had started playing music in their early teenage years as a way of passing the time in a town where there was not much else to do, especially after they got fired from their lawn-mowing jobs. Every day after school they went to Patrick's father's garage and made up songs together. 'We never even thought of ourselves as a band,' Dan said, poking at the cucumber floating at the top of his Pimm's. 'There was only two of us, and normally you have four guys in a band. We were doing it for fun.'

With Akron, Ohio having a limited supply of music on offer, both boys turned to their father's record collections for inspiration. Patrick's dad liked the classic rock of Led Zeppelin, The Rolling Stones and Cream, and Dan's had a lot of the blues legends on vinyl: Son House, Robert Johnson, Muddy Waters, Sonny Boy Williamson. 'I loved the sounds all the old blues guys were making so I just copied them,' he said. 'It was a case of repetition reaping rewards: I would listen to the record, try and play it, get it wrong, and listen to it again. Eventually I understood what it was they were doing.'

Instead of taking an academic approach to wailin' the blues, Dan bought a series of videos featuring footage of the blues guitarists playing live and studied what their fingers were doing. 'If you watch them enough times, and then listen to the records, you can work it out,' he told me. 'At first I didn't know the names of the chords or the techniques that they were using – that came later. But it was so cool to manage to make a noise that sounded good, even if I couldn't play the song that it was a part of, that I got hooked on to the guitar. That's all it was – and is.'

There were other people for me to look to for inspiration. I liked the British singer Polly Harvey's style of playing: she made a primeval sound on songs that are structured around a few simple chords. I suspected that she wasn't doing anything too complicated. But then Harvey is musical: she started out playing the saxophone in pubs in her native Dorset as a teenager and by the time she hit her twenties she was proficient in a dozen different instruments. On one album, 2004's *Uh Huh Her*, she played everything bar the drums. It was about two days after picking up the guitar that I met Harvey in London. She's a sweet, quiet woman who was encouraging about my new pursuit, so I felt that I should ask her about her own approach.

'I never go near the guitar when I'm not recording or playing live,' she said in her soft, precise Dorset burr. 'I've never practised scales in my life. If I'm going to write a new song I'll sit with the guitar and play around until something comes out that I like, and I'm not following any particular rules of harmony while doing that. And I've never studied music, not wishing to disturb what comes naturally and haphazardly.'

She had a song I liked called 'No Child of Mine'. It consisted of an acoustic guitar and her voice and it sounded simple. 'That song only has three chords,' she told me. 'I could show you how to play that in half an hour.'

Inevitably, I mentioned my attempts to master 'You Can't Always Get What You Want', and how it sounded so different when I played it. 'But that's exactly how I started writing songs,' she replied. 'I would try and copy famous songs that I liked, and when I got frustrated because they didn't sound right

I would put my fingers in slightly different positions to see what happened. If you do that you'll be writing songs in no time. The next thing you need to do is get some four-track recording equipment and start singing into it.'

Now that was going too far. Learning the guitar may have been a folly, but it was a noble folly. Trying to sing would simply be cruel to anyone within earshot. 'None of my favourite singers can really sing – Bob Dylan for example, or Leonard Cohen,' said Polly. 'Nick Cave was great until he learned how to sing, at which point he became a bit of a boring crooner. Music is all about creation, and the expression of what's inside, and it's not about perfection. Keep on with that guitar.'

I kept that in mind as I plodded my way through *The Guitar Handbook* on a grey, supposedly summer morning. Being faced with mathematical disability wasn't pleasant, but I found it hard to believe that a technical mind was really needed to play the guitar. Later that afternoon I called Doyle, who never struck me as being academically inclined, and asked him if he understood music theory. 'Of course I do,' he claimed. 'What happened is that people started making music through trial and error, and a system of rules was then developed to give structure to what they were doing. But you don't have to be Einstein to play the guitar, man. All you need to understand is that these scales were made to describe certain styles of playing, so now you can use those scales to make it easier to play those styles. The pentatonic scale is just a series of notes that form a blues and rock sound. Learn to play a few songs first and then you'll see how the notes fit together.'

Slowly it began to make sense. I learned that the note you begin with, the root note, defines the scale. The cosmic law of harmony decrees that the fourth and fifth notes in the scale sound good when they follow the first one, so if you play the note of C you can follow it with the notes of F and G. There is a thing called a relative minor, and to find it you take the root note of the scale and move two notes back, which for C is A. That, I believe, is the most basic rule of music.

Living in the flat above us in North London was our friend Liam Watson. Liam had built his own vintage recording studio, complete with a mixing desk salvaged from EMI's Abbey Road studios and authentic pre-decimalization recording equipment. The studio, and Liam, achieved a degree of fame in 2003 after the American guitar and drums duo The White Stripes recorded an album there for a few thousand pounds that went on to become a number one smash hit all over the world. But before it was deluged with rock hopefuls searching for a bit of that White Stripes stardust, Toe-Rag Studios in Hackney, East London was something of a home for the freaks and misfits of the musical world. One of these – who Liam held up as the best musician he had ever worked with – was a man called Teddy Paige.

Liam had discovered Teddy Paige playing rockabilly at a London pub. He was an enormous middle-aged man with a beard who dressed as a medieval troubadour, complete with tights, little pointed shoes, a felt hat and a leather tabard. He lived in a hostel in Soho and spent most of his days busking, playing early music on a lute. He kept to an authentic meat-only diet and wore his medieval gear all day, every day. The sight of Teddy cycling down Denmark Street had earned him the nickname Medieval Knievel.

Teddy's roots were revealed to the handful of people in London who knew him after he walked into Sounds That Swing, a rock'n'roll record shop in Camden, and asked for a 45 made at Sun Studios in Memphis, home to Elvis Presley, Carl Perkins and so many other rock'n'roll greats, by its catalogue number. The man behind the counter had recognized the number as belonging to 'Cadillac Man' by The Jesters, a rare slice of rockabilly from 1966. Asked why he wanted it, Teddy said: 'Well, I guess I made it.'

Teddy Paige was a teenage prodigy from Memphis, Tennessee. He went to school with Jerry Phillips, the son of Sun's founder Sam Phillips, who got Teddy a job at the studio as a tea-boy, but his wonderful guitar playing – intricate, harmonious, rooted in the blues – saw him promoted to session guitarist on records by Jerry Lee Lewis and Carl Perkins. He was there in the sixties when visiting musicians such as Etta James, Paul Simon and James Brown's band ('man, those guys could play!') swung by, and he went out on the road with the Memphis R&B stalwarts Booker T. & The MG's, taking the place of regular guitarist Steve Cropper. He helped build the guitar that Elvis played on the '68 Comeback Special. He cornered Chuck Berry in a phone booth to ask him which key 'Baby Doll' was in. ('He said it was C. I said it was E flat. He told me to go away.')

Teddy formed his own band, The Jesters, and recorded 'Cadillac Man'. It wasn't a hit, and it was the only single The Jesters ever released. Teddy did cut a few other tracks under different names – 'Frank, This Is It' by Jellean Delk & The Casuals was a tear-jerking R&B number featuring a local black teenage girl and Teddy on guitar and songwriting duties – but nothing he made ever got anywhere. When Sun Studios was bought up and moved to Nashville in 1970 Teddy came as part of the package. Then in 1972 something happened. It's unclear to this day, but it seems that Teddy had an argument with Jerry Phillips and stormed off, never to be seen again. A decade later word got out that he had been one of the victims of the Jamestown, Guyana tragedy in which cult leader Jim Jones committed mass genocide by making his followers drink strychnine-laced Kool Aid. The truth about Teddy, however, was far stranger.

Teddy had left America for Europe, where he took up the life of a medieval troubadour with no fixed address. He slept under the stars in France and played in castles in Spain. He persuaded a series of women to make his jester's outfits for him and he picked up the lute. I heard from a Swedish busker who remembered being with Teddy in a bar in Switzerland and going to the toilet only to return and find that Teddy had been busy attempting to convince the guy's girlfriend to run away to the South of France with him. 'It was always better to keep moving and not be tied down,' Teddy told me about his itinerant days in Europe. 'Trouble comes when you get stuck in one place. As long as you can still pick up and go, you stay free.'

Trouble did indeed start for Teddy when he came to England in the early nineties and settled in Nottingham, originally arriving in search of centuries-old folk songs and the myths surrounding the Robin Hood legend. He found himself a council flat and a three-foot sword, a nod towards medieval authenticity that was somewhat lost on the authorities. He bought a four-track recording machine to lay down some of his lute tunes and augment them with rockabilly sound effects. He ended up having to leave Nottingham after barricading himself in his flat to resist eviction, and then he travelled down to Bath where he busked and lived in a hostel. London followed a few years later.

A few months after recording some of his songs with Liam Watson at Toe-Rag, Teddy disappeared. No one in London seemed to know where he was and months passed without news. Then it finally came – from the BBC. In January 2003, a man dressed as a medieval troubadour had been arrested in Hastings,

South-East England, for attacking his neighbour with a sword. The neighbour's arm had almost been chopped off. Teddy, who was going under the name Count Macdonald and claiming he was the rightful heir and laird of the great Macdonald clan of Scotland, had complained about the noise coming from his neighbour's bedroom. After his complaints had been ignored one time too many he went on a crusade with his sabre. Following a spell in jail Teddy was sent to Ashen Hill, a maximum security psychiatric institute in East Sussex in the south of England. Given a life sentence, he was to remain there indefinitely.

Liam and I made a day trip to visit Teddy at Ashen Hill and it was tragic to see his medieval finery replaced by a blue towelling tracksuit, his big hairy belly poking out through the gap between the top and the trousers. He was a gentle, slow-moving bear of a man and it was hard to imagine him turning violent, but the sword incident was not the first. 'I've had nothing but trouble since I moved to England,' he said, shaking his hairy head, his sad eyes staring at the institutional lime-green of the heavy-wear carpet in his unit's common room. Behind us a middle-aged man was telling one of the nurses how once he mastered jiving and singing on ice, he would be performing at all the theatres in the West End. 'Beatings, fights and arrests. They sure got me good this time.'

In his slow, low voice, Teddy told us the story of his life. 'I never could stand acid rock,' he said, his fingers in his ears, on why he left his former life as a professional guitarist in America. 'I think the electric bass destroyed music. That's a real turkey of an instrument. Music went downhill in the sixties and it never recovered.'

He explained that he had no time for what he called the 'perversion' of electric guitar music: distortion, effects pedals and volume over skill. He liked a purer form; either twelve-bar blues played on an acoustic or rockabilly on a big, reverberating electric guitar like a Gretsch. He had spent his teenage years collecting rare blues records and they represented good music as he saw it. So when music moved into an era he felt he couldn't be a part of, he left for Europe to create his own medieval utopia.

'Often I only made enough money to buy either cigarettes or food,' said Teddy. 'But the costume seemed to help, and every now and then I would get booked to play a party and make more money from that.' With no other possessions, his home was in the guitar and the lute. 'It was complete freedom. No one could pin me down. I had a few girlfriends – they came and went – but as long as I kept playing I never really felt lonely.'

I was hoping to learn something from Teddy's playing, but he wasn't really capable of explaining his techniques and I wasn't a sophisticated enough player to learn just by watching his fingers move. Although he was a brilliant guitarist, it seemed that he couldn't decide on the best way to approach the instrument. He said that the beginner must learn the structure and theory of music in order to understand it, and then he said that all the great guitarists taught themselves without any formal training. He was happier talking about his life than he was about his music.

Teddy let the guitar pick up where he left off. He strummed the old strings with such tenderness that it was tough to reconcile the incarcerated minstrel before me with the bearded giant of fearful wrath and might who had almost hacked his techno-loving neighbour's arm off. His playing was transcendent: it took us all to another place and transformed the cold white walls of the high security psychiatric home into rainbow tapestries. For a brief moment, Teddy was the epitome of the working man staking his claim in the celestial firmament. If only he wasn't locked up, he would be the spiritual inheritor of Django Reinhardt's gypsy guitar.

Meeting Teddy Paige was sad but inspiring. Until his wayward character had proved too much for the authorities to cope with he had lived a life of real freedom, and either through choice or necessity he had escaped from the materialism and neurosis of bourgeois life that weigh so many of us down and root us into being prisoners of our own pointless fears. Much of Teddy's lifestyle was a product of mental health problems – he suffered from manic depression – but I couldn't say that his life of near poverty was any worse than one ruled by colour supplements, mortgages, trips to out-of-town furniture stores and worrying about what other people think of you. Not long after seeing Teddy I heard about a riot at a discount furniture store on the outskirts of London, where shoppers went on a frenzy of bargain-hunting violence. They had ended up attacking each other with dining table chairs at knockdown prices. Teddy was certainly no madder than they were.

As I got into the routine of the evening back at home, with children's baths followed by stories followed by the inevitable refusal to get into bed, I decided to do something that I had never done before.

From the outside, my life might have seemed bohemian. I had no employer, my family lived in one big room, and we had always put curiosity about life over financial security. But it was conventional, really. NJ stayed at home with our two kids while I went out to the office I shared with other freelancers and stared at a computer screen all day. The sedentary reality of how most of my working hours passed was much the same as the average office worker. Research was carried out, words were written and invoices were sent. There was the one o'clock break and the cheese ploughman's from the local sandwich shop. I had created this routine of my own choice. When people have nine-to-five jobs they dream about the supposed freedom of being freelance, of the decadence of spending an afternoon in the cinema or letting a lunch dissolve into dinner. The reality is that most freelancers think they're going wild if they take their coat to the dry cleaners during working hours.

The following Monday morning I fought against it all. I put the guitar in its case and took the bus up to Hampstead Heath, the huge hilly park in North London that is the closest the city gets to a piece of countryside. With its beech tree woods and muddy streams, the Heath has a Blakeian tranquillity, especially on a weekday morning at the end of July after days of heavy rain, when it is almost empty and the earth is thick with moisture and things that crawl. I was going to play to the logs, and the trees, and any birds that cared to listen in.

Just as the lute was a symbol of cosmic accord in Renaissance Europe, so my guitar would chime with the music of the spheres in twenty-first-century London. The guitar was to provide an escape from a world of familiar routes and heads turned towards the pavement. People looked up to musicians because they were apparently free of the concerns that engulf the lives of so many of us. Davey Graham sounded like he had surrendered to an extreme form of eccentricity to follow his muse. Presumably Django Reinhardt never worried about which bank account he should open. Teddy Paige used the guitar to remove himself from all the usual problems of life. Admittedly, he replaced them with a whole new set, but at least they were interesting problems.

Now that I had a guitar, I too would be released from mind-forged manacles. My stage would be the land, my audience the animals of the forest.

Deep in the heart of the Heath is a clearing in a wood of

beeches where there is one solitary hollow tree. It has always been one of my favourite places, not least because climbing inside a tree is one of the great joys of childhood that one should never feel the need to grow out of. It was here that I had come as a teenager with friends to smoke joints and then feel slightly guilty about it when some small children appeared and wondered what the smell was. I had taken Otto to this tree and he had loved it; one Saturday our entire family had had a picnic inside it. This was to be the spot that would inspire my new guitar-liberated life.

I climbed in through one of the holes at the side of the trunk and strummed my way through 'You Can't Always Get What You Want'. Continued practice to the point of NJ's nausea had meant that I had pretty much mastered it in a basic fashion. It sounded nice in the acoustics of the hollow tree. Dappled sunlight broke through the canopy of branches above and a dog barked in the distance. The laminated back of the guitar sat on my lap, and I sat in the ancient grooves of the gnarled old tree, and it was good.

This would be the ideal way to prepare myself for the concert in five months' time. I could come here every weekday morning and it wouldn't even matter if it were raining because the tree would protect me from the elements. In such a setting it would be easy to develop one's own unique style, and no doubt the spirits of the forest would lend a helping hand in providing inspiration. When I was a twelve-year-old boy I had gone on a weekend break with a friend whose father lived in Dorset. The boy's dishy elder sister had befriended some hippies who lived in a log hut in the woods. They had constructed their own stage for mini-festivals, and in their encampment they had set up what seemed to my impressionable mind to be the perfect life. One of the hippies, Spider I think it was, sat under a tree and strummed his guitar while the elder sister closed her eyes and moaned in far-out communion. In all the years since I had held that image in my mind as something I would like to immerse myself in one day.

It was almost perfect. But as is so often the case when nirvana is in sight, along comes dirty reality to pull you down. An acrid whiff of dog shit had been dancing lightly around my nostrils ever since I got inside the tree. I assumed that there must be a bit on the bottom of my shoe, but couldn't see any. Then I realized. I was sitting in it. What kind of a dog climbs inside a hollow tree, finds a nice reclining spot on the inside trunk, and crimps one off? It was all over the seat of my jeans. I tried using a stick to get the worst of it off and only succeeded in getting it on my hands. The foul smell of an evil mutt's arse-paste dominated everything.

I put the guitar in its case and headed towards a nearby pond to wash my hands. In order to get to the water you had to walk a few feet into muddy banks, and, being ill equipped to deal with anything other than concrete beneath my feet, I had not thought of changing my footwear – black leather slip-on brogues – for this rural outing. In my desperation to rid myself of the demonic stench of canine turd I didn't think for a minute that these shoes might get stuck in the mud. My right shoe sank into the cold, wet swamp and stayed there when I pulled my leg up to release it. Yanking the shoe out of the mud resulted in my knee falling into it. Entirely defeated, I sat down in the pond.

There was no point enduring this torture any more. I had played guitar for all of ten minutes before being assaulted by mud, water and faeces. I plodded through the woods, cursing and thinking about Django Reinhardt looking suave as he played his custom-built Maccaferri on the steps of his caravan, a benign smile coursing the line of his moustache, and wondered how my noble efforts could have gone so wrong.

That night, NJ and I went into our little basement room. She read and I strummed away at the guitar. There is a song that Dylan wrote and The Byrds covered on their country-rock album *Sweetheart Of The Rodeo* called 'You Ain't Going No-where'. At that time The Byrds had two master guitarists among their number: Roger McGuinn, whose 12-string electric Rickenbacker gave the early albums by the sixties LA band their unique jingle-jangle sound; and Gram Parsons, the short-lived country-rock pioneer who created what he called 'cosmic American music' – white country with the depth of feeling of black soul. With these two in their ranks, The Byrds were capable of incredible things. But *Sweetheart Of The Rodeo* was the album on which they stripped things down. 'You Ain't Going Nowhere' is a beautiful lament made of three chords: G, A minor and C. Pete Millson had shown me how you could link them with a simple rhythm.

While NJ sipped at a glass of bourbon with ice and read David Niven's memoirs, I had a go at the rolling, gentle sound of 'You Ain't Going Nowhere'. Something happened: I could play it. Pretty much anyone, after a couple of hours' practice, can play it too. Once I got going I couldn't stop. I must have rolled over those same three chords for an hour.

'That's a lovely sound,' said NJ with a smile, and went back to reading her book.

Ordinary people with a natural tendency towards sanity and guilt, who do not have any particular musical talent and who do not have the character to liberate themselves from normal routines, can still express something profound with the guitar.

That realization came on a Monday night. The following

Sunday we went for a walk and a picnic on Hampstead Heath, as we often do, settling on a patch of grass under a tree without too many stinging nettles and no dog shit. Otto attempted to ride his bicycle down a hill on a path nearby. Pearl tried to fight her way into a large packet of crisps. NJ, in her suede waistcoat and long skirt, looked like she was posing for a fashion shoot for a 1974 edition of *Vogue*. I played my guitar. It was pleasant to sit there with my family, making simple music.

We had packed up and were about to leave the Heath when something happened that ensured I could never abandon this journey I'd now begun. I was pushing Pearl in her pram, three carrier bags and a guitar case hanging off its handles, along a path that is lined by a series of ponds. This is the busiest section of the park, and on that Sunday there were couples, old ladies, joggers, screaming children and dogs filling up the path. Otto was moaning about wanting to go on my shoulders and NJ was dragging his bicycle, when we heard the familiar sounds of a crumhorn and a cittern, those medieval instruments I had seen Circulus play a few weeks earlier. Michael Tyack and Will Summers were walking towards us, Tyack in a black frock coat and wide-brimmed hat that made him look like a seventeenth-century witchfinder and Summers in a purple velvet cape and hat, playing a fanfare for their approach.

They were on their way to a musical picnic deep in the woods of the Heath, at a point that was said to have particular earthly significance because of its cross-section of ley lines. It sounded tempting but it was a fair walk and the children were tired. Tyack asked me how I was getting on with the guitar.

'It's been slow, but at least I can play something now,' I told him, and got the guitar out of the case to demonstrate. I knocked out 'You Ain't Going Nowhere'. After a couple of rounds Tyack joined in on his cittern, which is much smaller than a normal guitar but, with its four courses of strings, can still make quite a noise. He added a different melody that was based on my rhythm. Will Summers nodded his head a few times before accompanying us with some vigorous blasts on the crumhorn. It was my first jam: an outdoor medieval/country strum that sounded so much better than the sum of its parts. Playing with two excellent musicians certainly made my own contribution sound good.

We played kneeling down on the grass, a few feet away from the path. A little boy ran past with his fingers in his ears and an old lady who had been feeding the ducks shook her head in theatrical horror, but everyone else smiled as they went by and a few even stayed a while. A middle-aged woman in an Indian skirt and beads started dancing barefoot until a fast-moving Staffordshire bull terrier tripped her over. Otto sat down and quietly watched, stunned into silence and contemplation by the event. Pearl even seemed to be appreciating it in her own infant way. It was a perfect moment, and one that was impossible to repeat, capture or exploit.

Chapter Three

The People's Guitar

'It's all folk music.' That's a phrase you read a lot in interviews with musicians. They are probably referring to the fact that a blues man whose name escapes me once said that he hadn't heard of any music that wasn't made by folk. (I have – music made by animals such as birds and whales.) But it's not true. Classical music, for example, is not folk music because it utilizes complex structures that are not about a single voice reflecting on their situation or the world around them. Jazz is not folk music because it works so much in the abstract. And the vast majority of rock isn't folk either because as soon as most guitar-based bands develop a certain degree of proficiency, they want to show off their new skills with endless guitar solos. Fretology – the advanced science of the electric guitar – is rather like having a modern car equipped with every gadget and status-enhancing addition but without a decent engine inside.

I loved the fact that I could play The Byrds' version of Bob Dylan's 'You Ain't Going Nowhere' despite being such a novice, and that Roger McGuinn, who having played since the age of twelve was, by 1968, at the height of his powers, chose to stick to the song's three-chord sequence because the sentiment he wished to convey desired it. Three years previously McGuinn was combining John Coltrane's modal lines with

Ravi Shankar's ragas and reinterpreting them for a 12-string electric Rickenbacker on 'Eight Miles High', but for 'You Ain't Going Nowhere' what was needed was simplicity. The song is guided by the same spirit as Christianity, Islam, Buddhism and pretty much every other world religion: the idea that we need to take our own egos out of the equation in order to see what's necessary, to make a real contribution, and to focus on the core of value in what we do. That's not to say that, come the big night of the debut gig, I didn't expect an onslaught of screaming fans, record company executives and beautiful groupie chicks to collapse after my 38-minute solo induced mass hysteria through every inch of whatever mega-stadium I'd be playing in. But right now I liked people who kept it simple.

The acoustic guitar was made for folk music. In the troubadour tradition that Django Reinhardt and Teddy Paige were a part of, young men and women sought to express something about their world through their voice and guitar. Often a few well-strummed or picked chords were enough to act as vehicles for the words. For the same reason that nineteenth-century Europe saw a boom in the guitar being used by the common man and woman – because it was affordable – so did the twentieth century see a new generation of people who wanted to explore, live cheaply, and comment on what they found out there. The guitar was the only instrument for the job.

America was the place for the twentieth-century's acoustic guitar revolution. It was a new country, with all the problems and advantages that brings. The ancient cultures – India, Africa, Europe and Russia – have musical traditions that are complex and weighed down by centuries of shared experience. But America, historically speaking, is fresh. It can produce simplicity without affectation. And the country's size invites travel. A guitar is light and cheap enough to take on that journey.

Because the acoustic guitar was so central to American folk music's image of itself, the arrival of the electric guitar in the middle of the twentieth century became a political issue. At the 1963 Newport Festival of Folk and Blues songwriters like Pete Seeger and Phil Ochs sang earnestly about banning the bomb; two years later Bob Dylan appeared at the same festival with The Paul Butterfield Blues Band and an electric guitar and Pete Seeger – Mr Peace – was trying to pull the amplifier plugs out of their sockets. The king of folk purity was Seeger's old travelling partner Woody Guthrie, who had journeyed through the dustbowls of Depression-era America to sing songs that championed the underdog, mocked the establishment, and could be learned by anyone with an acoustic guitar in a matter of weeks. He became a symbol of all that was good and wholesome at a time when the electric guitar was celebrating the modern age. The traditional folk crowd hated rock'n'roll and the materialistic world of girls, cars and electric guitars that went with it, but the appeal of folk music is its simplicity and honesty, not the type of guitar it is made on. As a protest song, 'Satisfaction' by The Rolling Stones has stayed the course far better than 'We Shall Overcome'.

Nothing beats an acoustic guitar to get going on because it is self-contained. An electric guitar needs an amplifier, a power supply and, preferably, a bassist, drummer, a lead singer and an audience to go with whatever you play on it. An acoustic guitar can be used to make music anywhere you want, from a bedroom to a desolate hillside to a railway station. Following my disastrous attempt to sing to the logs of Hampstead Heath I still wanted to go in search of the folk music traditions that grew out of this freedom.

I heard about a festival in Cornwall called Tapestry Goes West. Held in a re-creation of a Wild West town near the wilds of Newquay, the festival was an offshoot of a night in a working man's club in London that NJ and I sometimes went to. It was small-scale – only a couple of hundred people were expected – with a rock, folk and country line-up of mostly unknown bands. It was organized by a plasterer from Camden in North London called Barry Stillwell, who was doing it all on so little money – there was certainly no corporate sponsorship, nor was it wanted – that Barry had pawned his vintage Fender Telecaster to pay for the advertising posters. Circulus were on the bill, bringing their medieval folk fantasy to the West Country, and that was good enough for me. It was decided that the whole family, plus Doyle, would go down to Cornwall for the festival in search of the ancient folk spirit of the acoustic guitar. So we packed up guitars, children and tents (and Doyle), and made the seven-hour drive from London to Cornwall.

It didn't get off to a good start. After a night of heavy rain, the hillside field that was to be the campsite was sodden and muddy; Circulus had already managed to get their car stuck in a bog after deciding they couldn't be bothered to make the quarter-of-a-mile walk from the car park to the campsite. Doyle's tent wasn't a tent at all: it was a Wendy House (his mother had packed it for him). Our tent had the small but significant problem of missing one of its poles, which meant that it stood rather limply. I told NJ and Otto that if we all ensured that we slept right in the middle of the tent and didn't touch the sides all night, we should be fine.

We headed down to the festival site. It really was an authentic cowboy town complete with saloon, sheriff's office, jail and cantina, where a large Cornish woman with enormous pink plastic-framed glasses served deep-fried chips and greasy burgers in polystyrene containers. Some dour Cornish cowboys fired off cap guns upon our arrival, which excited Otto. We

wandered around the Wild West set until we found the stage
for the bands.

A death metal band were leaping around the stage as the lead
singer growled 'Fuck you all' into his microphone while the
guitarist was bent double over his instrument, his long hair
fringing the floor. Otto started headbanging in the large empty
space in front of the stage. Pearl burst into tears. It came to an
end when the guitarist took his black Gibson Les Paul and
raised it above his head as if he was about to sacrifice it to the
crazy gods of endless noise. He started twirling it around and for
one hopeful moment I thought he was going to ram it into the
amplifier, but he brought it down and made do with carefully
leaning it against the amp to create a screeching feedback that
lasted for about ten seconds before the sound was cut off. Then a
Cornish cowboy got up on stage and announced that certain
people had been seen urinating in the bushes rather than in the
designated overflowing urinals, and if these renegade pissers
were caught a posse of yokels would round them up and drive
them out of town, to fend for themselves in the wilds of the
nearest dual carriageway.

Things improved after the death metal lot cleared off. As the
sun went down the extremely muddy members of Circulus took
to the stage, and Michael Tyack's cittern made an ancient hum
against the backdrop of the fading Cornish light. With songs
about magical creatures and brave deeds by knights in suits of
rusting armour Circulus seemed like the very best kind of folk
band, celebrating the mysteries of history and the lineage of
English music while never taking anything too seriously. It felt
suited to the environment that, despite the best efforts of the
redneck nerds who ran the place, was as provincially English as
they come.

Circulus improved all of our moods and from then on

Tapestry Goes West did indeed feel like a proper folk festival. There was no backstage area and no distinction between the bands playing and the audience, which was mostly made up of people in bands anyway, and guitars dominated. Some children who turned out to be brothers and sisters called Kitty, Daisy and Lewis played heartbreaking country-folk songs on a big old Gibson acoustic guitar, harmonica and accordion. By nightfall our own children needed to sleep and it was obvious that my plan of us all bedding down in the tent was not being received warmly by the rest of the family, who took the car to go to NJ's parents' house about half an hour away. So Doyle and I, now very drunk, made the most of the campfire scene that developed after the bands had stopped playing.

There were three or four campfires up on the field with the tents, each with its own atmosphere. At the first we arrived at a loudmouthed Irishman was singing rude ditties in a belting tone with accompaniment from a man with two sticks and a biscuit tin. It was an impromptu show for the Irishman's talents and the spirit of folkie democracy was not to be found. Doyle wandered off, and eventually I did too – it becomes quite hard to leave a campfire surrounded by people you don't know for fear of looking conspicuous – to find my friend stumbling about in the dark.

'I went to a fire at the bottom of the hill but nobody would talk to me,' said Doyle, who was much drunker than I was; you could tell by the way his eyeballs were heading off in different directions. 'Come on and join me so I've got someone to talk to.' We stumbled down over myriad guy-ropes to find about ten people standing around discussing politics in an earnest fashion. 'This fire's surrounded by a bunch of geeks,' shouted Doyle. 'Let's go.'

The third campfire was much better. A skinny man with

glasses was standing up and playing rock'n'roll and blues on a battered guitar while everyone else was sitting down and singing cheerfully. Confusingly, Doyle shouted, 'This fire's so gay,' which got him a few stern looks, before concurring: 'It's gay, but it's warm,' and he collapsed next to it. The wood smoke and tinny acoustic guitar went well together, and someone was passing round a bottle of Jack Daniel's. I wanted to get up and have a go at the guitar but did not feel ready to face an audience yet, albeit a very gentle and small one. Two longhaired girls were swaying as they sang the words to 'Sloop John B'. It was a mellow scene. Then the man with the guitar said: 'Does anyone else want a go?'

Doyle galvanized himself into action. After a couple of botched attempts he managed to stand up and put the guitar around his neck. He strummed loosely before closing his eyes and, in a high, croaky voice, singing the words to the chorus of 'Proud Mary' by Creedence Clearwater Revival. At first the hippies around the fire did their best to sing along. Then it became clear that Doyle was only going to sing the chorus, again and again, with the odd line from one of the verses transplanted into it. He sounded like he was crying, although this was just his drunken attempt to inject some emotion into the delivery. After a while he reduced the song to its core: the line 'Rolling, rolling, rolling down the river' over and over again to an open strum on the guitar. Its owner began to twitch nervously. Nobody was singing along any more. People were looking sober, even worried.

Fifteen minutes later Doyle stopped singing altogether, although he continued to mouth the words. His feet remained firmly planted in the same place, about a foot from each other, and his mouth and fingers were the only part of his body moving. One by one, people were leaving the campfire. On more than one occasion the owner of the guitar hesitantly tapped Doyle on the shoulder, but he got no response. Every now and then Doyle would sing a random word from the song. Finally it came to an end. 'It carries on a bit longer but I've had enough,' said Doyle. 'You can't expect me to play all night.' Everyone had gone apart from the guitar's owner and myself.

The songs that dominated the campfire sessions at Tapestry Goes West were all by Bob Dylan. I came late to Bob. With the exception of *The Basement Tapes*, the rough collection of songs old and new that he made with The Band at their house in Woodstock, upstate New York in 1967 that was eventually released in 1975, I couldn't be bothered with him at all until a few years ago. He was clearly a genius, but that doesn't mean one necessarily wants to listen to him when '1969' by The Stooges is so much more happening. The earnest older kids at school always liked him, and you could be guaranteed to find at least one Bob Dylan album alongside *Legend* by Bob Marley, *Bridge Over Troubled Water* by Simon & Garfunkel and *Making Movies* by Dire Straits in the record collection of every square in town. Dylan was so much a part of the classic canon that it didn't seem like you had to go near him. But you can ease into Bob and come to him when you're ready – he will be there – and as soon as I picked up the guitar he made perfect sense. Whether he created his music with an electric rock band or on an unaccompanied acoustic, he really did make folk music. Whatever instrument he played was only there to act as a vehicle for words that tore deep into what it means to be alive and curious.

The Basement Tapes is one of those records that make you want to learn how to play guitar. Before NJ and I had children we used to go to a dilapidated little cottage in a village called Battlesden, about fifty miles from London. Our friend Stacey's long-divorced parents had rented the cottage since the sixties and they still only paid £10 a week for it. There were three rooms on the ground floor of the cottage: a tiny kitchen with an ancient stove that leaked so much gas that striking a match to light it meant a blast in your face that burnt off your hair; a living room with a fireplace that had to be lit immediately upon arrival to clear the house of damp and heat up the water for a bath the following morning; and an always-freezing back room filled with books and cardboard boxes that revealed hidden treasures for anyone with a passing interest in the 1960s and 1970s. In one such box was a stack of scratchy vinyl and in another was a Dansette record player that, with a bit of tweaking, worked. On the weekend we discovered these Rosetta Stones *The Basement Tapes* was the only album that got played. It provided the perfect soundtrack for a world of nature and friendship, of chopping logs before burning them to keep warm and boiling water in a kettle to brew tea in a chipped brown pot, where a bottle of cheap whisky, some tobacco, good friends and a chair to sit on were all that was needed to be at peace with the world.

The Basement Tapes sums up the appeal of the folk guitar, even though it also has a seesawing organ, clanking drums, Dylan's nasal, frequently sarcastic whine and Robbie Robertson's softer, sadder voice. But the songs, from a sing-along about an apple suckling tree to a story about going to see a prostitute and hoping that nobody finds out, all have the spirit of a guitar at their core. They sound like they were made for the joy of making music together and they probably were, given that they were recorded on amateur-quality home equipment and not released until eight years after the session. You wanted to be there with them, amongst the nice old instruments and the creaking floorboards, were it not for the fact that listening to the record in Battlesden was just about perfect anyway.

On those weekends none of us – Stacey, her boyfriend Will, NJ nor myself – could play guitar. Cranking the old Dansette into action was enough back then, but now I can see how great it would have been to have a guitar with us. I hope one day to go back to Battlesden, with a few of the songs from *The Basement Tapes* under my belt, and sit next to that fireplace in the old armchair, and bore everyone to tears with endless renditions of them.

As far as learning the guitar is concerned, folk music is a good place to start because it does not place an emphasis on virtuosity or knowledge. The singer-songwriters like Dylan and Leonard Cohen played imaginative but straightforward guitar to get their words across, and the folkies didn't emphasize difficult sequences but the value of droning notes, minor chords and repeated motifs. I still needed a way of approaching folk guitar myself, though. Then I struck gold. I was idling through a creaking second-hand bookshop in Highgate, North London, when I came across a book called *The Penguin Folk Guitar Manual*. On the first page was a line drawing of a bearded hippie, who looked rather similar to the one in *The Joy Of Sex*, holding an acoustic guitar. The book was written by John Pearse, who turned out to be a Welshman chiefly responsible for turning a generation on to the joys of the acoustic guitar in the mid-seventies through his BBC television series *Hold Down A Chord*. While Ralph Denyer's *The Guitar Handbook*, although thorough and informative, appeared to insist you had to learn about all kinds of complicated things without ever actually telling you how to knock out a tune, Pearse's *Folk Guitar Manual* broke everything right down and took the reader through each step as if its author was right there with them, and the end result was a song you could play. 'Got that? Good,' he encourages after some of the exercises, optimistically

assuming that every single person who uses the book will
indeed get the hang of playing the guitar as long as they follow
his step-by-step approach. 'You're doing really well. I think
you're ready to move on to the next exercise.' One might take it
as patronizing; I found it reassuring.

Pearse tells you everything, from holding the guitar the right
way to the length your nails should be. There are several pages
devoted to playing a single chord (G). And there are songs along
the way as you learn each new step – the first, 'Three Blind
Mice', consists of three chords that anyone could play, even me.
I don't know if I could get away with including 'Three Blind
Mice' in my set list for the big show in four months' time, but it
was good to have it in the can (perhaps for the encore). Pearse
came across as a nice old hippie, too: the kind of uncle you
dream about having, who would have had a stack of great
records, some underground comics like *The Fabulous Furry Freak
Brothers* and Robert Crumb's confessionals of misadventures
with Amazonian beauties, and if you're really lucky, a stash of
marijuana in his basement den. What better person to guide
you through the guitar and perhaps even life itself?

In the preface, Pearse explains how he got frustrated at the
thought that although his television show reached a wide
audience, he could not be there for every person who wanted
to pick up the guitar. People often didn't have access to a
teacher, and if they did that teacher might be set in their ways
and not open to new approaches. Pearse was, back in the
seventies, there to help. He would be patient with you as
you admitted that, two months into learning, you still had
nothing more to show for your efforts than the opening bars to
'You Can't Always Get What You Want' and the three-chord
strum of 'You Ain't Going Nowhere'. That evening I picked up
the guitar and followed Pearse's instructions to the letter. 'Don't

move your hand, just move your fingers,' said Pearse as I struggled to get from G to C in time. (I imagined his voice to be a slow and reassuring Welsh burr, slightly muffled through his beard.) 'OK, relax your hands for a moment, get up and walk about the room for a few minutes, make a cup of coffee, straighten out those cramped finger joints. When you're ready, try again.'

'Ah, you're right! That's much better now!'

'Who are you talking to?' asked NJ, who had sought solace from my guitar's invasion of her peace in the novels of E. F. Benson.

'My new guitar tutor,' I told her.

'You're taking this whole thing too seriously,' she said, before digging herself further into the chair and doing her best to ignore me. 'Can't you give it a rest? It's impossible to concentrate.'

Despite everything that has happened in the last hundred years or so people still like to play the acoustic guitar, and I wanted to talk to someone of my own generation who was following its tradition. (After all, technology has taken us a long way from the folk boom of the sixties, yet people are still making a living by playing guitars. The worst concert I ever went to consisted of a man staring at a laptop and I have no desire to see someone 'playing' a computer ever again.) I had been listening to an American singer called Chan Marshall, who performs under the name Cat Power. The Atlanta, Georgia-born Marshall made sweet songs that sounded like the product of an unhinged personality. The guitar was the most suitable tool to get her message across: there was no virtuosity in her playing, but it wasn't trite either.

Chan Marshall seemed like a good person to pick up a few

tips on the guitar from, so I managed to blag an hour in a hotel
room with her when she was in London. A pretty thirty-year-
old with long hair, a sexy southern drawl and a flirtatious
manner, she wasn't the most stable of people. Every incident
that she recollected seemed to end in disaster. She picked up
and put down a few times the guitar that she had in the corner
of the room, but never actually played it. She was in the middle
of an endless tour that sounded like it took in half the world.
'What else am I meant to do?' she said, when I asked her why
she was undergoing this gruelling endurance test. 'My boyfriend left me for another woman. What else am I meant to do?'

It became clear that Marshall belonged to a folk music
tradition of tragedy and heartache. 'I was working as a waitress
in Atlanta when my boyfriend passed away and I completely
lost my mind,' she said, staying under the covers of her bed and
smoking one cigarette after another. 'Then my best friend died
of Aids . . . Everyone I loved in Atlanta was on heroin and it
was really awful and gross so I went to New York . . . I got a job
in a restaurant because my boyfriend was fucking the owner, a
married woman with two kids, when I thought he was just
fucking me . . .'

Compelling and tragic though Marshall's misadventures
were, I was more hoping that she might let me in on the
secrets of her craft. I asked her but she either ignored or didn't
hear my request. Instead, she told me about her relationship
with the instrument, and about her musical career, which she
claimed was something of an accident. Having lived an itinerant childhood at the behest of her hippy mother, she settled in
Atlanta as a teenager and joined the city's underground music
scene. At the age of sixteen she bought a Silvertone electric
guitar because she had a crush on the guitarist of a local band
called The Flat Duo Jets, who had one. For years the guitar

served only as an ornament, propped up in the corner of Marshall's bedroom but never touched. 'All these guys would come round and say: "Yeah, I can teach you everything you need to know in three weeks," ' she said, affecting a deep, macho tone. 'But I only bought it because I loved Dexter from The Flat Duo Jets. One afternoon I was bored, so I picked it up. Then I got thinking: "This isn't so hard . . ." ' Then she disappeared into a taxi to be whisked off to a television studio and I never saw her again.

A bit closer to home was Mr David Viner, a young man from Finchley in North London who was busy singing and playing his guitar anywhere that would have him. Viner had made a great album at Liam Watson's Toe-Rag Studios called *This Boy Don't Care*, in which he sang songs about his troubles with women, his fantasies about killing people, and stories about sailors returning home after seven years at sea to find their wives married to other men. His lyrics had a dark edge but the songs were quite innocent, really, and most consisted of nothing more than Viner accompanying himself on an electro-acoustic guitar. Much as I liked the modern American folk singers, I could relate to Viner more, and there was something very British about his attempts to sound like a world-weary man with lines on his brow that have been chiselled by tough experience despite being a privileged Jewish boy from Hampstead Garden Suburb. A few days after my aborted attempt to get a guitar lesson from Chan Marshall, I gave him a call.

He was happy to drop by our flat with his guitar in hand one afternoon, after our telephone conversation had revealed a shared love of English acoustic players like Davey Graham and Bert Jansch alongside American blues singers such as Mississippi John Hurt and John Lee Hooker. I was older than Viner, and once you get over thirty it is almost expected of you to develop an interest in dead blues men, but Viner was only twenty-four, so his musical tastes were a little more surprising. 'When I was seventeen I discovered my uncle's record collection,' he said by way of explanation. 'All these great old records had so much more depth than whatever it was my friends were listening to at the time, and the music still seemed relevant. People don't really change that much, after all.'

Viner was a pleasant fellow; a laconic man with a dry sense of humour and what seemed like enough patience to deal with my pedestrian approach to the guitar. I was keen to encourage him to be another teacher for me, and as an unemployable youth without any real responsibilities he had the luxury of being able to spend five hours of every day sitting at home and practising. His songwriting technique involved exploring the instrument for a couple of hours until he came up with the bare bones of a melody, which he then put lyrics to. He demonstrated a few tunes he had fashioned recently.

'I learned strictly from listening to records,' he said. I told him that I wasn't good enough to listen to a record and be able to copy whatever it was they were doing. 'Well, neither was I, really,' he replied. 'But you can get an idea of the rhythm and the strumming. The problem was that I really liked the sound of finger-picking and I had no idea how to do that. I went to a guy who runs a folk club in Crouch End and asked him for a couple of lessons. He asked me what I could play and I ran through a Big Bill Broonzy piece I had learned. He shook his head and said: "No, that won't do at all." So he showed me a few exercises and after a few months I got the hang of playing an alternating bass line, which makes all the difference. Then I went back to the records and I could copy them much better. I think that's the best way of approaching it.'

I demonstrated to Viner my mastery of 'Three Blind Mice',

using John Pearse's excellent three fingers-and-thumb technique. 'That's good,' he said, unconvincingly, 'but it will sound really good if you use an alternating bass line.' He explained that this meant hitting the lowest string with your thumb, playing the three top strings with your fingers, and then playing the second lowest string with your thumb, thereby creating a driving sound with a lot more flavour and rhythm. I tried it. It wasn't so hard. 'See? It sounds really varied but you're not actually doing very much.'

All the songs I had learned so far consisted of three chords. This was meant to be the irreducible amount of skill you needed to play guitar and, according to the punk-rock ethos of 1977, there wasn't much point in learning anything else. But it might get a little boring to play the same three chords for the rest of your life. 'Three chords is enough to do something, but if you add a minor chord you can make it so much more interesting,' suggested Viner. The minor chords, which are created by taking one of the notes in a major chord down a semi-tone, have a melancholic, softer quality and give a completely different colour to a song. Folk music depends heavily on the use of minor chords.

'You don't really have to go mad and play all kinds of weird chords,' said Viner, picking out a few notes on his battered guitar. 'I would have no idea where a G major fourth was, for example, and I still stick to the twelve principal major and minor chords in the first positions. You can also completely change the tone of a song by moving it up a key. There's a song by a blues guy called Reverend Gary Davis that I moved up from C to D and it was completely different. But, then, why stop anywhere? You can keep exploring the guitar for ever and ever. I've got by so far just by knowing the standard chords and adding bits with my little finger.'

If humans had only three fingers on each hand most folk music would not exist. Nearly all standard chord shapes use the first two or three fingers and leave the little finger free. But if you play a standard chord and then add the little finger somewhere you can often get a great spooky sound that instantly creates images of dark-eyed maidens with long plaited hair prostrating themselves before a sacred stone while a group of children wearing horses' heads dance around a maypole nearby and a toothless undertaker cackles as night falls on an unkempt graveyard. It doesn't always work, but pressing down the little finger to add another note to an open chord can really do some remarkable things. You need to know a certain amount of structure to be able to play the guitar, but you can also create a lot of music just by exploring the instrument at random.

Then Viner played, without any prompting from me, his own take on Davey Graham's 'Anji'. He had worked out how to do it by listening to versions of the song by Bert Jansch and Simon & Garfunkel. It is said that there was a period in the mid-sixties in England when you could walk down the hallways of any student union and you would hear someone attempting to play it. Mastering 'Anji' is one of the folk guitar rites of passage and it remains one of the best songs ever written. It sounds melancholic and evocative, it utilizes many techniques of guitar playing like bends, hammer-ons and pull-offs, and it requires the player to keep a bass line going at the same time as a melody. In other words, it's bloody impossible. It was the first song Viner ever learned to play the whole way through, or at least he claimed it was. I wondered if I really would be able to play this song when my six months were up.

Viner tried to demonstrate how 'Anji' was played – and the frustrating thing is that the entire song is based around the

chord of A minor, making it, in essence, very simple indeed –
but I couldn't begin to get my fingers to do all the things they
needed to do. Viner realized this and gave up trying to show
me. 'It's going to take some time to play "Anji" because you
have to do two different things at once – the rhythm on the bass
strings and the melody on the treble – but you'll get there if you
keep at it,' he said. 'My only real advice about the guitar is to
keep going for more than three months. That seems to be the
cut-off point because it's around then that people get good at
playing one song and never do anything else. I remember how a
friend at school could play the theme tune to James Bond really
well, and he left it at that. It's so liberating to be able to play, to
learn new things and keep going for ever – there's Hawaiian
guitars, slide guitars . . . it's an endless journey.'

Viner was a good person to talk to about the folk guitar,
not just because I liked his style, but also because he was
trying to make a living from it, constantly doing shows and
writing songs and surviving on the little money he made from
gigs. When he came over for that afternoon in September
2004 he was, admittedly, yet to take over the world – his
album had sold around seven hundred copies – but he was
original and he had talent. He was thinking about buying a
motorcycle with a sidecar for his guitar to get from one
performance to another. He had played at The Royal Festival
Hall, one of London's most prestigious venues, and he was
dealing with the problems of being a young folk and blues
singer playing to audiences more used to rowdy rock'n'roll.
'People talk a lot during my gigs,' he said with a sigh. 'I
suppose they've gone out to drink and have a good time so
you can't really blame them too much, but it does get
annoying. I used to shout and tell them to shut up, but
now if it gets really loud I just try to play louder and shock

them into listening. Mind you, often I can't even hear what I'm doing. I need a sound man. And a roadie, a masseur, a chef, groupies . . .'

I foresaw another problem to my proposed live performance, which was now only four months away. People like Cat Power and Viner had presence and charisma and that was just as important as the music they were playing. I had thought it would be enough to learn the guitar and get up on stage. But you had to write songs – that meant not just coming up with the music but thinking of some words, too – and you had to talk to the audience, draw them into your world, and amuse them. I hated all that. When I was at school in an English class I used to be terrified if it was my turn to read from whatever book we were studying at the time. I could never have dreamt of getting up in front of the entire school and doing some sort of turn as so many of my fellow pupils did. I was not – am not – a natural performer.

There was hope, though. Viner was an affable, smart and reasonably normal young man, and quite shy really. He managed to find something within himself to make an impact on stage. He admitted to still finding the whole thing terrifying, stating that he had never been so scared in his life as when he took to the stage at the Royal Festival Hall, where there was twenty feet of emptiness on either side of him and a huge auditorium full of people before him. If you could play in a place like that and rise to the occasion while still keeping the excitement you get from discovering something new on the guitar in your living room, then magic could happen.

Viner had showed me a technique to be getting on with – the alternating bass line – but that evening a strange and rather self-indulgent depression set in. The usual ritual of getting the children to eat something and then go to bed passed without surprise or incident. Otto rubbed his pasta into the table and had a bit of a Victorian moment when he insisted on calling me Father (it didn't last). Pearl ate some of hers and threw the rest on the floor, and then they both demanded to watch a feature-length cartoon called *Lilo & Stitch*, which, incidentally, has some great guitar sequences: the story of a lonely little Hawaiian girl who adopts a genetically created alien built to destroy everything, it's a sweet film about friendship and family. When Lilo is feeling sad she listens to Elvis Presley records and Stitch, being super-intelligent, picks up the guitar and learns to play 'Burning Love' in about five seconds. It put Otto in a good mood and he went to bed peacefully. Pearl followed soon after. NJ and I went into our basement at about nine o'clock, as we did every night, and I picked up the guitar. I was running over the same chords I had been playing for the past two months. The simplicity of the guitar is a potential pitfall: it can stop you from progressing.

It was a rut. I would pick up the guitar, put it down, stare at it, pick it up again, and let it rest on my lap. Those three chords I kept playing sounded good together, in the same way that some cheddar cheese, a dash of pickle and two slices of bread will make a good sandwich, but the glory of this classic combination fades when you have it for lunch every day. I've seen it happen: people get so attached to a certain style of dress or a certain routine that they favour them to the exclusion of everything else and they go mouldy. Such self-imposed constrictions eat into the soul. I put the guitar down and NJ put her feet up on my knees.

'What are you doing?' I asked, pointing to her feet.

'What does it look like I'm doing?'

'That space is reserved for my guitar.'

'You love that guitar more than you love me,' she sniffed.

I didn't, but it tormented me as much as NJ did. It wasn't a case of being a beginner and not being able to do much; it was more the feeling that I didn't have the imagination to really explore the instrument and express myself through it, which was the whole point. And thus my romantic dream of being like the people I admired, of liberating myself with the guitar, could never happen. I wasn't free to sleep in the hay of an abandoned barn where the stars shone through the broken thatches of the roof and the wind cried through the old oak trees outside. I couldn't sing for my supper in little bars in Italy and Spain or write odes to the spiders that crawled out of the logs by the fire where I sat and played. Like most other people in the world (including the country singer Merle Haggard, who wrote a great song about it), I had to be a working man damn near all my life.

It took a little reflection to realize that my dissatisfaction was born of vanity. I thought about all the different people I had played guitar with so far. Not a single one of them had the same approach. Doyle, the drunken wild man whose nights out generally end up with his having one less tooth in his mouth, only ever tried to emulate seventies rock songs exactly as they were first played; Pete Millson, whose idea of going wild involves taking his wife out to the local Pizza Express once a month, never tried to play anything that had been written before but let a pleasant and imaginative if unchallenging melody fashion itself in the moment. I was only depressed at not being able to conform to a shallow image of bohemianism. No two people on the planet are the same. The folk guitar can be used in the same way as a pen or a brush or a voice: as an extension of what it means to be human. There's no point in feeling bad about your lack of ability or imagination. As long as you stick with it, inspiration will come in some form. But you do need to push yourself into new directions every now and then. It was time to look beyond the cheese and pickle of the three chords I knew and take a flight into the cosmos. For this, I would need to have a good pilot or two to guide me on my journey. I knew where to look.

Chapter Four

The Cosmic Guitarist

Ever since lutenists strived to play their instruments in accordance with the divine symmetry of the universe, the guitar and its ancestors have been involved in a process of cosmic exploration. While nothing beats knocking out 'Wild Thing' by The Troggs at the end of a drunken night (it's easy: you play E, A and B, and back again until the chorus, which is E, G and F), there is something to be said for searching a little deeper with the instrument; tapping into sounds that forge an expanded consciousness. Just as the Hare Krishnas you see chanting down the high street are transporting themselves to the outer reaches of the universe through their saffron-clad tambourine and drum bashing, so the mind-expanding guitarist raises him or herself out of their bedroom with the week-old unwashed teacups on the floor and into the astral plane.

Three months after first picking up the guitar I was beginning to get somewhere. I had calluses on my fingertips, I knew a few basics about music theory and I could play some songs that sounded quite nice on my Walden: 'You Ain't Going Nowhere', a Jimi Hendrix-style version of 'Hey Joe' but without the difficult parts, John Pearse's 'Three Blind Mice' and of course 'You Can't Always Get What You Want'. I had even written my own song, which consisted of all the above thrown together in a haphazard fashion. I knew enough to fuel my enthusiasm, and even if there wasn't much time to play – about an hour a day, in-between the children going to bed and NJ and I falling asleep in our armchairs – certainly nobody had to tell me to go and practise.

Guitarist magazine had a few handy tips about chord changes, damping and page after page of 'tasty licks' transcribed by tablature that I could never bother to decode. Doyle, Pete Millson and Michael Tyack from Circulus were the friends that had shown me tips, and Polly Harvey, The Black Keys and Mr David Viner were among the professionals that had imparted knowledge on their own approach to the guitar. Even Ralph Denyer's *The Guitar Handbook* was beginning to make sense, although I still wasn't sure what a suspended fourth was. What I needed now was a deeper understanding of what the point of playing guitar was in the first place.

Something that Polly Harvey had mentioned was the value of the beginner's mind, of being prepared to come to the instrument with a freshness that allows you to learn new things. The beginner is in an advantageous position: only the severely deluded would think that they know too much to learn when they know nothing. A divine spark is within us all, but it can get buried under the layers of knowledge. Playing guitar requires an open mind; what is known in Buddhist thought as carrying an empty cup. The story goes that a nineteenth-century Zen master called Nan-Nin was visited by a university professor hoping to learn from him, but the professor talked so much that Nan-Nin could not get a word in edgeways. The Zen master poured a cup of tea until it flowed over the table. 'What are you doing?' said the professor.

'Like this cup, you are full of ideas,' said the master. 'How can I teach you unless you first empty your cup?'

My first step towards understanding the beginner's mind was reading *Zen Guitar* by the late Philip Toshio Sudo, a Japanese-American guitarist who had applied Zen philosophy to learning the instrument in a way that valued understanding over knowledge. Sudo's message was that in order to really learn anything, you have to remove your ego and take on the mantle of the student.

Sudo's book doesn't give any factual advice, but it helps one to build confidence. Until now I had had a mental block about tuning the guitar. All of my life I have been told that I am tone deaf, mainly because it seems that my singing voice is not particularly pleasant to the ears of some of the less enlightened people I know, including my wife, my children, and everyone else I have ever met. But Sudo states that anyone who can tell the difference between the bark of a dog and the chirp of a bird can tell the difference between a higher pitch and a lower pitch. He also states that you must learn how to be in tune with the instrument itself because every guitar has its own idiosyncrasies. And ultimately, the only tuning that really counts is the one that resonates with your soul; the tuning that brings mind, body and spirit together in harmony. Joni Mitchell writes songs by taking the guitar out of standard tuning and twiddling the strings in order to throw the sounds open into the cosmos. 'Then when you discover something that has an element of divine intervention,' she has said of the process, 'it's like a blessing.' Sudo hit the nail on the head about the bigger meaning of guitar tuning: 'A player must be clear of internal static such as impatience and frustration. Otherwise the spirit frizzles like a radio slightly off dial.' It is the moment when your spirit is uplifted that counts.

I began to think about the guitarists that I liked to listen to and what they were doing. I love The Velvet Underground, and

Lou Reed's guitar playing on songs like 'All Tomorrow's Parties', 'Sunday Morning' and 'Foggy Notion' is imaginative and full of feeling. Anything from The Rolling Stones's golden period of 1968 to 1972 is great, and Keith Richards never does solos that stray outside of the parameters of the song. His genius is economy: on the immortal 'Wild Horses' Richards creates shifts in mood by switching the order of the chords G, B minor, D and A minor. Marc Bolan's guitar has a fantastic sound. Chuck Berry and Bo Diddley never abandon the rhythm. Even hugely skilled players like Bert Jansch, Joni Mitchell and Roger McGuinn, who make full use of the intricate delicacies and possibilities of the acoustic guitar, rarely play an excess of notes. Jimmy Page is an inventive guitarist, although he lost it for me when Led Zeppelin became a vehicle for him to show off his ever-expanding skills. Jimi Hendrix, the greatest electric guitar player of all time, who played lead and rhythm at once and did things that nobody else has ever come close to, wasn't promoting his ego so much as being open and creative. All of these people are – or were – connecting what's inside them with wider forces.

There is another guitarist who does it for me. Johnny Marr reinvented guitar-playing when he emerged in the early 1980s with The Smiths. I had no idea how he played songs like 'What Difference Does It Make' and 'Please Please Please Let Me Get What I Want', but I remember thinking at the time that I had never heard anything like it. His playing is never bombastic, while still having a shed-load of attitude and invention, and it reflects the uncertainties that colour all of our lives.

In my search for a master who might understand the cosmic relevance of the guitar, I decided that it would be worth trying to talk to Johnny Marr. Two weeks later I was on a train to Manchester, my Walden in its solid body case in the luggage

rack above me. It felt surreal – an absolute beginner travelling
from the south to the north of England on a bright Friday to
have a lesson from one of the greatest British guitarists of all
time – but I kept in mind something that Neil Young had said.
'I like to play with people who can play simple and are not
threatened by other musicians thinking they can't play. And
that eliminates 99 per cent of musicians.' I wasn't worried if
Johnny Marr thought I couldn't play. I knew I couldn't.

Johnny Marr had suggested meeting in Night And Day, a
venue, club and café-bar in the centre of the city that is
something of a focal point for Manchester's music community.
In the high-ceilinged and almost empty room, where wooden
tables bore the stains of a thousand spilt beers and leaflets on the
bar gave support to small-scale local bands and events, Johnny
Marr arrived, his still youthful face smiling under a thatch of
Beatles-like black hair, although he must have been in his
forties. 'Let's go downstairs,' he said, 'and I can show you a few
tricks that will take years off your learning.'

In the basement, next to a large and rather noisy industrial
boiler and a broom cupboard, were a table and a couple of chairs
that would serve as our classroom. 'I've had enough of the smoke
and mirrors of the world of rock music,' said Marr, a quiet man
until fired up by the thing that has absorbed him since the age
of eleven. 'Right now I'm interested in what can be expressed
with the six strings of an acoustic guitar.'

This was good news, as the electric guitar was a world I had
not yet plugged into. He told me to show him what I had been
doing, so I got the guitar out and drove home – yes, that's right
– 'You Can't Always Get What You Want'. Nerves made it
sound worse than it usually did, and remembering the evocative
sound that Keith Richards makes when he plays it, I wondered
if my guitar was really up to the job. Quite possibly Johnny

Marr might be offended to have to dirty his fingers on such an inferior product. He nodded as I played and said that I had a good feel for the guitar, which was generous of him. Then he took it off me and ripped into an incredible version of 'Gimme Danger' by The Stooges. Perhaps it wasn't the Walden that was the problem after all.

'A friend of mine who heard me play "Gimme Danger" pointed out that it was pretty similar to "Toys In The Attic" by Aerosmith,' he said as The Stooges's dirty rock classic came to an end. 'Check this out.'

He blasted through another monster riff so enormous that it sounded like longhaired troglodytes had carved it out of stone 20,000 years ago. Then I realized what was happening: despite being one of the greatest guitarists the world has ever known, all he really wanted to do was show off one of his favourite riffs, which he had probably learned at the age of twelve and subjected his family to night after night. The excitement he had when he first got the hang of it was being relived and it didn't matter that his current audience consisted of one late developer. 'I never needed any encouragement to pick up the guitar,' he shouted over the rock surge, 'I couldn't wait to play. I was told to turn the amplifier down because my little brother was trying to get to sleep in the bed next to me.'

I got the impression that Johnny Marr would not have noticed if he was in a prison cell or The Ritz; with a guitar in his hand he was like a kid in a sandbox, wanting for nothing. 'I know I may not seem it, but I'm actually quite a sensitive guy,' he said, when 'Toys In The Attic' came to a dramatic end. 'And I'm really bored by the whole macho rock posture because music means more to me than that. There are things that can be done with an acoustic guitar that are far more interesting and expressive than anything that can be done by standing around with four geezers in leather jackets. I'm searching for something a little cosmic right now, and I've realized that I would have to live several lifetimes before beginning to understand the possibilities of a guitar.'

Marr gave me advice that was both practical and philosophical. He suggested getting new sounds by playing in an unconventional way. When you first pick up a guitar you learn the open chords: finger shapes on the first three frets of the neck that relate to the strings that are played open. Marr's discovery was that you could play the same chords in different places on the neck with remarkable results. If you made the shape of, for example, a C chord and moved it up two frets, you got a D that sounded strange and unique. I tried it. It worked!

Then he suggested playing in the dark. 'If you ever get stuck, turn off the lights and play with your ears because that returns you to the pure state. Right now you're in a wonderful position because you have a sea of possibilities in front of you, whether that means learning how to play "Cosmic Dancer" by T-Rex or one of John McLaughlin's most intricate pieces. When you're working with something you don't understand your mind and your ego are taken out of the picture. When you discover a chord that sounds nice you don't think: "That's a bit gauche," or "That's been played too many times before." It sounds good to you in a pure way.'

I tried playing a few other principal chords further up the neck, as Johnny Marr had shown me. 'You're holding the neck all wrong,' he said. 'Why is your thumb sticking up in the air like that? You're not trying to hitch a ride.' He used physical force to reposition my hands. 'Think about what you're doing. Concentrate!'

'But my fingers aren't going where they're meant to.'

'That's what practice is for.'

There is no getting round it: endless repetition is the key to playing the guitar. 'Tighten your mind,' says Philip Toshio Sudo. 'Don't ask, practise.' 'The only opponent is within.' Practice overcomes self-consciousness, as repetition results in the muscles developing their own intelligence to the point where thought and action are simultaneous, just as in typing and driving. I was reminded of my ongoing attempts to master 'Get It On' by T-Rex, which is a simple song but requires precision if it is to sound right. After Pete Millson had shown me the basic moves, another guitarist-playing friend of mine came to the house and we did 'Get It On' together. After a few false starts I played the best version I had ever done. We managed to get into the groove of the song; to stop thinking about hitting the right notes and let the rhythm dictate our movements. In a simple way, that was the essence of the cosmic guitarist, or the zen guitarist, or whatever you want to call it: letting thought be replaced by something more profound.

'I've got another key bit of advice,' said Johnny Marr. 'Why use a thousand words when fuck off will do? That's not to say you should try and be deliberately philistine because that would be false, but it's important to know how much or how little is needed.'

He went on to talk about two of *his* favourite players. James Williamson was the guitarist for The Stooges, Iggy Pop's wild delinquent garage band, when they came over to London with David Bowie to record *Raw Power*, their third album, in 1972. The Stooges had taken basic garage-rock into a whole new territory back in their native Ann Arbor in Michigan when they used the blues and rock'n'roll sound to express something about their dysfunctional lives, and in doing so they became the perfect rebellious rock'n'roll band: more street-tough than The Rolling Stones but just as romantic. James Williamson had poured his dementia into some remarkably threatening songs like 'Gimme Danger' and 'Raw Power', which are complex and full of attitude. 'I knew I was on the right track when I heard *Raw Power* because it sounds like me when I was young, trying to combine the stylings of The Byrds with The Patti Smith Group. I love James Williamson's playing because it has all the invention and endeavour of Jimmy Page without being too technical, and all the swagger and attitude of Keith Richards without being too sloppy.'

Marr's other great inspiration is the Scottish folk guitarist Bert Jansch. 'It's beautiful music because it's soulful, and his music is not about being academic. One thing that Bert and I have in common is that we hardly ever play an existing song when we pick the guitar up, and we never play one of our own. I just grab whatever is in the air and improvise until it forms itself into some sort of a shape. You know that you can express yourself through the guitar, so the technicalities are just like unlocking the Rubik's Cube. A guitar is there to capture something that is in the air, and when you hit the right moment it's an experience that borders on the mystical.'

I didn't have any problem in approaching the guitar as a mystical quest. Until the age of twelve my family had been a bourgeois nuclear unit: our working-class parents had worked hard to go to university and become middle-class professionals. They got a mortgage, moved to the status-conscious London suburb of Richmond, saved the pennies to send my brother and I to private school and generally made a clean break from the problems of their past through education, books and a Victorian home décor scheme. Then they went mad. My mother discovered feminism in a big way and decided she had had enough of being a wife and mother, while my father found eastern spirituality. I would return from an afternoon spent riding my bicycle in the local park to see the living room filled with large Indian women and wispy English men and women all dressed in white, staring towards a pinpoint of light in silent contemplation of the eternal nature of the soul. A few years later I would come home at four in the morning to find my father meditating in the kitchen. Although I'm too of the world to ever live my dad's ascetic lifestyle – he has given up the material and sensual world in order to search for spiritual communion – I appreciate the wisdom that he has passed on to me about the eternal nature of the soul. For that reason I was ready to view the guitar as something much more than a block of wood with six strings on it.

Although I appreciated Johnny Marr's philosophical theories about the guitar, I still wanted to learn how to play the thing. His fingers were moving so fast on so many notes that I couldn't possibly see how I could ever replicate that. 'The dexterity is a byproduct of just having fun with the guitar,' he told me. 'It's not important – what you should think about are the eureka moments when you suddenly discover different ways of playing the thing. It's like kicking a football. You don't think "How the fuck am I going to dribble?" every time you go near a football. You just kick the bloody thing. Any flash stuff comes when you're in the flow.'

Once you know the rules, life can be made much easier by ignoring them. 'If you don't like a note, don't play it,' he said. 'You can play chords in unconventional ways in order to free your fingers up and all of a sudden the guitar has expanded hugely. A mix of logic and excitement has inspired everything I've learned.'

I still had the problem of my fingers not going where I would like them to go. My big difficulty was changing from an open chord to a barré chord, where the index finger is pressed down

across all the strings on one of the frets. 'Then why do you have
to do a barré chord?' said Johnny. 'Just don't play the strings
that don't go with the sound you're making. Don't play what is
too difficult until you're ready, and do whatever is pleasing to
your ear.'

Although most of Johnny Marr's life has been dedicated to
the guitar, he has never had any formal training, and he has
developed his style through imagination, not intense dexterity.
The son of an Irish road builder, he grew up as part of a large
family in Manchester where the men worked as labourers. His
interest in guitars was not shared by anyone else. Whenever a
guitar came on the television one of his parents or brothers
would call him, and each year the triangle-shaped boxes underneath the Christmas tree got a little bit bigger.

By the time Johnny Marr was a teenager his main concern,
along with learning how to roll the perfect joint and having a
girlfriend, was working out how James Williamson played
'Gimme Danger'. 'You're fourteen or fifteen and you've got a
leather jacket, and all you can think about is how one of the
coolest riffs of all time is made, which sounds sleazily druggie
without being pointless – it's suggestive of other worlds rather
than of some bloke dribbling. I was on the bus when I realized
how it was done – by altering a few conventional chord shapes.
It's all about finding the right chords to make a big noise while
freeing up your fingers so that you can do things on your own.
That's the reason why I sound like two guitar players. I
reconfigure the conventional chords so that I can play tunes
within the chords themselves.'

Johnny Marr grew up in the seventies, too young to be a part
of the guitar culture where men like Jimmy Page and Black
Sabbath's Tony Iommi were heroes to a generation of longhaired
youth, and at exactly the right age to make sense of punk, but

with too expansive a mind to buy into its puritan ethic. 'I loved the iconography of the rock guitar age but the music wasn't enough. What drove me crazy were things like the outro to "Metal Guru" by T-Rex, or the sweet spot in the chorus of "All The Young Dudes" by Mott The Hoople where the melody changes from major to minor. I was walking into bus stops every day that song was in the charts. Whatever it was that happened in that second was sublime, and after hearing it my life was totally and utterly out of balance because reality was two-dimensional by comparison. So I had to play the guitar to try and find that sublime moment in "All The Young Dudes". If I hadn't, and if I had done what my old man does – going out and digging holes with a jackhammer – I would have led a pretty confused life.'

I tried to imagine a fourteen-year-old Johnny Marr – in my mind his head was exactly the same as it was now, but on a much smaller body with a giant pair of brushed denim flares – walking down a suburban street in Manchester, past the hole in the road that his father was mending, dreaming of playing guitar alongside Marc Bolan on *Top Of The Pops* and wondering whether he could get away with putting a bit of glitter around his eyes without getting beaten up by the local teddy boys. "Get It On" by T-Rex is lazy but perfect,' he said. 'Marc Bolan recycled Chuck Berry and Howlin' Wolf riffs and made them inauthentic by sticking a gothic minor chord in the middle of them, which no delta blues man would dare do for fear of being accused of homosexuality. Marc Bolan had a vulnerable appeal – he looked as beautiful as he sounded – and his records had men singing falsetto backing vocals. There was nothing like it where I came from and Bolan gave a promise of another world, which is the reason I'm here today.'

I would love to be able to play like Johnny Marr, but that

would always be impossible – and to an extent, asking him how to play guitar would be like asking him how I should live my life. All I could hope for were a few pointers that would help me find my own path. He was so accomplished that it was quite hard for him to demonstrate things that were simple enough for me to get my head around, but he did boil guitar playing down to its bare necessities. 'As long as you know four chords – and one of them has to be a minor as it's emotionally boring if you only play major chords – then you have enough to get going with. The thing to do is work out the building blocks and then do it on your own.'

He let me in on a few other secrets of the guitarist's craft. 'For whatever key you are playing in, the relevant open bass note will always sound good. And remember that the most important things about the guitar are discovery and mystery. By playing around with the standard chords – moving them up a fret, changing the fingering to let a bass note ring out – you make the possibilities limitless. That's how I came up with all the songs for The Smiths. Once you start developing habitual patterns, break them. I recently wrote a piece of music that was in a tuning I didn't understand at all, but it ended up sounding just like me anyway even though I was using a completely different language.'

I went home from Manchester that day with my head spinning with broken chords and unconventional fingering patterns, and I cannot claim to have understood half of what I had been told. But when I got home and thought about it, it began to make sense. Johnny Marr was urging me to explore the guitar and apply a bit of logic to making up my own language on it. The important thing is to keep an open mind.

Bert Jansch was a name that Johnny Marr kept coming back to as an example of a liberated, expressive guitarist who taps into something more interstellar than the standard blues and R&B licks. He had described the first time he saw Pentangle, Jansch's old group, on television in the early seventies. 'They were hunched over their acoustic guitars in plimsolls and odd socks, looking like the television performance was interrupting a drinking session that started two days earlier. This was the age of Deep Purple and Led Zeppelin, and of having an over-expanded musical vocabulary without ever actually saying anything. The impression I got of Pentangle was that all the other bands were regarded as utter lightweights, musically, physically, philosophically and lyrically.'

Jansch is something of a hero to a generation of guitarists who wished to explore the instrument in a non-linear way. Born into a working-class Edinburgh family in 1943, he first picked up the guitar at the age of seven and knew a few years later that he wanted to devote his life to the instrument. At seventeen he was travelling through Europe playing gigs and busking. He recorded his first album in the folklorist Bill Leader's kitchen in 1965, and became one of the leading lights of the London sixties folk scene that gathered around Les Cousins, a basement club in Greek Street, Soho.

I started to listen to Bert Jansch as a result of hearing people like Johnny Marr sing his praises, and the album that really blew my mind was 1978's *Avocet*. A series of instrumental pieces played with a band, *Avocet* is just a beautiful, evocative piece of music. It sounds like the soundtrack to a flight through the British countryside at dawn, passing over gnarled oaks and down rocky streams with not a pylon or a Little Chef to break the spell. His playing sounded like he was channelling into something that had always existed.

It was worth finding out if he would be prepared to show a novice like me a few moves, and for such a high priest of the guitar pantheon he was remarkably accessible. Bert lives with his wife Loren in a flat in Kilburn, where rows of acoustic guitars hang from the walls. When he isn't touring or making a record he spends his days getting up late and shifting himself from the bedroom to the living room sofa to play one of his many guitars until the evening. His life is entirely focused on the instrument. He's also a shy man who can express himself far more eloquently through music than he can through words.

Bert Jansch really did seem like a different creature. He is physically designed for playing guitar. The frog-like tips of his fingers are so enormous that he can play the A chord with only two fingers when most of us need to use three. Jimmy Page doffed his cap to the master: 'At one point I was absolutely obsessed with Bert Jansch. When I first heard that LP [Jansch's 1965 debut], I couldn't believe it. It was so far ahead of what everyone else was doing. No one in America could touch that.'

As is so often the case with people who have an honest love of the guitar for its own sake, he liked the fact that someone was coming to him and asking to learn, and he was only too happy to let me come over for an afternoon lesson. He began by showing me how you can make the most of simple movements – you can play a single chord and create a whole sequence simply by finding small variations within that chord. He showed me how you can do something called peddling, in which you play an open string constantly against a series of other notes that fluctuate slightly – this is the basis of a lot of Led Zeppelin's *Stairway To Heaven*. He played what sounded like intricate pieces that only involved moving a single finger up and down the neck. The mystical secrets of a master guitarist were being revealed to me in a basement flat in Kilburn.

I wondered if Bert Jansch had special super-ears. 'There's a note on your guitar that's really bugging me,' he said as I strummed the strings wildly, and he isolated the string that was, unbeknownst to me, very slightly flat. 'I only go to a certain point in theory before I cut off,' he said in his quiet way. 'Since string was invented, and it was taut and vibrated, these sounds have existed, but the theory that we use to map out music only goes back to Bach. Before him, the pianos or harps were made using untempered scales – they were not tuned to an equal temperament with one another. It was Bach who turned music into a fantastic science.

'The reason the guitar has been so successful is because it is so versatile,' he continued as I tried my hand at peddling. 'A blues player like Mississippi John Hurt, and a classical guitarist like Julian Bream, are chalk and cheese, even though they are related. Classical players don't know how to bend strings and it was only when the blues came along that that became a technique. Then along came Jimi Hendrix and everything changed for ever.'

Bert Jansch's playing – otherworldly, timeless and eastern-influenced – belongs to the ancient traditions of the oud, and the player that opened Bert Jansch's young mind was Davey Graham. Graham combined blues techniques like walking bass lines with the Indian classical style of droning to make music that, in the early sixties, sounded like nothing that anyone in England had heard before. Graham had lost an eye as a child after he stuck a pencil in it; and it has been suggested that his transcendental exploration of music was at least partially a result of his visual impairment.

I could now see that it was not by chance that 'Anji' had set me off on my path. A line was being drawn connecting all the players that I liked and that line was leading to one mysterious figure. Jansch confirmed that he was still alive, although he could not vouch for Graham's accessibility or even sanity. It had

been a long time since Davey Graham had made a record and he
hardly ever performed live; few promoters would book him
because there was always a strong chance he would not turn up.
Jansch still saw him every now and then, and told me that he
was living in a one-bedroom flat in Camden, North London,
still chasing after experiences and wisdoms a long way outside
of convention. 'He's a very charming man,' said Jansch, 'but he's
not with the rest of us for most of the time. If you talk to him
about the guitar he's fine but when you go into any other aspect
of normal life you lose him.'

'Can you tell me how to play "Anji", then?' I asked him.

'Are you planning to stay for the rest of the week?' he replied.

As well as writing the immortal, if elusive, 'Anji' when he
was barely out of his teens, Davey Graham diverted from the
standard 'Spanish' tuning that guitarists generally use – E, A,
D, G, B and E – and made up his own, the most famous being
D, A, D, G, A and D. 'He invented that tuning in order to play
eastern style music on the guitar, and now all the Irish players
use it,' said Jansch. 'As soon as you start playing around with
tuning you open up another universe as far as the guitar is
concerned. When you play eastern instruments like a dulcimer
or an oud, you play the melody on one string and the others are
used as drones. With DADGAD it's the same – you can play a
melody on a single string because the rest of the strings all relate
to each other.'

Bert tuned my guitar to DADGAD and something remarkable happened. All I had to do was strum it and that was enough
to create an ancient sound reminiscent of a thousand pilgrims
chanting in prayer and devotion to a distant god.

He explained how most playing was really about getting the
right feel and atmosphere rather than hitting the right notes,
and how friendship is the key to the kind of guitar style he is

interested in. 'Unlike in the classical world, everyone I've ever played with has been mates,' he said. 'You have to have a certain sympathy with someone, and you absolutely *cannot* – or at least I can't – play with someone you don't like. It would never work because it would be reflected in the music. Johnny Marr, for example, comes from a similar background to me so it's easy for us to get along and do something good together.'

After hitchhiking down to London from Edinburgh in 1964, Jansch moved into a flat with his friend and fellow master guitarist John Renbourn. Alongside Davey Graham, their big inspiration was an American guitarist called Jackson C. Frank. Frank had come over to England with the money he received in compensation for being the victim of a fire at the age of eleven, which had left one side of his body badly scarred. He had chosen London as the place for adventures with his new-found wealth because he wanted to buy a Bentley, but he quickly became a regular at Les Cousins, enticed the singer Sandy Denny into being his girlfriend, and recorded his one and only album, *Blues Run The Game*, in 1965 with a then-unknown Paul Simon as producer. 'He was my favourite player of all time,' said Bert. 'If I had the time I would learn every song from that record as it is so magical.'

Blues Run The Game was not a hit beyond the tiny world of London's hip folk scene, and when rock took over folk in the public's tastes Frank returned to America. After losing his son to cystic fibrosis in 1971 he fell into a deep depression. He was in and out of mental institutions for much of the 1970s, and in 1984 he was discovered living on the streets of New York. He died in 1999, crippled, impoverished, blind in one eye after being shot a few years earlier, and almost entirely forgotten. Frank's album is so rare that when it was released on to CD Jansch had to lend the record company his copy of the vinyl album for the cover artwork.

Jansch played me a song by Jackson C. Frank called 'Milk And Honey', which was later covered by Sandy Denny. It was eerie and beautiful. 'This isn't complicated, but it's delicate,' said Jansch. 'You could certainly learn how to play it, but it's the feeling that counts, not the notes that he's picking out.'

Everything I had learned had been about the left hand, which picks out the chord shapes and notes, and all I had done with the right hand was strum, either with the back of my thumb or with a plectrum. I hadn't given timing much thought as the less I consciously tried to keep time the more I seemed able to do it. I noticed that Bert played with a weird claw-like metal ring on his thumb called a thumb pick. 'I got that because of the blues player Big Bill Broonzy,' he explained. 'When I was sixteen I went to see him play in Paris, and because he was black and playing in a dark nightclub this white thing on his thumb stood out a mile.'

It was the Spanish classical guitarist Andres Segovia who said that the guitar is like an orchestra. The player can modulate the guitar so that it sounds like different instruments, and it is possible to play a melody with an accompanying bass line as 'Anji' has proved. So far, my strums had had the effect of making the guitar sound like a rubber band and a stick, but Bert showed me something that changed everything. 'There was an American woman called Elizabeth Cotton who invented claw hammer,' he said. 'It's a right-hand technique that involves plucking two strings simultaneously and alternating between two bass notes.'

Once again, Bert played something that sounded like it was far beyond my reach. But with a patience that began to wear thin because I kept getting it wrong again and again, he showed me how claw hammer worked. In an hour or so I had got the hang of it. It's just a simple finger pattern, but it allows you to find variation and richness in a single chord. Once you start changing chords you have an entire symphony going on.

I could have stayed all day, and would quite happily have slept in the garden if Bert would show me a few more finger-picking techniques the following morning, but it became clear that it was time to go. Before I left he told me that rock'n'roll is all about keeping the rhythm and only involves hitting a couple of strings most of the time, and that jazz guitar, the most difficult of all the styles, is about starting the chord from a different note to the one you might expect. Before I left he played me a piece of music to show how much the unaccompanied guitar was capable of: a recital by the great classical guitarist Julian Bream. 'We played it at our wedding,' said Bert, as the delicate strings of Bream's guitar were plucked from the stereo. 'My wife wanted Metallica. Sometimes you have to put your foot down.'

Johnny Marr wasn't the only famous guitarist to worship at the mind-expanding altar of Bert Jansch and Davey Graham. A couple of days after talking to Bert I heard that Devendra Banhart was in town. This young Californian singer-songwriter was living a real hippy bohemia: he travelled constantly and played a show every night, sometimes on his own and some-times with a full band, while writing surreal and frequently nonsensical songs that might possibly hint at the secrets of the universe. NJ and I went to see him play in London with a chaotic bunch of men who looked like they had been picked off a New York welfare line's junior division: stumbling drunkenly on stage with bushy beards and thrift shop clothes, they played skilfully but irreverently, frequently stopping mid-song to talk nonsense – one of the four guitarists spent ten minutes con-ducting a rambling ode to Maker's Mark, his favourite whisky, in which he claimed that the distinctive red wax that seals every bottle is lovingly hand-crafted by apron-clad beauties in the American countryside. He almost started crying.

Devendra Banhart was so great that I had to get him to give me a guitar lesson, and he seemed so friendly up on stage that I couldn't believe he would refuse me the pleasure. He didn't. On the afternoon after the concert he met me in the London offices of his record company. He would have looked saintly with his white turban, flowing white lunghi, large beard and patient brown eyes were it not for the fact that he had a raging hangover. I told him that, for such delicate music as his, it was good to see that his backing band appeared to be a complete bunch of clowns. 'Oh yeah, brother, those guys are all goofs,' he said, the American vernacular standing against his swami-like appearance. 'That's why I like them.'

He was surprised that I wanted to learn from him, claiming that he wasn't a good guitarist at all. I explained that I liked the way he created a simple drone: I understood that he was generally only playing two or three chords, but that the way he made so many musical possibilities within those chords was inspiring. 'Well, there's a reason I play like that,' he began. 'When I started, I had a guitar without any strings. This was when I was thirteen, and I just felt the frets and the wood and got used to it. That went on for a month. Then I bought one string, a high E. I played that for a month. Next month, another string. There were two months with those two strings. It feels like only recently that I actually played with all six strings. I developed really cyclical patterns because of that process.'

Devendra taught me how to play a song by Ella Jenkins called 'Wake Up Little Sparrow'. It was only made up of two cords, an E minor and A minor, but the way in which he picked the notes gave it a pleasingly cyclical drone, and even more pleasing for me was the fact that after a few false starts, I could play it. 'That's it!' said Devendra, with a little laugh. 'Don't pay attention to what your fingers are doing exactly as it doesn't matter if they don't always do the same thing. The important thing is to keep the rhythm. There you go, you see! That's awesome.'

Devendra had only ever had one lesson – at McCabe's Guitar Shop in Santa Monica, which his father had taken him to. He learned how to play some Beatles songs. He had also learned that good quality does not necessarily make for good music: some of his favourite guitarists were African musicians who, due to economy, played on very cheap electric guitars and produced a high, cheerful sound as a result. He talked about the life of being in a band, and it didn't sound as much fun as I imagined: he explained how the long bus journeys were soon boring and smelly and everybody got on each other's nerves a few dates into any tour. 'So what becomes the joy is playing guitar, which is why we improvise on stage rather than try and recreate everything note for note each time. Elizabeth Cotton would call the guitar "my joy". She would come back from work and play guitar as her reward, so it was never anything but a pleasure for her. That's how I feel about it. Playing guitar – and now I only get to play it when I'm actually on stage – is my joy, my freedom. The rest of the life that goes with being a musician is work.'

His advice was to learn a few chords and add little bits to them, just as Bert Jansch and Johnny Marr had suggested, rather than try and play lots of difficult chords in all kinds of awkward places. 'Hey, have you ever heard of a song called "Anji" by this cat Davey Graham?' he asked. For the next half hour he tried to teach me how to play it. We got as far as the opener and the bass line that underpins the song, and I left with the knowledge of how it is done but not the ability to do it. He was very calm as I continually hit the wrong notes and cursed every time I did it. 'You know what you do that is awesome?' he said. 'You say shit every time you get it wrong rather than "I'm sorry," which is what most people say. That is much more honest and more respectful both to me and the guitar.' I couldn't see the difference myself, but it made me feel slightly better at my failure to even begin to play 'Anji'.

I left to allow Devendra to fly off to Spain and continue his everlasting journey, and felt that I was one step closer to using the guitar in a way that seemed worthwhile. I did not have the skill, time or inclination to become a super-fast virtuoso, but I still wanted to make music that could take me, and who knows, maybe one day an audience however small, somewhere outside of the mundane. At least I knew how the bass parts to 'Anji' went and could practise them when I got home. That was a start.

Pete dropped by one quiet Tuesday afternoon, when the allure of the guitar prevented me from being able to get on with earning money. Pete never takes too much prompting to favour a guitar session and a cup of tea over making a living, so although he could not forgive me for having a one-on-one tutorial with Johnny Marr he was prepared to swallow his envy and run over a few of the secrets that Marr, Jansch and Banhart had imparted. He analysed what Johnny Marr was saying about taking a chord and moving it up the frets while playing the open string that related to it, and discovered that he was describing a power chord: a distillation of a standard chord into a pattern that emphasizes its key characteristics. So for 'Gimme Danger' and 'Toys In The Attic', Johnny Marr had turned whatever had originally been played in a complicated way into something easy – something even I could play.

Pete ran through the riff of 'Toys In The Attic', and it turned out to be very simple – it just required three moves – but what was important was what you did with the right hand. You had to strike out big sounds and kill them a second later. It took a bit of practice, but eventually I got it. Ever since I started shaving I have had sideburns that would not look out of place on a guitar-toting rock hairy. Now, finally, I had a sound worthy of them. At the end of each blast of 'Toys In The Attic' I could not stop myself from raising my arm, Pete Townshend-style, and pointing my finger at an imaginary audience.

'Wait until you play that on an electric guitar,' said Pete. 'That's what it's made for. The true power of rock will be revealed to you in all its Neanderthal glory.'

This was something, of course, that had to happen. Soon.

Chapter Five

Disaster

The more I learned about the guitar, the more it became obvious that if I was ever really going to understand it, I had to explore America. It was in America that slaves and settlers created the twin forces of blues and country music, and it was in America that Les Paul nailed some pick-ups and strings on to a piece of wood in 1941 and invented the first solid-body electric guitar, leading to the production of Gibson's Les Paul model a decade later and giving rock music its one essential ingredient.

What is remarkable is that the roots of the popular music we listen to today – rock, blues and soul – are found in Tennessee and the Mississippi Delta, a poor and backward section of a country that holds such cosmopolitan, epoch-defining cities as New York and Los Angeles. The South is a long way from either of those places, and it is still held in a fair degree of contempt by the liberal North. Mississippi in particular has never recovered from the economic wreckage it suffered after the Civil War, when poor farmers were separated from the means of production and had to rely on more prosperous states for their sufficiency. The race problems of the South have been well documented, to the extent that most white southerners are truly sick of being stereotyped as bigoted hicks. This barren, impoverished, divided and derided land would be the fertile breeding ground for the music that has defined the twentieth century.

The guitar has been at the centre of the music of the South. It offered a chance to transcend race issues, with the southern white rock'n'rollers learning their craft from the black share-croppers they grew up alongside. Robert Johnson, Charley Patton and Son House pioneered the blues on cheap guitars, and Elvis finally landed a recording deal – after over a year of trying – at Sam Phillips's Memphis Recording Service (later Sun Studios) when he and Scotty Moore knocked out the old Arthur 'Big Boy' Crudup song 'That's Alright Mama' on their guitars during a break in rehearsals for soppy ballads. When Mississippi country boys like Muddy Waters and B. B. King rode the train to Chicago in search of work they took electric guitars with them and started a new style of music as a result. Nobody could have expected Robert Johnson to lug a Steinway piano to the crossroads at Clarksdale in Mississippi to sell his soul to the devil, and Hank Williams just would not have looked the same if he was bowing a cello between his legs, rather than having a big old acoustic guitar hanging above his groin.

Three months into my guitar odyssey, most of the songs I could play were by American bands from the 1960s: 'You Ain't Going Nowhere' by The Byrds, 'Hey Joe' by pretty much everyone, and two classic but easy garage-punk tracks: 'You're Gonna Miss Me' by The Thirteenth Floor Elevators and 'Can't Seem To Make You Mine' by The Seeds. 'Anji' was written by that habitué of the twilight English musical nether world Davey Graham, but I couldn't actually play it, despite my continuing efforts, so that didn't count. American guitar music has permeated so much into our consciousness that a guitarist would have to make a concerted effort *not* to play anything that was coined in America – or stick to Spanish classical. All of the music I was attempting to play was a branch of a tree that grew from the trunk of the blues and country that came from the South.

My first spur towards going to America came from a chance meeting with Roger McGuinn, the 12-string Rickenbacker-playing former leader of The Byrds and one of my favourite guitarists. For the last few decades McGuinn has spent much of his life touring the world with his wife Camilla, building on the jingle-jangle style he developed with The Byrds and playing traditional folk songs alongside Byrds classics and new material, and he was passing through London. Roger and Camilla turned out to be an easygoing couple, so I asked if I could come and see them some time in America to talk about guitars. My dream was that Roger would show me how to play 'Eight Miles High' by The Byrds, one of my favourite songs and, as far as I could tell, a difficult piece of music to master. They told me that as long as I was prepared to make the journey down to Orlando, Florida I was more than welcome.

This cemented my resolve to further my knowledge of the guitar with a trip to the States. The plan was to take in as many aspects of American guitar culture as I could in the space of two weeks – the maximum amount of time I could get away from the wife and kids without NJ going insane – which isn't long to penetrate the core of the greatest musical revolution of the twentieth century, but at least it was something. As well as getting a few tips from Roger McGuinn in Orlando, Florida and any living blues man I could find in the Mississippi Delta, there was Nashville, home of country music, and the rock'n'roll soul town of Memphis to take in. I had also heard about a garage-punk festival in New Orleans, where sixties one-hit wonders The Seeds, the greatest two-chord simpletons of them all and a huge inspiration to anyone with limited skills, talent and imagination would be performing in some capacity.

If there were time I would head out to New York where, incredibly, Les Paul was still going. At the age of eighty-nine he was playing at the Iridium Jazz Club in Midtown Manhattan at eleven o'clock every Monday night. I contacted the club and asked for an interview. No problem, just hang around after the set and you can talk to Les as much as you like, they said. So with this excuse to extend the trip to New York I would of course follow in the footsteps of Jack Kerouac, Andy Warhol's superstars, Sid Vicious and even The Stooges's James Williamson and book a room at the famously decadent Chelsea Hotel. The history of the American guitar was waiting on the other side of the Atlantic.

There was one more crucial element to my American guitar odyssey. The myth about Robert Johnson selling his soul to the devil is the most powerful and evocative episode in the history of the guitar. It is taken so seriously that blues historians have fallen out with each other over the location of the crossroads where Johnson made his deal with the horned one. Convention has it that it took place at the junction where Highway 61 meets Highway 49 on the edge of the town of Clarksdale, where Johnson stayed for a while, but purists have decreed it to be a more desolate spot. I suspected that when Johnson's former master Son House began the rumour about the Faustian pact he was using an allegory, but I was still prepared to believe that Johnson really did sell his soul, and hoped to find out more. I was thinking about this when I went to get my hair cut by, as luck would have it, a total blues bore. Needless to say, he was a middle-aged man, and I should have guessed by the way his hair was styled into a pointlessly defiant quiff that I was asking for trouble by mentioning my forthcoming adventure. He went on to lecture me on half a dozen well-worn blues clichés including the one about Robert Johnson. I questioned its veracity. 'Robert Johnson could hardly play the guitar, and two weeks later he was better than everyone,' he said, with such vigour that he almost cut off my earlobe. 'How do you explain that? Even if he practised fourteen hours a day without a break he couldn't be so good in such a short time.'

The so-called two weeks was, in fact, a year. You can do a lot in a year.

But I had been practising steadily for three months, and was still subjecting 'Hey Joe' to a punishment worse than hanging every night. Maybe the barber had a point about Robert Johnson after all, and something more than mere practice was needed. Then it dawned on me. Why couldn't *I* sell my soul to the devil? Then I might actually be skilled enough not to make a total mockery of a live performance in three months' time. My soul was as good as the next man's. I didn't see why I shouldn't go to those crossroads in Clarksdale and give the devil whatever he wanted in exchange for the meanest licks this side of Jimi Hendrix.

Before abandoning all that is good in the Mississippi Delta, however, it was time to meet one of the premier blues men of the Thames Delta. John Moore was a guitarist in the eighties alternative band The Jesus And Mary Chain and has played solo and in other bands ever since, but his heart lies in the blues. When he was an eleven-year-old middle-class boy from the Thames Valley a family friend named Peter Banham gave him his collection of blues records, ostensibly to hide them from the bailiffs after Banham's business went bankrupt. Fortuitously, John had recently picked up the guitar.

'Peter Banham was a sharp-suited young man who my father knew from his involvement in the Wokingham Liberal Party,'

John told me when I went to see him at his flat in Kilburn, just down the road from Bert Jansch's. I had brought over a bottle of wine and looked forward to learning some blues licks from John, a dapper, bright and sardonic man who I had met through my brother. 'I thought he was the coolest person in the world. He smoked cigarettes, he wore great clothes, and he played the blues. So when he gave me this huge pile of rare records by Lightnin' Hopkins, Muddy Waters and Howlin' Wolf, and then taught me how to play them, it was like every boy's dream.'

John unearthed a reel-to-reel tape recording he had of himself doing a rendition of 'I Just Want To Make Love To You' – at the age of eleven. It was quite hard to be convinced by the sound of a polite, unbroken voice telling the listener that he wanted to lay it on them right there and then, but it was a remarkable piece of social history none the less. It was John's first ever performance. 'From then on it was only ever blues and early rock'n'roll for me. I had to have a Gibson ES 125 with a P90 pick-up because that's what Chuck Berry played. Then when I was sixteen I persuaded my mother to take me to the Mississippi Delta.'

Moore, his mother and Peter Banham embarked on one of the most bizarre family holidays of all time. Taking the last of the economy flights run by the 1970s airline entrepreneur Freddie Laker, they went on a tour of small Mississippi towns in search of the birthplaces of blues and rock'n'roll legends. 'I made her take me to Magnolia, Mississippi, because that's where I heard Bo Diddley came from, and Rolling Fork where Muddy Waters was born. If I saw a shack with a black guy playing guitar on the porch I would drag my mother in there to meet him, and once these people got over the shock of realizing that we weren't looking for directions to the nearest Holiday Inn they were almost always fantastic. I asked any black guy over the age of sixty if they knew Muddy Waters and of course they all said that they did.'

John got his first lesson in the realities of playing guitar for a living through his blues obsession. In the same year as his trip to the Delta he went to see the rock'n'roll pioneer Bo Diddley play in a tiny pub called The Half Moon in Putney, Southwest London. The Half Moon has a capacity of around a hundred, but at the end of the 1970s this was the kind of place the man behind such classics as 'Mona', 'Say Man' and 'Who Do You Love' was reduced to playing in. John went with Peter Banham to the gig and the pair managed to get backstage and talk to Bo Diddley afterwards.

'We were taken upstairs to the dressing room, which was just a pub function room with flock wallpaper, and then ushered over to this huge, muscular guy. I told him that I had been to Mississippi in search of his birthplace and he was very friendly after that. He asked me if I played guitar so I did a few runs for him, and he showed me how to get that Bo Diddley sound. It's all about using unusual tunings. It was only ten minutes of his undivided attention but that was a lifetime for me, and it was also the turning point: from that moment on I knew that I wanted to be a guitar player for the rest of my life.'

John Moore did go on to become a guitar player, albeit not for a blues band. By the late 1980s, when he was in The Jesus And Mary Chain, he had embraced the rock'n'roll accessories of black leather, sunglasses and drugs, and after spending an evening with him, it was clear that the image that goes with the guitar was still as important for him as actually playing the thing. 'The guitar is sexy,' he said. 'They move in a great way, and the shape you make when you play the guitar is a wonderfully erotic shape. You can imagine lots of kids playing a tennis racket in front of the mirror, but there can't be too many of them who pretend to be, I don't know, great violinists. And the guitar as we know it is an American instrument. What's the English equivalent? The lute, and that doesn't sound so good through a Marshall stack.'

I learned a few other things about the guitar from John that night. I learned that bad guitar playing could be just as interesting as good guitar playing. We listened to David Bowie's 'Young Americans', on which Carlos Alomar's guitar is so hopelessly out of tune that you begin to wonder just how much cocaine everyone involved must have been taking not to notice it, and yet it does nothing to detract from the uplifting power of the song. I learned that when you are in a reasonably big band – and at their height The Jesus And Mary Chain were selling out 3,000-capacity venues – one guitar could never possibly be enough. It is expected that you will snap a string or at least go out of tune after bashing the instrument for a couple of numbers, and all you have to do is stick your arm out and another one will appear. And I learned that people in bands are not always the best people to learn guitar from because they are consummate show-offs. I should have realised this when I met Johnny Marr. Much as I tried to get John to slow down his blues licks so that I could copy them, he was insistent on running through them at hyper speed to add to the impressiveness of it all. By the time I got home I felt that I had learned everything about the guitar from John except how to play it.

The next few weeks were spent waiting excitedly for the big trip that would take in these icons of American culture I had read about all my life. In the meantime, practice was needed for the forthcoming gig, which, due to my total lack of ability to sing or play guitar with any real finesse, was going to need some support from the people who had helped me along the way so far. Pete was a great guitar player and I knew that I could rely on him, but I didn't feel that the pair of us would be enough. He had the skills, but he didn't have the bite. We needed a woman to sing the songs for us and give a focus for the audience – I wondered if the foxy French girl in Circulus would agree to do it – and we needed a touch of disorder to add to our acoustic whimsy. It had to be Doyle.

Doyle was my first teacher. We liked the same kind of music and I loved the guy, however much he annoyed me. Frustratingly, he was being rather elusive. He had somehow convinced a nice young Japanese woman to be his girlfriend and now he was increasingly hard to pin down. It seemed that at the age of thirty-four, he wanted to domesticate himself. It was hard to believe. This was the man who, when we went for a week's holiday to the Czech Republic two years previously, took three items with him in his holdall: a dirty, flattened toothbrush, a hardback dictionary, and a huge illustrated book from the 1950s called *Torture Of The Christian Martyrs*. (He claimed that he was researching a screenplay into the subject and needed a dictionary to help him with some of the more arcane words used in the book. I never heard about that screenplay again.) He had no change of underpants – three days into the holiday he turned his pants inside out and four days after that he disposed of them entirely. They may well still be stuck to the branch of the tree he threw them into, which can be found near the railway line somewhere between Prague and Český Krumlov.

With his tendency to froth at the mouth on most Saturday nights and his penchant for less than successful chat-up lines ('I've never seen a grown woman naked' never failed to confuse and alarm the chosen subject of his amour), Doyle could strike the casual observer as the ultimate unreconstituted man. He is actually one of a kind, witty and astute, and the perfect example of someone who has found solace from his troubled life in the guitar. The son of an Irish father and a Madeiran Portuguese mother, Doyle is the eldest of four children who grew up on an estate in King's Cross, one of central London's sleaziest and most depressed areas. His father was – is – a severe alcoholic who never worked. The welfare money intended for the family mostly funded his endless, sometimes violent drinking binges, and he had enough of a problem to be classified as mentally unstable and frequently sectioned. The house had no furniture as everything was inevitably sold down the pub. Doyle came home one day to find his dog won by a neighbour in a bet. When he was ten he worked as an assistant to a King's Cross priest, chiefly so that he could escape from his chaotic household.

At the age of sixteen he stole his first guitar. He claimed it was a gift from God. He was walking home early one morning when he passed a house with a living-room window open and an Ibanez guitar just inside it. He decided that if he could find a stick to prop the window open, the guitar was meant to be his. The stick was only a yard away from where he was standing.

I met Doyle two years later, at a sixties club in London called Creation. He had discovered the same garage bands as I had, but while I merely listened to the records while staring for hours on end at the pictures of a spotty geek in Cuban-heeled Beatle boots from 1966 who I idolized as the coolest cat on the planet, he actually bothered to learn what these teenagers were playing (it wasn't hard). At that time nobody knew where Doyle lived and he didn't reveal too much about his background. He would turn up for an evening at somebody's house on a Friday and leave around lunchtime on Monday. The shared flats of pretty much everyone I knew had at least one item of Doyle's clothing in it for most of the 1990s. He did officially have a job, working in a shop on the Holloway Road that sold candles and potions to North London's followers of an Afro-Brazilian folk religion, but he very rarely turned up to it. When everyone else had finished the party, slept off the hangover and gone to work, Doyle sprinkled a little speed on to his cornflakes and tried to nail another sixties classic down pat on his or somebody else's guitar. Playing guitar is like meditation, or, I'm told, fishing: it is a peaceful way of cleansing your mind of trivial matters and focusing on something that feels more eternal. The guitar was Doyle's passport to a better world.

My own background couldn't be more different. I grew up in a pleasant if dull suburb, in a semi-detached house with liberal values and a Volvo in the drive. But Doyle and I hit it off instantly. He's one of the funniest people I have ever met, albeit one of the most maddening. A few days before my so-called blues session with John Moore, I finally convinced Doyle to get round to buying a guitar in preparation for what would now be not only my, but also his, debut gig. (He claimed that he had once played guitar in the bar of a hotel in Bayswater in front of five Korean tourists, but I had no evidence of this.)

'I've got to get a small guitar,' he told me. 'They're not easy to find.'

'Why do you need a small guitar? You're not *that* small.'

'They're perfect,' he said. 'You need something that travels well. And they're very fashionable. All the trendsetters have got them.'

It took him a while, but Doyle found his small guitar. It was terrible. At first I thought it just went out of tune quickly, but then I realized that it was terminally out of tune: the neck did not have a harmonious relationship with the body. It wasn't cheap, and the brand – Tanglewood – is said to be a good one, but I have never heard anything so awful in my life, apart from the screech my daughter lets out when her older brother yanks her doll away (she's adorable otherwise). Doyle was a skilled enough player to get some semblance of a song out of the small guitar, but it wasn't easy.

'I must have knocked it again,' he muttered, hopelessly fiddling with the tuning pegs. 'The bloody thing keeps going out of tune.'

We ran through 'I Can't Seem To Make You Mine' by The Seeds, before Doyle recalled the time he spent living in a trailer park in Kentucky where the local kids had found a new way of getting a cheap high: sticking their heads in microwaves and nuking themselves. It was said to be even better than crystal meth.

Later that night Doyle showed me how to play one of the best American garage songs ever written. 'I Never Loved Her' is the B-side of the only single by a band called The Starfires. Released in 1965, it is pure garage attitude distilled into two-and-a-half minutes of restrained, perfectly formed aggression. Through a very simple progression of barré chords and a lead lick on a second guitar, the growling yet whiny singer starts by telling his friends to quit bugging him about the girl who has dumped him. He goes on to tell them in an angry snarl that he only took her home from school one day because her house was on his way; that he only took her for one ride in his car, and they didn't even get very far. Then, when it hits the chorus and he sings in a much sweeter, more plaintive voice about how he never loved her, it's clear that the poor kid has had his heart trampled by some tough chick that probably ended up with the captain of the football team. It is a work of brooding downtrodden genius, and it doesn't take long to master (E, F sharp, G and back to E, and then B, C and A for the chorus). We decided that we would play it at the gig. As we ran through it with controlled tension,

I felt like I was sixteen again. Then Otto came along and grabbed the neck of the guitar and I was reminded that I wasn't.

The disaster happened later that night. I had organized the trip to America – I would drive through the South before flying from New Orleans to New York – and take the guitar with me. The Walden was beginning to make sense. It may not have been the best guitar in the world, but it was the one I was learning to play on and I had no problems with it. I couldn't really tell the difference between the sound of a £5,000 Martin and my £160 Walden anyway, at least not if it was me doing the playing. That evening I sat in our low-ceilinged basement, where the damp spots are covered by stacks of magazines and where flakes of house debris fall on to the CDs every time the wind blows down what was once an old chimney, and practised the claw hammer technique that Bert Jansch had showed me. I had got the hang of it and it was sounding pretty good. I could happily jump from one chord to another, moving a single finger to completely change the mood, and it felt like I was making music for the first time. Even NJ didn't seem to mind.

'That's nice,' she said with a peaceful smile, before going back to her book.

It may not sound like much, but for a thirty-four-year-old man who has been told all his life that he is tone deaf, and who spent his musical education banished to a back room and told to keep quiet, it was the world. Pete, Doyle and I were going to form a great new band with our blend of curly hair, imperfect yet manly appearances, repertoire of originals and rock classics from the sixties and seventies, and virtuoso guitar playing.

Then I did something extremely silly.

Just as we were going to bed, NJ asked me to put two mattresses that were leaning up against the basement wall into a back cupboard. I put the guitar down by the wall next to the mattresses and picked them up – they were heavy together, but I reckoned I could get the job done in one go. I have never been a practical man or a particularly careful one. I wasn't watching where the backs of those mattresses were going.

It was only after I had closed the cupboard door that I saw the guitar. It had been knocked to the floor and had landed face down. The neck was at a forty-five-degree angle to the body and the break was so deep that it had splintered the sound hole. It looked so mournful, with the strings, once so proud and taut, now flaccid and impotent. I had to stare at it for a while before really accepting that the guitar was broken. Smashing it up in a Pete Townshend-style fit of auto-destruction would have been all right, but crushing it with a mattress was tragic. I picked it up and pulled at one of the strings. It let out an eerie, defeated moan. I tried pulling the neck back, thinking I might be able to glue it back together, but it was impossible. A wonderful musical instrument had been transformed into trash and it had happened at a critical juncture in my learning, just before I planned to embark on the ultimate journey of discovery.

I consulted Philip Toshio Sudo's *The Zen Guitar* for help. It didn't appear to have a chapter on what to do when you wreck your guitar in a domestic environment. I wondered if this was a message from God warning me about impending vainglory, about the humiliation that would inevitably occur when a thirtysomething father of two entertains axe god fantasies in front of a paying audience. God knows there were more important things to concern myself with. NJ had been having a tough time of it since the kids came along. She worked in fashion before she became a mother, and doing two-day-long shoots for little money didn't blend well with changing nappies and entertaining toddlers. As a result, she had taken up the domestic duties in our family and they didn't satisfy her intelligence or curiosity. I had a responsibility to cover the bills and the rent, spend time with the children, and exercise the British man's basic right to go to the pub and moan into his beer every now and then. Ever since Otto was born we had never had enough money to relax and take it easy, and holidays were only ever tacked on to work assignments. This guitar obsession had come at the wrong time. Plus, I had never picked up a guitar when I was younger for a good reason – musically, I stank. It was nice of Johnny Marr to offer wise words of encouragement. It was great that Bert Jansch could give up enough of his time to show me how to do claw hammer. But surely the shattering of the guitar was a message from God to stop this nonsense, just as the presentation of Doyle's stolen Ibanez had been a message for him to start.

As I got into bed that night I couldn't even tell NJ about what had happened. I couldn't bring myself to say to anyone that my guitar was now broken because that would confirm that it really was. It was ridiculous to mourn over a cheap guitar that, with a bit of prudence, could be replaced easily enough, but it felt like the end of an era. After three hours of staring into the black of night, I had to wake up NJ and tell her.

She rubbed her eyes, rolled over, and mumbled into her pillow: 'This doesn't mean your adventure is over.'

Chapter Six

A Byrd Takes Flight

There is an unfortunate side to human nature that wants to discourage those who would embark on a new adventure. The only person to actually suffer from my going to America was NJ, who would have to cope with looking after two children on her own, but she encouraged my dream wholeheartedly on the proviso that I didn't cop off with any Yank chicks. Doyle was full of enthusiasm for the trip and even went so far as giving me the names of some friendly, if slightly frazzled, trailer-park residents from Kentucky should I happen to pass that way. But others warned me that my longish hair and apparently less-than-macho appearance might result in my death or the loss of a limb at the very least. 'They're really weird down in Mississippi,' said one friend. 'Don't stop in any small towns.' 'If you go even slightly over fifty-five miles an hour the cops will haul you over, plant drugs on you, and throw you in jail,' claimed another. 'Act tough at all times,' was a piece of advice I heard more than once. 'You will be flying into Florida in the middle of a hurricane,' said one particularly silly person. 'For God's sake, change your travel plans immediately or you will die.'

What on earth were they talking about? I ignored such nonsense as the dampening outpourings of jealous minds, kissed the family goodbye, and boarded the plane with 'Anji' spinning through my head and adventurous notions in my heart. On 24 September 2004 I took a United Airlines flight to Orlando, Florida by way of Washington, DC.

During the hour's stopover in DC, I decided to call Roger McGuinn's wife Camilla to check that all was OK for the following morning. Over e-mail conversations she had invited me to come in the morning and stay for lunch. 'Will, I'm really, really sorry to do this to you,' she began, 'but we're going to have to leave early tomorrow morning. I don't know how long we can spend with you.'

'What the hell are you talking about?' I snapped. 'I've just travelled halfway across the world to talk to Roger. I can hardly turn round and go back now, can I?'

'I appreciate that,' she said, calmly. 'But have you not heard of Hurricane Jeanne? It's expected to hit Orlando tomorrow and it's going to be the worst we've had in years. We have to leave because our house is likely to get destroyed and it will be too dangerous to stay.'

'Oh. Well in that case . . .'

Maybe I should have checked the weather forecast before I left after all. On 25 September 2004, Hurricane Jeanne hit Florida with the force of a Category-Four storm. At 9am that day, it was 190 miles offshore. By midnight it would suck Orlando into its vortex of freak weather chaos. Roger and Camilla suggested that I arrive at their house as early as possible in the morning as they needed to leave by midday to drive out of Florida safely and go straight up to New York. An estimated three million people would also be heading on to the highway and it was a case of stay put or get moving: there would be no time to shake hands with Mickey Mouse while Hurricane Jeanne was raging. The plane arrived in Orlando around mid-night. After picking up the hire car and trying to get my head around American automobile technology – what kind of neurotic vehicle won't start until you've buckled up? – and getting lost about five times, I made it to the Best Western on International Drive, a large and ugly collection of motel-like rooms built around a little swimming pool and a greasy restaurant. Nobody at the hotel seemed too concerned about Jeanne, but since it was going to be their fourth hurricane in six weeks I suppose they were weathered to such things. I asked the lady at check-in what I should do: stay for the night and leave in the morning or stick it out for my intended three nights.

'Oh, you'll be just fine staying, hon,' she said, chewing gum as her fingers tapped out a staccato rhythm on the computer keyboard before her. 'Just stock up on snacks and water, don't leave your room for forty-eight hours, and stay away from all windows.'

I got two hours' sleep that night. In the morning I drove to Roger and Camilla McGuinn's house, which was down a tree-lined cul-de-sac about five miles away from where I was staying. It wasn't the kind of house you would have expected a psychedelic folk-rock hero to live in – in fact Orlando, with its stretching lines of chain hotels and supersized theme parks, was not the kind of city you would place him in either. It was a huge mansion complete with shiny white pillars and a manicured lawn. Camilla, a handsome black-haired woman with an air of brisk authority to her, came out of the house as I rumbled into the drive. She apologized for the fact that she had to cut short the visit, but said that I could spend the next few hours talking to Roger. She led me along the marbled floors of the house to Roger's den, a small room filled with banks of technology and two or three guitars hanging from every wall. It looked like the perfect place for a rock musician, his youth behind him, to spend his days in a world of solitary musical exploration.

Roger was looking good and healthy for a survivor of one of
the most important bands of the American sixties revolution.
Unlike The Byrds' co-founder David Crosby, he was not fat and
clinging on to what was left of his long grey hair, but then he
hasn't spent most of his adult life taking as many drugs as he
possibly can. He had his cocaine period in the mid-seventies,
but ever since the turn of the 1980s, he has been clean living,
Christian, and touring as a solo artist with Camilla at his side.
While the emotional Crosby is a rock wild man – and he
remains a freedom-loving, politically committed, probably
spoilt, but undoubtedly charismatic, product of the age he
helped define – McGuinn was always a more fastidious soul:
reserved, detached and principally interested in practising
guitar licks and dabbling with new technology. The genesis
of 'Eight Miles High', the avant-garde pop classic written by
McGuinn, Crosby and Gene Clark in 1965 that helped invent
psychedelia, illustrates the difference between the two. While
most of us have assumed that 'Eight Miles High' is about the
reality-expanding power of LSD, McGuinn claims that it is in
fact an ode to the joys of international air travel. Crosby's not so
sure. 'Of course it's about drugs. We were on drugs when we
wrote it.'

McGuinn is a sweet man, not a feral one, and it seems that he
likes to stay in control. Even back in 1967 – the year that he and
fellow founder member Chris Hillman chucked David Crosby
out of the band – McGuinn was writing anti-drugs songs:
'Artificial Energy', from the album *The Notorious Byrd Brothers*,
tells of a drug-freak who ends up killing a homosexual in a
speed-fuelled psychosis, and photographs from the late sixties
and early seventies show McGuinn looking pensive and cautious
beneath his long hair and groovy beard. *The Notorious Byrd
Brothers* also features 'Wasn't Born To Follow', which became

one of the most famous and iconic songs of the sixties after it was used as the theme to the film *Easy Rider*. Even in this hippy anthem McGuinn sent out a message of innocence, not decay: it suggested the possibility of a good life, lived on one's own terms, which McGuinn has adhered to ever since. Given that he spends most of his time on the road, he has never stopped in the search for America that was at the heart of *Easy Rider*.

In 1965 only The Beatles matched The Byrds for invention and impact, and much of that was down to what McGuinn did with his 12-string Rickenbacker. McGuinn, Crosby and Gene Clark started playing together at an LA folk club called The Troubadour in 1964. Coming out of folk music, but inspired by The Beatles, the trio grew their hair into Prince Valiant bowl cuts, recruited Michael Clarke and Chris Hillman on drums and bass – the former on the strength of his Brian Jones-style mop top – and hired a manager, Jim Dickson, whose friend Bob Dylan provided a rich source of material for the band to cover. In January 1965 The Byrds – or rather Roger McGuinn and a bunch of LA session musicians – recorded 'Mr Tambourine Man'. When the single came out on the Columbia label six months later it brought overnight fame. The Byrds played at the LA club Ciro's, where Dylan, Peter Fonda and Jack Nicholson took the spaces at the front of the stage and Sonny and Cher skulked in the back, taking notes. They hung out with the city's pre-hippy hippies at the studio of a bohemian sculptor named Vito and had Bryan MacLean, guitarist of Love, as their ultra-handsome roadie. They were the coolest band in America. 'Backstage at The Troubadour one night, I had Dylan on my right and Spector on my left,' McGuinn told me that morning. 'Spector leaned over and said: "You're in with the in-crowd, man."'

I wanted to know how Roger McGuinn got into the guitar in

the first place. Born James Joseph McGuinn in Chicago in 1942, he had a childhood generally free of any musical interests. 'I had heard the pop music of the time and it didn't impress me, and my brother had a plastic accordion but that was as far as my musical knowledge went,' he said. 'Then in 1956 I heard Elvis Presley's "Heartbreak Hotel" on the radio and something clicked. I had to get a guitar for my fourteenth birthday. I taught myself lead licks from listening to records and sounding them out – I couldn't even play chords. Years later, when I met George Harrison, we compared notes on how we learned to play and discovered that we both learned the same lick at the same time, which was a song by Gene Vincent called "Woman Love" that was the flipside to "Be Bop A Lula". There was a break in it that we nailed by trial and error, so you could say that the guitarist in Gene Vincent's band The Blue Caps, whoever he was, was my first guitar tutor.'

The guitar dominated McGuinn's teenage years. He went to the general store to buy lyric sheets to songs by Elvis Presley, Gene Vincent, The Everly Brothers and Carl Perkins, and learned that rockabilly and rock'n'roll were easy to play: they are blues-based, generally using three major chords and only occasionally adding a minor or passing chord. Then at around sixteen he started attending after-school sessions at a Chicago institute called The Old Town School of Folk Music. Folk guitar is more complicated than rock'n'roll, especially in its use of the right hand. When McGuinn heard The Beatles combining the two styles, a world of possibility was opened up to him.

'The big distinction I heard in The Beatles was that they were using passing chords, I guess because of their experience as a skiffle group,' said McGuinn. 'They brought those passing chords into rock'n'roll, which hadn't been done before. So really The Beatles invented folk-rock and The Byrds just picked up on it. I imagined that they knew how to play mandolin and bluegrass banjo, which they didn't, but they were certainly using styles like the dorian mode and various others that were more interesting than straight rock'n'roll patterns . . . things that went off the beaten path and which had only been used in folk and jazz before.'

It gave me hope to discover that a guitarist of McGuinn's calibre never really had any formal training. He only ever took a few lessons, and learned most of what he can now play by slowing down vinyl records and working out what the guitarists were doing by ear. I told him of my struggle to understand much of Ralph Denyer's *The Guitar Handbook*, and of how I was intimidated by musical theory because my own musical education had been so poor that I left school not even knowing that there are eight notes and twelve tones. (I only discovered this when I picked up the guitar.)

'Don't let the academic part of music destroy your love for it,' said McGuinn, when I told him about my technical insecurities. 'You can forget about the academic side that confuses you because it's not that important. I think it's better to learn the songs you like and have a heart for the music. Once I went to lecture a high-school group alongside the classical conductor Zubin Mehta, and I told the students that I had made number-one records and been a rock star despite the fact that I really don't know how to read music. Zubin said: "I think that is *so* disgusting. You're telling these children not to learn to ever read music, which is the most important thing in the world." But from his perspective, that was true: You can't be a conductor unless you read music. But you can certainly play rock'n'roll and folk.'

The Byrds created their unique sound, which fed into their image, ethos and pretty much everything else that made them, because of the brand of guitar that McGuinn used. F. C. Hall, the owner of Rickenbacker guitars, had brought out an electric 12-string in the hope of cornering the folk market, not realizing that no self-respecting folkie would be caught dead with an electric guitar. In his error F. C. Hall made folk-rock happen, providing both George Harrison and Roger McGuinn with the guitar that dominated so many of the songs of The Byrds and The Beatles.

A candy-apple red Rickenbacker was hanging from one of the walls, and my thoughts turned to my favourite Byrds song of all, 'Eight Miles High'. If I could learn how to play that song, with its Indian raga-like drone and free jazz opening sequence, my life would surely be complete. It's rumoured that McGuinn and David Crosby introduced John Lennon and George Harrison to the sitar when the four were sharing a bathtub in Los Angeles in 1965, high on acid, but while Harrison used the sitar on the song 'Norwegian Wood' there are no Indian musical instruments on 'Eight Miles High'. That sound came from the guitar.

I hedged around the subject by asking McGuinn how he came up with 'Eight Miles High'. He explained that at the end of 1965 The Byrds had taken a Phillips reel-to-reel tape recorder on tour with them. They only had one tape: on side A was *India* by John Coltrane, and on side B was an album by Ravi Shankar. 'We played it constantly, so by the time we got back to LA, "Eight Miles High" is just what came out. And when I first bought the Rickenbacker I learned a jazz scale and practised it for hours, which is what the opening sequence developed from. I was copying Coltrane, and the reason it sounds like a raga is because Coltrane was copying Indian music. It's actually really simple in its chord structure, even though it sounds so angular and modal.' I thought about the strange intro to the song, which didn't seem too simple to me, and asked McGuinn what notes he was playing. 'I can't tell you because I'm not sure, but we can go through it if you like.'

McGuinn reached up and brought the Rickenbacker down from the wall. It's a strange guitar: despite having twelve strings it has a very narrow neck, meaning that chords are often played with fewer fingers than you would normally use. He ran through 'Eight Miles High'. 'I'm a little rusty,' he said, knocking out about ten notes a second. 'I'm just riffing in E minor,' he explained as his narrow fingers danced up and down the neck. I didn't see how he could be riffing in E minor when he wasn't actually making the chord of E minor. 'All the notes I'm playing are in the scale of E minor. I'm playing E minor, an abbreviated F sharp minor, then G, then D and C. That's it, and the break is just a vamp in E minor.'

'What's a vamp?'

'It's bouncing backwards and forwards in a slight chord change,' he explained. 'This song is really easy and it's fun to play too. I'll give you the tabs if you like.'

He went to his own website and printed out the tablature for 'Eight Miles High'. There wasn't half as much to it as I had thought, and here is where, for me, the heart of guitar-playing lies. The best players really do seem to do a lot with a little, and even though they have good technique, they realize that technique is only the road map that helps you arrive at your destination. 'Technique without feeling is fluff – it's nothing,' said McGuinn. 'You can be the fastest player in the world but if you haven't got a feeling and a love for the music it's worthless.'

I gave 'Eight Miles High' a go. There was no point in trying to do the intro – that would take months of practice – but I attempted the main chord sequence, and created a sound that faintly resembled the song. As his wife Camilla battened down the hatches of their pink mansion and packed the van in preparation for a swift escape from a terrible hurricane that would hit in but a few hours' time, Roger McGuinn was teaching a stranger from England how to play one of the most iconic and perfectly realized pop songs of the sixties.

Realizing that it wasn't as supremely, impossibly complex as I had thought was another myth about the guitar shattered. Beefed up by this discovery, I wanted to show McGuinn my mastery of 'You Ain't Going Nowhere'. 'Check it out,' I said as I strummed my way through G, A minor and C. I could play it pretty well now. 'This is one of my favourite Byrds songs, and yet it's only three chords.' I nodded my head and swayed my knees as I demonstrated the song to the man who made it famous.

'Um, actually, it's four,' he said in his polite, breathy way. 'You're missing out the D that comes after the C. But you've almost got it, and you're right that you can do a lot with three or four chords.' He took the guitar from me and played it as it should have been played rather than the way I had confidently been doing it for the last two months. 'You should let your love of the music you want to play guide you, and once you get the hang of the basics you can add a few techniques like hammer-ons and pull-offs to add flavour. It's like spicing up your cooking, but still using the basic ingredients of meat and potatoes.'

McGuinn compared learning to play the guitar with learning a language: once you understand the dialect, what you do with that knowledge is where the art comes in. Outside the little room a palm tree was bending into itself while a spectral mist of rain fell from the gothic reds and greys of the sky, but I only noticed it after McGuinn had taught me the rudiments of scales. 'Scales are just a series of notes that relate to each other,' he explained. 'And it's worth learning a few because then you can stick one into the middle of a guitar solo and it always works. Here, try this one.'

He got me to play a major scale mixed with a minor scale, and although I played it far too slowly there were the beginnings of a musical sequence there. At this stage in my playing I hadn't really thought of doing solos because I wasn't really into the whole solo culture. The usual guitar heroes like Eddie Van Halen and Steve Vai had never done it for me, technically brilliant though they might be. The people I really admired, like Jimi Hendrix and Bert Jansch and of course Davey Graham, never seemed to be showing you how fast they could hit the notes, although realistically their entire career was based around playing solos. I also dug the understated playing of Steve Cropper of The Memphis soul band Booker T. & The MG's, who always played with tight perfection, but never sacrificed the song to his own moment in the limelight. I asked McGuinn if I really needed to learn scales if I wasn't turned on by fret masterwork.

'Scales can be useful because it's good to have a large vocabulary in order to express yourself,' he explained, taking back the Rickenbacker to knock out another lightning-fast rendition of the opener to 'Eight Miles High'. 'But I agree that a lot of solo rock guitar playing takes a very superficial approach to music.'

McGuinn's gentle nature came through in his attitude to the guitar. 'The guitar has been my friend and a source of great comfort and excitement through the years,' he said, casually picking random runs as the wind outside made the house rattle ominously. 'I love playing and I do it for fun. I never let it become drudgery and if I get fed up with it I'll put it down and do something else for a while. But I got to a point a while ago

where my interest in doing new things waned and I was happy
with that jingle-jangle style I developed with The Byrds. It
makes me feel good to play it and people seem to like it so I
don't really see the point in changing that.'

He showed me how the jingle-jangle McGuinn sound is
created. With a series of open strums and upstrokes, he uses a
combination of flat-picking and finger-picking: he has a metal
finger pick on his index finger while holding a plectrum with
his thumb and index finger, so he's playing two styles at once to
get that rich vibration. This invention was born of necessity:
when The Byrds did their sets at Ciro's in the mid-sixties they
had to perform five times a night without a break and McGuinn
did not have a chance to stop playing and change from finger
pick to plectrum. So he combined the two.

I remembered that I was without a guitar. I had heard about
these guitar supermarkets in the US, where racks of every guitar
ever invented and a few that were about to be invented lay in
wait for you to be seduced by their bright colours and handsome
sunburst finishes. McGuinn's Rickenbacker was a thing of
beauty, and considering the company custom-built it for
him it was also unique. Yet there were plenty more guitars
on the walls of his study that didn't have the material splendour
of the Rickenbacker, but weren't without their own merits. He
took down a huge, battered old nylon-stringed guitar that he
had recently bought for $25 in a garage sale. It had a soft and
subtle sound, and my version of 'You Ain't Going Nowhere'
sounded good on it. I asked McGuinn's advice on what guitar I
should buy.

'Takamines are OK and you could pick one up for about
$600. There is a Yamaha that is a knock-off of the Martin D-28
and it sounds just as good, but because there's snobbery about
Yamahas in the guitar world they sell for much cheaper. The

Japanese bought a lot of our spruce and rosewood in the seventies and eighties, and as the quality of wood and the workmanship define the quality of the guitar, many of the Japanese copies are superb. I play a Martin, and you can't go wrong with one of them, although you do pay a lot for the name. How much were you thinking of spending?'

'I'm prepared to go all the way up to $300.'

'Hm. Maybe you don't need a Martin at this stage in your development. You don't want a cheap guitar that's going to be hard to play or that goes out of tune the whole time, but there are certainly advantages in starting off on something inexpensive. Leadbelly was one of the great country-blues pioneers and he played a Stella, which had a real funky sound to it. That's why the blues men started to bend the strings: they wanted to get more out of a note on guitars that weren't generally of the best quality.'

I would have stayed in McGuinn's guitar universe all day if I could, but the palm tree outside the window was bending ever further and Camilla's footsteps outside the room were increasingly emulating the pitter-patter of the falling rain. Roger and Camilla had been on the road for most of their adult lives, and as far as I know they still are. With a guitar as his reason for leaving the house, McGuinn has spent an average of six months a year travelling the world since he was sixteen. He told me how he gets bored at home within two weeks of returning, and how he has grown to love a life of maid service, eating out, and not having to do any housework. The couple travel in a van equipped with a tracking system, a fridge, a television and DVD player and satellite radio. But there are hassles, too: the security obsession that has gripped America since 9/11 means that he has to take off half his clothes to get through any domestic flights, and American highway patrolmen like to do random shakedowns every now and then. A month before I met Roger and Camilla they were pulled over in Pennsylvania by a policeman who claimed that they had drugs when they didn't. 'America is much worse than Europe now,' he said as he packed the Rickenbacker in its case, 'but I'm not going to stop doing what I do because of that. My hero is the great Spanish classical guitarist Andres Segovia. He was booked to play Carnegie Hall at the age of ninety-four and the only reason he didn't show up is because he died. That's my plan.'

Camilla and Roger asked me what I was thinking of doing. They explained that if I left it too late I would be sitting in traffic for hours on end while the hurricane got ever nearer. I told them that I would like to go to Nashville but it was too far away. 'Nashville is a good idea,' said Camilla. 'If you try and stop anywhere in Florida or Georgia all the hotels will be full. You can get to Nashville in twelve hours if you do it in a solid run.'

She made me a travel survival kit. It contained two bottles of water, two bars of chocolate, a large bag of cashews, three tins of salted almonds, some mixed fruit and nuts and Roger McGuinn's latest album. We went outside to look at the rain. 'This is classic pre-hurricane weather,' said Camilla. 'The rain is really light and misty. I think this one's going to be bad.'

With hardly any sleep, no road map and no idea of what to expect next, standing outside Roger and Camilla McGuinn's big beige house in a Florida cul-de-sac and discussing the weather before taking off on a mammoth journey felt rather surreal. 'You know, while we were waiting for "Mr Tambourine Man" to be released, and we weren't sure if it was ever really going to happen, Dino Valente suggested that we form a group for which we wear spacesuits and sing into wireless microphones as we float around the room,' said Roger McGuinn, looking up at the shifting sky. 'I almost did that, but at the last minute I decided to stick it out with The Byrds. I'm glad I did.'

Chapter Seven

Nashville and Memphis

It was a strange drive to Nashville. The tolls were open, the big wide interstate highway was busy but calm – Americans are easier, more patient drivers than Europeans – and all that was heading in the opposite direction were fire engines. Every radio station I tuned to talked about the hurricane. I left Roger and Camilla at one o'clock and went back to the hotel, packed my few possessions and got the white Chevrolet out on to the road and moving without a break for the next five hours. At the side of the highway you could see houses being boarded up and men and women lugging cardboard boxes into trucks as their children hopped about nearby. It was a Saturday and the roads would be closed by Sunday, when the hurricane was expected to be pulling Florida apart.

I escaped in time and saw nothing of the devastation that was to come, save for the blanket television coverage I watched in a hotel room in Nashville of cars floating down streets, advertising hoardings smashing into buildings and newscasters in windcheaters attempting to stay vertical and shout something about the bravery of the local community as the winds howled around them. A lot of the footage was coming from Orlando. I stopped for a late lunch in a diner somewhere in Georgia, where large men with moustaches sat hunched over plates of grits and fried eggs and made jokes with the two waitresses. 'You from the north? New York? Chicago?' asked the younger waitress. I told her I was from England. 'England! But that's so far!'

Even when I was still many hours away from Nashville, country music took over the radio waves. The daylong 'Led Zeppelin from A to Zee' radio show in the northern part of Florida gave way to a George Jones special. Giant billboards decorated the highway offering a glimpse into the major concerns of the population: there were signs for 'adult' recreation centres with pneumatic blondes licking puffed-up lips next to signs for Bible sales and pro-life organizations with smiling foetuses waving their tiny, morally unquestionable paws to the motorists below.

I came into Nashville at one in the morning and trawled through the chain hotels that dominate the highways on the neon outskirts of every American city and town: Days Inn, Best Western, Hyatt. They were all full. I pulled up in the parking lot of a Red Indian-themed corporate motel with a sign outside bearing the legend 'We welcome the Macon Girls Of 55!!!' and went into the reception only to be told by a smiling concierge that none of their 2,576 rooms were currently available. The Macon Girls of 55 must have stayed healthy in the years since. It was hard to work out where everyone came from. I'm used to London, where every street, restaurant and pub has people in it and you can walk from one to the other in minutes. In the American South there are vast tracts of land with not much in them at all, and if you want to go from your house to the nearest bar you probably have to use your car. At night the outskirts of Nashville were eerie: the mass of bright colours, high above one's head, shone down on a concrete world free of people, and yet in the giant hotels the rooms were full.

Country music was created in this environment, where

travelling is a dominant part of daily life and the sheer amount of space creates the suggestion of possibility. The reality is that possibility is limited in the South. So the road offers some kind of escape, and the fleeting romance of greasy truck stops, giant flashing signs with at least one letter in every word missing and the sins or salvations that are offered underneath them made country what it is.

The romanticized ideal of a good and wholesome life started, on record at least, when the Maces Springs, Virginia-based Carter Family headed for the town of Bristol for an open-auditions recording session in 1927. The Carter Family combined the styles of the day – blues, gospel, vaudeville – to make what was then known as hillbilly music, and they created a rural fantasy in their songs. At the height of the depression A. P. Carter sang songs that gave reassurance in despair and preached of the strength one can find in acts of piety. Maybelle Carter developed the guitar technique that helped define country music, playing a melody on the bass strings while maintaining a rhythm on the treble. As her son-in-law Johnny Cash said: 'This style was to be imitated to the note by literally thousands of guitar players.'

Just before I left for America, Michael Tyack of Circulus had shown me how to play the Maybelle Carter way. It gave a nice bluegrass style, but this was the length of my country music-playing knowledge. Nashville seemed like the obvious place to learn a bit more. I imagined a town filled with wooden houses where men in dungarees plucked at guitars at every street corner while their gap-toothed wives danced a jig by the watering hole. I also needed to pick up a new guitar. Failing to buy one in Orlando due to freak weather conditions might have proved beneficial. What better place could there be than Nashville, if not in a pawnshop then in a famous second-hand store like Gruhn Guitars?

So far all I had seen of Nashville were highways and towering neon signs, but this was not the hour to worry about authenticity: right now I needed somewhere to sleep. Six chain motels in I found a run-down place not far from the centre called The Knight's Inn. It was cheap and the overweight manager with a ponytail and moustache was friendly. When I told him about my plans to buy a guitar he excitedly related his story of how he found a '51 Gibson in the attic of a woman from his church whose house he was clearing out following the death of her husband. 'It was the most awesome moment in my life, second only to the time I quit drugs and became a Christian.' After a long treatise on why Led Zeppelin were the best band ever he let me go to the motel room, past the group of rowdy rednecks doing a shouted version of Queen's 'We Are The Champions' in the bar and the two teenagers in the parking lot daring each other to hold firecrackers in their hands for the longest before they exploded.

The room smelled of desolation. A small clock radio with cigarette-sized holes melted into its plastic casing was nailed to the table at the side of the bed, and I couldn't stop it from making a low but insistent buzz. Stale cigarette smoke and ash had sunk into the hardwearing fabric of the carpet and the durable green and yellow shades of the walls were murky and stained. Outside I could hear the sudden pop of firecrackers followed by cries of 'OW!' It was a lonely adventure I was on, and without a guitar the neon strip lighting of the bedroom shone with sleazy solitude. It was two in the morning: it would be after nine back home. After grappling with the insolently mundane complexities of the American telephone system and the barrage of inappropriately enthusiastic recorded voices telling you that you have not achieved your goal of making a call, I got through.

NJ was in tears. For the last few months she had been working as a stylist to an up-and-coming fashion designer: it had been London Fashion Week just before I left and she had put many hours into helping design the collection he was showing. The show had gone well but the designer was unhappy: he felt that it was NJ's vision up there on the catwalk, not his own. So he sacked her.

'But he can't sack you,' I told her. 'He wasn't paying you. You were working for free.'

'That doesn't make me feel much better,' she sobbed.

She was inconsolable. She was stuck at home with two small children, cut off from her friends by domesticity, and the one thing that had given her a life outside of the home had been taken away from her. The designer and his team had been her friends; she felt betrayed and rejected. And she had been sick with worry about the hurricane. I told her I was fine; I was in Nashville.

'Oh baby,' she squeaked, managing to stop crying for a little while. 'I miss you so much. I even miss listening to your guitar. I wish I was there with you in Nashville.'

I looked around the room, noticing for the first time some graffiti on the wall that said 'Shoot, junior done took the truck', and wondered if she really would have liked The Knight's Inn that much. But life didn't seem fair on NJ, and the fact that I had left her to cope with her misery all on her own must have made things so much worse. In a moment of pretension, I thought of all those women left behind by guitar men who were too selfish to forgo their dream of a free life. The women guitarists that broke through were often the same. Joni Mitchell gave her child up for adoption to become a superstar, and later split up with Graham Nash, whom she was in love with and who loved her, because in her contentment she couldn't write good songs any more. I told NJ that I loved her and turned off the light. All that was left was the radiation of neon.

The next morning I headed into Nashville's downtown area, a grid of smart streets with tall buildings that it's easy enough to walk around. The streets were empty. I parked the Chevrolet behind Gruhn Guitars, which turned out to be closed. Inside the tall building, which stands on the corner of 4th and Broadway, I could see beautiful second-hand models by Gretsch and Guild; oversized peacocks of guitars in bright red and blue. They held such authority that they seemed to suggest owning one would take you halfway towards being the real thing. That's the trap they can tempt you into, of course – the world is full of people spending two thousand dollars on the same guitar that Keith Richards plays, forgetting the fact that Keith Richards's genius is only in part down to the scratches on his Telecaster and the raggedness of his hairstyle. But standing outside Gruhn Guitars and looking in to this world, you could see how easily temptation can take hold.

It was ten in the morning and the streets were filling up with crowds heading in one direction. They were mostly white, mostly in shorts, and frequently large. There is a street in Nashville called Broadway that is at the city's commercial and entertainment hub; maybe here I could find a guitar or at least something for breakfast. Only the souvenir shops were open, all with the usual Elvis figures with bouncing heads and Jack Daniel's T-shirts. Famous shops with great storefronts like Hatch Show Print (the USA's only remaining wood-block advertisement printers) and Robert's Western Wear were shut. The Charlie Daniels museum on 2nd Avenue – Daniels is the longhaired country-rock fiddler who scored a massive hit in 1979 with 'The Devil Went Down To Georgia' – was open, but it turned out to be just another souvenir shop.

I heard music coming out of a dirty-looking bar on Broadway called Tootsies Orchid Lounge, and went inside to find a middle-aged man with an enormous grey permed mullet – a tumble of perfectly aligned waves cascaded down his back while the rest of his hair was short and neat – sitting on a little podium, playing his guitar and singing well-worn country songs to three tourists at the bar. The place smelled of bad beer and cleaning products and it looked like it was only open to squeeze some cash out of the undiscerning. The bartender broke into a well-practised smile. I got out quick.

Everything else was closed, and then I realized why. I was in the heart of the Bible belt on a Sunday. Most of the town was at church. The large people in shorts were going to a baseball game. Sport or prayer was the choice on offer in Nashville that day. I knew nobody in the town and had failed to arrange to meet someone who might illuminate me on the role the guitar had played in turning Nashville into what it is. I got in the car and drove up to Music Row, a neat residential area that is home to the city's music publishing firms. On the well-kept lawns of smart wooden houses were signs congratulating various singers I had never heard for selling 500,000 copies of their latest recording. In my ignorance I thought of country music as those soul-searing songs by Gram Parsons like '$1,000 Wedding' and 'She'; of Johnny Cash, middle finger raised and teeth clenched into bottom lip, entertaining the inmates at Folsom Prison. They have no place in Nashville.

Even the right-wing, moralizing image of country music is something of a smokescreen to cover the fact that the vast majority of the industry is simply about making money. The radio is dominated by insipid music that studiously avoids exciting anyone in one direction or the other. Even someone like Merle Haggard, often drawn as the archetypal redneck because of his blue-collar anthem 'Okie From Muskogee', belongs to a far wilder world than the one Nashville apparently likes to endorse.

I left Music Row and headed towards The Grand Ole Opry. The Grand Ole Opry had a lot to do with Nashville turning into a country music town. In 1925 the Tennessee radio station WSM launched the WSM Barn Dance. Uncle Jimmy Thompson played his fiddle and a harmonica player called DeFord Bailey established himself as the most popular draw; few of the show's listeners knew that the four foot ten-inch Bailey was black. Getting on to what became The Grand Ole Opry was the ultimate goal for any would-be country star: WSM used 50,000 watts to get out to most of the country and it was hugely popular.

Formerly in the central Ryman auditorium, the Opry institution was now a few miles out of town. Perhaps here I could get an idea of what it must have been like for Hank Williams's steel guitar to be blasting into people's homes all over the country, or for The Byrds to perform songs from *Sweetheart Of The Rodeo* to an audience who hated them for their long hair and infiltration of country values. The Opry took the music of Roy Acuff, Jimmie Rodgers and Hank Williams into little towns where no music was otherwise heard at all, and it introduced country to black and white audiences all over the nation. It was at the heart of American culture.

What a mistake that was. The Grand Ole Opry is now part of Gaylord Opryland, which is the Disneyworld of country music, a mega-resort complete with corporate entertainment suites, golf links, a mock Delta village, overpriced souvenirs, a huge hotel and a nearby showboat. What was I thinking? Any institution that had Richard Nixon at its inaugural opening wasn't exactly going to be inspiring. Owned by the massive

Gaylord Entertainment, Opryland is enough to put anyone off country for life. I found an opportune moment to cut short my guided tour through the auditorium and hall of fame and make a dash for it.

On the way back from The Grand Ole Opry, and lost due to the fact that I still hadn't got round to buying a road map, I passed through a black area that was what is known in America as a project. It was bedraggled, empty and poor, and the opposite of the image that Gaylord Entertainment presumably wished to project of Nashville. Back in England a few weeks later, I discovered that I was in the project that had been home to one of country music's pioneering figures: DeFord Bailey. Bailey joined the Opry at its very beginnings in 1925 and he was dismissed in 1941, a victim of the Opry's and Nashville's increasing professionalism. The reason given was that he did not learn new songs. The Opry's MC George Hay stated: 'Like some members of his race and other races, DeFord was lazy.' As Bailey died in 1982 I had no way of knowing the veracity of that statement beyond its obvious ignorance. But the gulf between the harmonica player's home and the money-soaked Gaylord Opryland suggested that the real reason for his dismissal was a little more brutal.

There didn't seem much reason to hang around any more.

The road from Nashville to Memphis is beautiful. Through the deep forests of Tennessee, Interstate 40 is a reminder of the inspiration the American landscape can provide. The wide road is home to proud, shining trucks and old-fashioned pit stops, and the pines that line it hide broken-down shacks and pillared mansions. It makes you want to write a song.

The idea of Memphis has figured heavier in my life than Nashville, and as I drove over those gentle hills I thought of the great music the city had produced: Elvis Presley, Otis Redding, Rufus and Carla Thomas, Booker T. & The MG's . . . rock'n'roll was born here when Ike Turner, the saxophonist Jackie Brenston and their band The Delta Cats loaded up their car with instruments and drove in from Clarksdale, Mississippi in 1951 to record 'Rocket 88' at Sam Phillips's recording studio. On the drive up, their guitarist Willie Kizart's amplifier fell off the top of the car, breaking the speaker cone. 'We had no way of getting it fixed,' Phillips told the blues scholar Robert Palmer. 'So we started playing around with the damn thing, stuffed a little paper in there and it sounded good. It sounded like a saxophone.' Phillips over-amplified the guitar to make a virtue out of its distortion, thus creating the rough sound that turned the blues into rock'n'roll. I had heard so much about Memphis, but my only visual image of it came from Jim Jarmusch's film *Mystery Train*, which paints a lifeless city filled with the ghosts of its former glories. One imagines that world-changing movements like rock'n'roll and soul were created in thriving activity and pulsating life; it seems they were really made to fill empty spaces.

Memphis is poor. I had no idea where I was once I arrived in the city, which is sprawling and even more devoid of people than Nashville. There are signs to historic places like Beale Street, the home of blues clubs since the 1920s, and Sun Studios, but I didn't find my way to anything that didn't look like suburban emptiness. I stopped to ask for directions at a gas station that must have been located in a dirt-poor area given the fact that the gardens of the collapsing houses had been turned into all-purpose dumping grounds. I parked the car in the forecourt and a skeletal man in ripped clothes pulled a shaking smile and said 'Hey there, big guy'. Another man, also in rags, managed a wave from his spot outside the gas station store's door. I asked to use the bathroom and the clerk gave me a key to enter the most disgusting room I have ever encountered. Shit was smeared on every wall. As for the toilet itself, it looked like it had got blocked up six months ago but nobody had bothered to tell the people that used it. As a European raised on American television shows where even waitresses have Manhattan loft apartments, one is not exposed to this side of the country's life.

It was a mission just getting from the bathroom to where the car was parked about ten metres away. The two hobos grabbed on to me and demanded money while younger men in baseball caps hanging around the store watched the scene with mild interest. One of the hobos began a story about needing to get a bus to see his daughter on the other side of town, but I suspected that city bus fares didn't cost ten dollars. I managed to get into the car but the two hobos were banging on the bonnet, demanding money and shaking desperately. I drove away in the hire car to see the ruined men returning with resignation to their place between the petrol pumps and the store.

Memphis, for all its fame, is a shabbier town than Nashville. It is also more charming. It isn't hard to find a run-down old diner with red leatherette banquette seating and a miniature jukebox in every booth, where a cigarette-smoking fifty-year-old waitress with a black-dyed beehive hairstyle will take your order for grits, scrambled eggs and fried potatoes and charge you three dollars for it, endless amounts of coffee included in the price. Some of the shop signs are the purest examples of Americana you can find anywhere, with the beaming optimism of the joined writing and stylized exclamation marks let down by the fact that six out of their eight neon letters no longer light up and haven't done so since 1973. The town is racially mixed, although the hobos that you find on every street are invariably black, male and middle-aged.

My guitar tour of Memphis began, naturally enough, at the tiny Sun Studios. But I wanted to go beyond the usual Elvis knowledge in the hope of understanding the part the guitar played in creating this culture. I had heard of a man called Roland Janes who had been at the centre of the golden age of Sun. He was the guitarist for the rock'n'roll firebrand pianist Jerry Lee Lewis, and he played on countless sessions for rockabilly and country stars like Billy Lee Riley, Carl Perkins, Charlie Rich and Charlie Feathers. Unlike most of the original Sun men he still lived in Memphis, and was said to be in charge of the Sam Phillips Recording Studio, the modern equivalent of Sun Studios, located just around the corner from Sun and still operating. He had been a friend of Teddy Paige. I wanted to find out what life was like for the guitar men back when rock'n'roll was born.

After satisfying my touristic urges by holding the microphone that Elvis Presley once sang into, I walked across the broken asphalt of the empty parking lots that connect Sun Studios with Sam Phillips Recording Studios a block away. It led to a dirty white door with no sign on it, but two buzzers that had come away from the doorframe and were hanging down limply by their wires. I was aware that no Elvis figure had come along in the last few decades to give Sam Phillips's legacy a much needed shot in the arm, and that since Phillips's death in 2003 the company had struggled, but this was shocking. There was no answer. The door was open so I stepped in, to see a dirty narrow staircase, its carpet worn through to the wood on most of the steps, leading to another battered white door. A dreadlocked young man appeared at the top of the stairs in a vest and underpants.

'Is this The Sam Phillips Recording Studio?' I asked him.

'Wha?' he said, rubbing his eyes.

'Er . . .'

Two skinny men with moustaches and mullets suddenly appeared behind me. 'Who's this guy?' said one of them with a hint of threat. I repeated my question to them. They looked at one another in cautious confusion, before one of them smiled and said to me: 'Y'all want the recording studio? It's right over the way there.' He took me outside and pointed to a large, rectangular, green building with a huge sign announcing it. I thanked everyone and waved goodbye, they all waved back and said 'You take care now and have yourself a good day,' and I crossed over the street. It took a few minutes for it to dawn on me, when I saw another group of hesitant youths arriving at the battered doorway, that I had walked into a drug den.

Roland Janes is a slow-moving man with a manner so dry it should be roasted on to peanuts. It appeared that he was the only person staffing the famous recording studio, and it was obvious that on the day I visited, there was rental time to spare. Janes had long since stopped playing his guitar. I told him that I was on a mission to understand the guitar and learn how to play it myself, and that I had come to America to learn the styles of playing I would need for my debut gig. He shrugged and said: 'You've either got a natural talent for it or you don't so nobody can show you how to play,' and I thought for a moment that the interview might be over there and then. Then he sat me down in the reception room and, though briefly interrupted by three big-hipped women wielding vacuum cleaners, we talked for the next two hours.

He remembered Teddy Paige very well. 'Didn't he chop some guy's head off?' he asked. I told him that it was an arm, and it wasn't chopped off, merely chopped at. He took in this information with a casual nod of the head. 'I always liked

Teddy, even though I found some of his views a little radical. Good blues player, though.'

Janes describes himself as 'a Roland of all trades', and he has been overseeing recording sessions since he opened Sonic Studios in Memphis in 1963, but it is as a guitarist that his place in history is assured. 'I did best on a Fender Stratocaster, although I had a Les Paul Custom for many years that I paid $350 for in 1958,' he told me. 'I never had a lot of guitars. I got one that I liked and stuck with it. We all did at Sun because there was never too much money around. Musicians and money is a bad combination.'

Janes was born in Arkansas in 1933 and raised in St Louis. His uncle played fiddle in a country and western band and Janes learned to play guitar by watching them. The family did not have a record player – very few people he knew did – and they did not have electricity, but a wind-up radio exposed them to country music on The Grand Ole Opry. He explained how he saw the rock'n'roll and rockabilly movement that he was a part of as a product of country boys moving to the city. All of the musicians he knew loved blues as much as they loved country. 'We didn't think of people as black or white – we were only interested in whether someone could play. And what we were doing was seen as this revolution, but we were never interested in rebelling against anybody. You could use a little bit of blues and what was then known as hillbilly music to go a long way.'

Janes got his first gig in 1956, playing guitar for the rockabilly singer Billy Riley. It was while he was with Riley that he developed a technique of playing two strings at once, creating a sound that wasn't country but wasn't blues either. He played with Charlie Feathers, the original hillbilly singer to combine blues with bluegrass, vocal yelps and a chopping guitar style, who was taught to play by a black Mississippi sharecropper and sometime truck driver called Junior Kimbrough. Feathers saw his style taken up by Elvis and brought on to a level he never thought possible. Then came The Rock'n'Roll Trio, a wild band led by the brothers Paul and Dorsey Burnette, who Janes played sessions with and subsequently recorded. The band are said to have created guitar distortion by sticking a screwdriver into the front of their amplifier, but Janes remembers it differently. 'We were always playing through mismatched amps because we couldn't afford to buy new equipment. We bought speakers from Radio Shack and put alligator clips on the speaker terminals, so the sound didn't come out quite as clear as it should.'

Everybody Janes knew, himself included, taught themselves how to play guitar in a haphazard way. I asked him if he knew how to read music. He wrote out the word 'music' and said that he could read it any time he liked. He wouldn't say if any sessions were more memorable than others because he claimed that after every session he ever played on, the guys would say, 'Man, that's going to be our biggest hit.' He spoke fondly of Jerry Lee Lewis. He talked of how The Rock'n'Roll Trio would never walk away from a fight, of how they had to be tough to play in the kind of joints that earned them their bread and butter.

It seemed sad that Janes no longer had any interest in playing guitar, and it was obvious that the studio could do with some more bookings. But he gave the impression of a man who had not moved on from the revolution he had been a part of in his youth. He said that his real respect went to The Rock'n'Roll Trio, one of the purest and most basic of all the fifties bands and far from the most famous. 'They were originals,' he said with quiet contemplation. 'Dorsey Burnette had his own style and he came up with licks that people are still copying today. There won't be anyone like those guys again.'

Memphis is a town content to trade on its memories. The Southside Church Of God In Christ pulled down the original Stax Records building in 1989 and in 2003 a museum was built in its place. In the bars on Beale Street bands play electric roadhouse blues the likes of which can also be heard in any branch of The Hard Rock Café the world over. Graceland is a ghoulish shrine to the money-spinning possibilities of the King's legacy. The great Memphis guitarists taught the rest of the world how to play the modern way – when The Beatles met Steve Cropper of Booker T. & The MG's in London in 1967, they stood before him in a line and bowed at the waist – but unlike less downhome cities like New York and Los Angeles, the music scene of Memphis, and the culture that surrounds it, is a backwards-looking one.

I needed to put myself into the present, what with Sun's premier session man having long since hung up his Les Paul and the city's other guitar greats either dead or in exile. Hope came in the form of the Gibson Guitar Plant, an imposing monolith of a building two blocks away from Beale Street surrounded by large clean parking lots and empty spaces. Thoughts of getting hold of a Gibson at a knockdown price were swiftly dashed: the factory's shop charges more than the average store because so many tourists are prepared to pay over the odds to buy a Gibson from the source. I couldn't begin to afford to buy a Gibson, but I thought I might be able to get a factory second at a reduced price. Who cared if there was a nick in the paintwork? I was politely told that no factory seconds existed. Prior to 1985 they were always available and made for a great bargain. Then two businessmen bought the company for $5 million. Desiring to increase profits they brought in a new regime: anything that was not perfect would be scrapped because it made better commercial sense to force someone who wanted a Gibson to pay full whack for it. When a mistake is made – and they happen every day, like they do in any line of production – the guitar is smashed up with an axe. Don't bother going round to the skip at the back of the factory to collect the pieces to build your own: a security guard is employed for the sole purpose of preventing people from doing just that. I know because I walked to the back of the factory to ask the guardian of the skip what she was doing there: she confirmed her purpose.

Under strict surveillance and for a ten-dollar fee you can undertake a tour of the huge factory. You could tell which employees were the master craftsmen: they were the middle-aged men with long hair or close-cropped afros. In the three weeks it takes to make a single guitar each worker has their own speciality, from cutting the wood for the body to doing the paintwork.

Gibson has three factories: one in Nashville, where all employees have to work for six months before moving else-where; one in Montana, where the acoustic guitars are made, and the one in Memphis that builds the solid-body electrics. My tour of the Memphis factory revealed a few other things about the world of guitar production. Women are always employed to strip the paint off a guitar because the job is so laborious that men are not considered patient enough to carry it out. The sanding is done – in Memphis at least – by huge and muscular black men because they are the only ones with the strength to hold the guitar in place as it hits against the enormous sanding wheel. And B. B. King, through his endorsement of the top of the range Gibson Lucille, has helped the company sell a lot of guitars.

The Gibson guitar factory not only illuminated me on the many details of guitar production, it also took me one step further to understanding the world of guitar obsession. Most of the people on the tour were middle-aged, white and male, and they had plenty of questions regarding the six-digit serial number of the 1959 Les Paul Special and whether the 1970 ES 330 really does have a neck that joins the body at the nineteenth fret. It's a world in which notions of authenticity and worth relate to the type of guitar you have rather than your ability to play it.

Back in London I found a book in the library that helped clarify the guitar fetish. Former *Guitar* magazine editor Ian C. Bishop's 1977 publication *The Gibson Guitar From 1950* unwittingly said as much about the mindset of the guitar-collecting obsessive as it did about, say, the Flying V ('it's aggressive phallic shape has made it popular with some sections of the guitar-playing fraternity'). 'I am writing this for all the many users of Gibson instruments who constantly bombard me, and the Gibson company, with questions concerning their guitars,' says Ian C. Bishop loftily, in the foreword to the book. 'I am continually surprised, even now, by the number of people who claim to have 1947 and 1948 Les Pauls and 1956 Firebirds and I hope that this book will finally lay these claims to rest.' Got that, you so-called owners of a 1956 Firebird?

Now I really had to get a guitar myself. The best place to go was said to be Strings And Things, a warehouse of a store on Madison Avenue about ten minutes' drive from the Gibson factory. It was staffed by mellow longhaired southern dudes with a laid-back approach to sales technique: after I told them I wanted an acoustic steel-string guitar, they took me to a large room containing about two hundred of them and welcomed me to take as long as I wanted and try as many as I liked. They weren't going anywhere.

I wasn't quite at the level of comparing serial numbers yet, but if it weren't for the $2,500 price tag that Martin D-28 would have been mine. I experienced a feeling I had not had since adolescence. When I was about eleven I discovered skateboarding and BMXing. The most exciting place in the world back then was a shop called Alpine Action in Notting Hill Gate, where a cool black dude, a hippy (they were rare in 1982) and a tattooed skater in a baseball cap swapped jokes, held court, and did their best to ignore the scores of pre-pubescents salivating over the stickers, videos and Powell Peralta skateboard decks. The shop was filled with magical objects like the Redline Flite Crank and the Kuwahara chrome-moly frame (expensive but dull bicycle parts). Even the crisp smell of chrome and oil was suggestive of barely imaginable excitement.

I had entered a world of sacred objects with high price tags once more. Still a novice, not only in playing but also in guitar knowledge, I found, the sight of all those Martins, Taylors, Takamines and Gibson flat-tops in one place intoxicating, and the distinctive smell and atmosphere – this time created by a dehumidifier and lots of polished wood – was just as evocative as that in Alpine Action. I started at the top and worked my way down. The Martins and Taylors sounded great, even when I molested them, but this was just window-shopping. I tried a Takamine, a Japanese brand, for $500 but I couldn't get a good sound out of it. Then I tried a guitar called a Seagull that sounded just right: gentle and melodious but loud and power-ful. It was really easy to play, a joy. And it only cost $199. It even had a nice wooden smell. I asked one of the mellow men about it.

'That's one of our bestselling guitars,' said the dude, whose name turned out to be Will. 'It's got a real sweet sound, right? That's because the solid top is made of cedar. A Canadian company called Godin makes it. They're real small and they set themselves up to make the best guitars at the lowest price. If you know a little bit on the guitar but you're still a beginner, that's a good choice.'

The more I played it the better it sounded. So many people had told me that Takamines are great, and surely that $500 model must have been a better guitar, but I couldn't get on with it. Giving Will a chance to make a higher sale, I asked him whether it would not be a finer guitar than the Seagull. 'It's a question of personal taste, man,' he replied. 'Also you have to remember that every guitar sounds and feels different, no matter what the brand or model. So you might play a Martin that doesn't feel right at all and another one that's like your dream guitar.'

The Seagull was the one. It would sound good with a glass of Jack Daniel's and a sleepy-eyed lady nearby. Will sold me an electronic tuner and a hard case to go with it, and I walked out of the shop feeling like a real guitarist. I hadn't felt on such a consumer high since I bought my first BMX bike twenty-two years earlier.

Later that night I went down to Beale Street to find a place to eat and hear some blues guitar clichés, and reflected on the thought that Memphis is a strange place. It has more churches per person than any other city in the union, but it has been a centre for sin and hedonism since the beginning of the twentieth century. It is at the heart of the Deep South and the race problems that have been a part of the region's history, yet it has been leading the way in integrated music since the beginning of the 1950s. It is a slow-moving place, from the way people talk to the amount of time it takes to get anything done, but it has produced the most passionate and frenetic cultural revolutions of all: soul and rock'n'roll.

In Nashville, men and women learned how to play guitar according to the rules. In Memphis they got it all wrong by playing broken instruments on badly set up equipment and invented new musical genres in the process. The history of music in Memphis is the history of mistakes.

I went back to the hotel early that night. I sat on the corner of the bed in an unremarkable room at the Best Western in downtown Memphis and picked out a claw-hammer pattern that Bert Jansch had showed me on the Seagull, and tried to imagine playing in front of an audience in under three months' time. I needed some kind of breakthrough if I was going to meet this challenge I had set myself. At the moment I was on a deadly plateau of entry-level playing and it was not enough.

Memphis was great. It had given me a guitar and revealed a rough and chaotic side of America that I had never been witness to. But it was time to go deep into the Delta. I would hit the crossroads and destroy myself for the secret of blues guitar. It was time to go to Mississippi, the birthplace of Muddy Waters, Howlin' Wolf, John Lee Hooker, and the blues itself.

Chapter Eight

Another Soul for Sale

The first time guitar-based blues made sense to me was on Highway 61, the road that travels from Memphis down to New Orleans. I was doing the three-hour trip from Memphis to Clarksdale. It is the straightest road I have ever seen in my life, and it is said that fifty-mile stretches of it do not deviate more than a foot on either side. It cuts through the flat expanses of Mississippi, where there really are cotton fields that form white expanses of the closest thing to nothing for miles, and where small wooden churches and decrepit shacks break up the monotony of the empty spaces. The familiar neon signs for McDonald's and Days Inn announce the arrival of each new town, but Mississippi is very different from anywhere I had been before. It is mystical in its bleakness. I saw a man with long hair and a beard wearing white robes and dragging a cross along the roadside miles from the nearest town and he didn't even look out of place.

On the way out of Memphis I stopped at a record shop to get some new albums for the journey. I bought *McElmore Avenue*, Booker T. & The MG's sophisticated and melancholic instrumental version of *Abbey Road*, which seems to be as much a product of Memphis as *Abbey Road* is of London. Steve Cropper's guitar playing is like the city itself: modest but proud. I also bought an album that pointed towards the direction I was heading in: *Most Things Haven't Worked Out* by the late Holly Springs, Mississippi guitarist and blues singer Junior Kimbrough. Kimbrough worked all his life and didn't get his first LP out until he was well into his fifties. The cover of the album showed a grumpy-looking man sitting down with his guitar, a cigarette hanging dispiritedly from his mouth, while two enormous women, their backs to the camera, appeared to be dancing behind him. He was sitting in what looked like a very rough bar and was most probably his own juke joint, where he performed on random Sundays to a crowd who found out about it by word of mouth. One of the tracks was called 'Burn In Hell', another was called 'Leave Me Alone'. The music was very odd. The songs were long and monotonous, mostly built around a single riff or a couple of chord changes, and the guitar was distorted and fuzzy. It sounded like Mississippi looked.

The simple guitar and drums-based music of Junior Kimbrough seemed to go on for ever with very little break in the regularity, just like Highway 61. I was vaguely aware of being hypnotized, or at least sedated, by the music and the landscape it came from until flashing lights surrounding an overturned truck pulled me out of my reverie. No doubt the driver, whose body I could see lying entirely still on the large grassy verge between the two lanes of Highway 61, had been lulled into a deeper calm by the road than I was. Junior Kimbrough's blues remained as straight as the white lines that stretched into the horizon.

Mississippi never had a chance. After the Civil War the cotton farms, which were dependent on the slave labour that was outlawed after the southern states were forced to return to the union, were separated from the factories that made use of their product, destroying the state's economy in the process.

Ever since then it has been fifty out of fifty, the poorest state in the USA and the most derided, too: the home of the Ku Klux Klan. It has also been home to an extraordinary number of musicians, mostly black and mostly playing the guitar.

The slaves of the South were denied drums and horns on the plantations they worked on for fear that they would send secret messages, but stringed instruments were seen as harmless. So they built guitars out of cigar boxes and baling wire, and by 1908 poor farmers were ordering steel-string acoustic guitars like 'the Toreador and 'the Serenata' from the Sears, Roebuck catalogue for $1.89. If you couldn't afford those there was always the option of making a diddley bow on the outside of your shack: two nails were hammered into the wall of the front porch and broom wire was pulled taut between them. A bottle or a rock was placed underneath the wire to form the equivalent of the bridge on a guitar, so moving the rock would change the tone. In this way the guitar was reduced to its heart. The butt of America produced the style on which almost all American music is based.

So came the blues, which owes pretty much everything to the cheapness and mobility of the guitar since its early practitioners were black convicts, drifters and poor sharecroppers without money and frequently no fixed address in the years following the abolition of slavery. In 1903 the bandleader W. C. Handy wrote of seeing a ragged black man at a Mississippi railway station, his toes sticking out of the tips of his shoes and his face expressing 'the sadness of the ages', playing a battered guitar by sliding a knife along its strings. The man repeated the same line three times – 'Goin' where the Southern cross the Dog' – and the result was, wrote Handy, 'the weirdest music I had ever heard'. It was also the most influential. The guitar music that we hear every day coming out of radios and record players, and in nightclubs all over the world – rock, soul and R&B – has its roots, however distant, in the blues.

That afternoon I pulled up at The Shack-Up Inn, a series of shotgun shacks on the old Hobson Plantation in Clarksdale that have been turned into rooms for rent. It's quite a place. A few miles away from the crossroads where Robert Johnson sold his soul to the devil, The Shack-Up Inn takes over a few acres of flat space near to an old silage warehouse, a cavernous barn called The Commissary that has been filled to the rafters with the physical detritus of twentieth-century American culture and turned into a live music venue, vehicles in varying states of decay including the seventies police car driven by Dan Ackroyd in the film *The Blues Brothers* (a present from the actor) and all manner of rusting farm machinery. The shacks themselves are welcoming and cosy – mine came with a guitar, a stack of copies of *Rolling Stone* magazine from the seventies and eighties, a fridge full of beer and pink gingham curtains that covered the tiny windows. It even had a porch with a rocking chair on it. The first thing I did was sit on that porch with a beer and play my new guitar. Looking out on to the highway a few hundred feet away, and the setting sun beyond, brought a romantic kind of desolate peace.

I went into The Commissary to see if I could meet anyone and have a beer. Mississippi people are so friendly that it is confusing: they say hello to you as if they have known you all your life. I got chatting to a guy called Ronnie Drew who, as luck would have it, based his life around the guitar. He ran a tiny shop in downtown (downtown? The whole place consists of only about ten streets) Clarksdale called Bluestown Music, where he sold second-hand guitars and the occasional new one, plus all the usual amps, leads and everything else you need to play. Unfortunately the shop averaged about one visitor per day and he couldn't make a living from it. So he paid a young man to keep the shop open while he worked as a financial adviser at the bank. 'Man, this job I got is getting me so stressed out,' he said, shaking his head at the row of whisky bottles behind the bar. 'They've got so much of this new Internet and e-mail technology that I don't know if I'm coming or going.'

Ronnie was a soft-spoken man with an easy manner, whose slightly long grey hair and sad eyes gave evidence to the fact that, despite his current respectable if frustrating position, he was very much a child of the sixties. He got excited when I told him that I had had a guitar lesson from Roger McGuinn. 'Damn, man, that is just so cool I can hardly believe it,' said Ronnie. 'McGuinn is one of the best guitarists ever, and The Byrds were just about my favourite band when I was a teen.' Ronnie was in one of the first-ever integrated bands in Mississippi, playing rock'n'roll and R&B at high school dances in the late sixties. 'We had three blacks and four whites in our band and I tell you we didn't even know what prejudice was; all we thought about was music. One time we were poisoned in a restaurant. Another time a white cop tried to run us over and broke my guitar. It was bad back then, man.'

Despite his natural grace and easy bearing, Ronnie Drew seemed to sum up the sadness of Mississippi, where charm and manners cover a suspicion that things can never really improve. We agreed that I would come and see him at his shop the next day, as soon as he could get out of the office (he reckoned around 4.30pm). I went back to the shack and sat on the porch to play guitar, which got the attention of a youth with a bleach-blond crew cut who introduced himself as the son of the cleaner. He had with him what looked like a toy electric guitar.

'Just got it in a pawnshop for fifty bucks,' he said. 'It's got a built-in amplifier.' He hit the strings and it let out a muffled electric sound. 'I only play metal. Y'ever hear of band name of Guns 'N' Roses? I learned a song they got called "Sweet Child O' Mine".' He played the intro. 'I performed that at school once when I was down in Florida. I dedicated it to the lead cheerleader who I was in love with at the time because I figured it might help to win her over. I never been so scared – I did it in front of the whole school by myself – and afterwards I even had teachers coming up to tell me how good I played it. No teacher had ever said anything nice about me before. Then the girl come up to me and shouted "You fucking idiot!" in my face. Then the bitch went and fucked my best friend.'

Over a few beers and under the light coming from the window of my shack, the teenager showed me how to play two of his favourite rock riffs: 'Sweet Home Alabama' by Lynyrd Skynyrd and 'Paranoid' by Black Sabbath. The latter wasn't really designed for a Seagull acoustic but it was a good learning exercise none the less. He also told a familiar story of a life lived on the edges of American society. He and his mother had travelled from state to state through the South, moving on at the point where another of her boyfriends became abusive or when he got into too much trouble at school for drugs or non-attendance. He said that now all he was really interested in was playing his guitar, and that his friends had worried about him when he told them he would rather stay in and practise than join them in the woods to unload a keg of beer from the back of a pick-up and get wasted. Despite his wild stories and muscular musical tastes he was a quiet boy, and he was happy to find someone to impart his guitar knowledge to. 'It's real peaceful here,' he said, looking around at the shacks and the old machinery. 'I hope my mom can stay here as I like it real good. Hey, what do you say we do a jam?'

He showed me the simplest of blues changes – E to A – and I

strummed the open chords while he laid down some lead guitar over the top. An hour later he sloped off and muttered something about having another jam tomorrow. 'I like playing the guitar a lot,' he said before he left. 'Watching TV is OK but I reckon playing guitar is even better than a good horror movie. If I had to stop watching horror movies or stop playing the guitar, I just about think I'd stop watching horror movies.'

Clarksdale is flat, regular and deadly quiet. When you pass someone on the street it is enough of an event for both of you to acknowledge one another. Since the Hollywood actor Morgan Freeman made it big he has been putting money into his home town, and now alongside the old juke joints Clarksdale has Ground Zero, a big graffiti-covered bar with live music on most nights. Otherwise there isn't too much going on. In the old station there is a German bakery run by pure-looking women in headscarves and no make-up who belong to an offshoot of the Amish faith (they thought the Amish were getting too liberal, apparently), and there is the Delta Blues Museum, which tells the history of the music of the region. The railroad tracks really do divide the town. On one side is the centre where the few shops and bars are, and on the other side is Martin Luther King Jr Boulevard, a rough street that courses through the black neighbourhood, where a lot of the houses are boarded up and young men stand around on street corners and stare at you.

Just outside the town, on the intersection of Highway 61 and Highway 49, is the place where one of the most important events in the history of the guitar is said to have happened. I discovered Robert Johnson when I was twenty. I had bought an album called *King Of The Delta Blues* that I had assumed was a collection of his finest recordings; it was years later when I discovered it was *all* his recordings. He only ever put twenty-nine songs down on to tape. There are just two existing photographs of him: in one he wears a suit and tilted trilby and sits smiling and cross-legged with his claw-like fingers tensed around the neck of a guitar. In the other he has a cigarette hanging from his mouth and he looks meaner, more troublesome. So little is known about his life that generations of music fans have reinvented him as the perfect blues man: an outsider beyond the reach of society and its oppression, who travelled the South to play guitar and make cuckolds of men all over.

The Rolling Stones played a wonderful version of 'Love In Vain', Johnson's story of 'following her to the station, her suitcase in my hand', as his woman boards a train out of his life, on their album *Let It Bleed*, although it says a lot about Mick Jagger that he read the lyrics to the song as '*a* suitcase in my hand', which changes the sentiment entirely. On the car stereo in Clarksdale, Mississippi the hissing, scratchy original sounded like it was soaking into every battered shack I passed. 'Hellhound On My Trail' came on, in which Robert Johnson describes being pursued by the devil, and his voice and guitar seem to erupt out of the land itself, with an unseen evil filling the wind and the trees with foreboding and threat. The music is so affecting that you cannot help but romanticize the man making it as a deep and restless soul embracing passion and despair and articulating suffering with wisdom. Who knows or cares what he was really like – he can't disappoint us now.

Robert Johnson was born on 8 May 1911 in Hazlehurst, Mississippi, the illegitimate child of Julia Major Dodds and Noah Johnson. The story goes that Julia's husband and the father of her first ten children, Charles Dodds, was a furniture maker who fell out with the local landowners and had to leave Hazlehurst, disguised in women's clothes, with a lynch mob on his trail in 1909. One by one Julia sent her children to live with their father in Memphis as she travelled from plantation to plantation for work, but Robert was the problem: as another man's son his existence prevented the family from reuniting.

He had taken up guitar by 1930, when he was living in the town of Robinsville and was already a widower after his sixteen-year-old wife died in childbirth. That was the year Son House arrived in Robinsville, and the older guitarist was to provide the material for the most enduring blues myth of them all. Son House told the folklorist Julius Lester about how, when he and his fellow musician Willie Brown played the Saturday night balls, Robert Johnson would be hanging around, trying to learn from them. In the break he would pick up one of their guitars while they were outside, cooling off. 'And such a racket you never heard!' said Son House. 'It'd make the people mad, you know. They'd come out and say, "Why don't y'all go in and get that guitar away from that boy! He's running people crazy with it."' Son House would take the guitar off Johnson and tell him to stick to the harmonica.

A year later, Son House and Willie Brown were playing in the town of Banks, Mississippi when Robert Johnson walked through the door, carrying a guitar. They teased him about still trying to play, and he asked to sit in Son House's chair so that he could show them what he could do. 'And man! He was so good! When he finished, all our mouths were standing open. I said, "Well, ain't that fast! He's gone now!"'

The story of Johnson selling his soul to the devil is usually attributed to Son House, but it might well have got confused with other Faustian pacts. The blues player Johnny Shines held Howlin' Wolf in such superstitious wonder that he suggested Wolf was a magic man who had done evil to get so good, and Tommy Johnson's brother LeDell told the folklorist David Evans that Johnson had said the only way to get really good on the guitar was to go to a crossroads with your instrument a little before twelve at night and wait for a big black man to walk up to you and take your guitar. He will tune it up, play a piece of music, and hand it back to you. After that you will be able to play anything you want, but you will also have a curse on you for ever more.

From 1931 on Johnson was a professional musician, travelling as far north as Detroit and New York, hitching rides on the back of pick-up trucks and hopping freight trains. According to Johnny Shines, who he often travelled with, he was a charismatic and popular performer, arriving in a new place and playing for tips outside bars and barbershops before landing a gig at a plantation shack or a house party where he would play anything from Bing Crosby to Jimmie Rodgers to Blind Willie McTell. He would also sing his own songs like 'Come On In My Kitchen', which with its overt suggestiveness would have got a few laughs. Shines claimed that Johnson was always clean and neatly turned out no matter how compromising his mode of transport had been that day. He was cool.

He picked up women along the way, including a midget in West Memphis. He left them where he found them. He preferred older women over the younger ones because they had money. Johnson was shy but direct: he would ask women if he could go home with them without ever trying to chat them up in the traditional sense. These always-short relationships came to an end with the return of the women's husbands or when Johnson hit the road again. The scattered accounts of Johnson piece together a picture of a sweet man who was rather immature and afraid of responsibility; who wanted to be looked after while not committing himself to anyone; who could articulate himself far better through his music than he could with conversation. Like so many other guitarists, in fact.

Johnson's recordings were made in 1936 by a talent scout

called Ernie Oertle in the Gunter Hotel in San Antonio, Texas. Over three days Johnson recorded sixteen tracks that used now-standard guitar techniques like a walking bass, designed to copy boogie woogie piano, in order to play lead and bass guitar parts at the same time. Songs like 'Kind Hearted Woman', 'Dust My Broom' and 'Cross Road Blues' were artful and poetic, evoking a world of experience. There was nothing throwaway about the songs. Johnson went to Dallas six months later for a second session. He made around $75 to $100 for the sum total of his recordings.

In the second session, Johnson secured his status as the devil-tormented blues man. Songs like 'Me And The Devil Blues' created the idea of his hedonistic life being lived on borrowed time, with the price to pay for such sweet sin coming soon. When he sings about having to keep moving to escape a hell hound on his trail you don't ever think he will succeed. In August 1938 he was playing at a dance in Three Forks, Mississippi, a village fifteen miles outside of Greenwood. A jealous husband gave Johnson a poisoned whisky and at around one in the morning he was taken to Greenwood. He died a few days later.

That afternoon Ronnie Drew taught me how to play the blues. We met in his tiny shop, where Epiphones and Rickenbackers await a new owner for years on end and where, a week before my own visit, the Irish singer-songwriter Elvis Costello had thrown a lifeline to the always-struggling shop by buying three expensive guitars. Ronnie had got out of the bank early – 'Hell, there's nothing ever going on there by mid-afternoon any how' – to give me a guitar session on the proviso that I played him the tape from my interview with Roger McGuinn. 'Hell, McGuinn, man,' he said, shaking his head slowly. 'That's about the best thing I've heard all year.'

Unfortunately my attempt at playing the blues was about the worst. I had got the hang of 'Get It On' by T-Rex early on in my guitar playing, which consists of E, A minor and G. As I understood it this was a basic twelve-bar blues pattern and I showed off my skills to Ronnie. 'That ain't happening,' he said. 'You should be playing E, A and B for the blues if you're in the key of E.' He showed me how to do that on three strings. It took about half an hour to learn and produced a chugging, train-like groove that will be familiar to anyone who has ever been in a bar in the American Midwest or in an American theme restaurant anywhere else in the world, or seen *The Blues Brothers*. It's really easy.

'There you go,' said Ronnie. 'Now you can be a rhythm guitarist. Hell, plenty of guys have put food on their plates on not much more than that for years.'

After an evening at Ground Zero watching a twelve-year-old girl on stage playing guitar like Johnny Winter, I drove the Chevrolet out to the Crossroads. I expected a lonely, isolated spot surrounded by flat expanses of cotton fields, where every ten minutes or so a giant lorry would roar past and cut through the darkness and the chorus of chirping crickets. What I got was a brightly lit intersection with a garage on one side and a row of fast food chain restaurants on the other. There was a stream of traffic and a dirty tin sign featuring two guitars crossed together, under which, in case anyone was left in any doubt, was the word 'Crossroads'. The immediate problem was where to stand to sell my soul. You simply can't hang about at the side of the road on intersections like this in the States, as you're likely to get either knocked over or arrested. The only possible place was the garage forecourt.

I got the guitar out of its case and waited for a large black man wearing a pinstriped, double-breasted suit and a wide-brimmed hat to come along and tune it up for me, flashing a toothy smile before breaking into low laughter, and hand it back, at which point I would be eternally damned and un-believably talented. I imagined sauntering on to the stage at my debut gig and watching everyone's jaws drop as I knocked out incredibly fast and complex riffs with haughty insouciance, perhaps with a cigarette hanging from my lips the way Robert Johnson had in the picture I had seen of him (I had given up four years earlier). But even standing in the forecourt wasn't easy: it was a Saturday night and the dangers of drink driving had not been sufficiently underlined by the Mississippi autho-rities. Huge pick-up trucks kept veering dangerously close, wherever I chose to stand. There was a group of teenagers on bicycles standing outside the garage shop and staring at me blankly.

Selling your soul to the devil is an intimate, personal thing, and this busy interchange did not feel like the most conducive place in which to do it, particularly under the glare of glowing neon signs. I tried playing the twelve-bar blues Ronny had taught me, but I could hardly hear it over the unyielding roar of the traffic. Hope arrived in the form of a tall, middle-aged black man who was wandering about nearby. He wasn't wearing a suit, but a T-shirt that hung loosely over his skinny body and a baseball cap perched on the top of his greying afro. He was clearly intoxicated, although I imagined the devil had no need to get drunk. He came up to me. 'Well hi there, sir,' he said with a smile that was toothy of a kind, except for the fact that most of his teeth were missing. 'Let me guess. Are you selling your soul to the devil?'

'Well, I . . .'

'The devil's done got tired of young men trying to skip on their guitar lessons,' he continued, still smiling. 'You must be the third this month. Say, you can get a cheaper lesson from me. You give me a cigarette and I'll show you how to do Muddy Waters. It's real easy!'

I returned to the Shack-Up Inn, deflated but somewhat relieved that I was still in possession of my soul. I also now knew how to play 'Mannish Boy' by Muddy Waters.

Chapter Nine

The Last Blues Man in Mississippi

Oxford, Mississippi is a smart college town at odds with the rest of the state. While the surrounding area consists of flat farmland with little more than juke joints and bars by way of culture, Oxford has large bookshops with creaking floors and deep sofas, coffee shops with plug sockets for your laptop, neat department stores and little record stores with jazz, classical and all the arty alternative releases. The home-town of William Faulkner, it has a central square of park benches and restaurants, where car drivers are politely asked not to stay for more than two hours, although there is no suggestion that anyone would do something as inhospitable as towing your car away should you exceed the preferred time. This was where I had arranged to meet the two men who ran a raw blues record label called Fat Possum.

My first experience of the blues came in the form of Sonny Black's Blues Band, a covers outfit that my secondary school drama teacher played bass for. They did a set at the 1987 Folk and Blues festival held at The Maltings in Farnham, Surrey, where a noticeboard with leaflets about yoga classes and toddlers' painting workshops was on a wall next to the coffee counter (50p with two plain Digestive biscuits thrown in). Four large, balding, middle-aged men with friendly faces and eyes like black buttons pushed into dough played 'Sweet Home

Chicago' and 'Smokestack Lightning', while a woman with a Tibetan-style multicoloured hat danced with her three-year-old girl at the front of the stage and our biology teacher, who was the organizer of the event, tried to stop her wayward son from lighting a joint in the corner.

Since I've been learning the guitar I've come to understand that The Sonny Black Blues Band, which was made up of normal men holding down jobs to look after their families, played the music they loved as a positive way of enlivening the toil of existence. At the time I thought they stank. I hated the blues because it seemed so staid and unimaginative. It was the soundtrack for pizza restaurants in English suburbs modelling themselves on Chicago speakeasys. It was what American politians played in the background as they were inaugurated into the Senate. It's taken me a long time to realize that this distaste for blues was based on the image that came with it.

Fat Possum were on a mission to return blues to its original spirit, to take it out of the museum and the theme restaurant and inject it with some life and dirt. They searched through rural Mississippi in search of authentic, undiscovered, preferably living blues men. The only problem with this noble quest was that their artists kept dying. Fat Possum were just managing to get Junior Kimbrough out to a wider audience when he died in 1998. A blues guitarist called Charles Caldwell had spent a lifetime working in a factory after his early attempts to make it in the music business ended in failure. He decided to make another go of it in 2002, when Fat Possum took him into the studio to record his first album at the age of sixty. He died the following year. One of their few still-living artists, Nathaniel Meyer, keeps ending up in jail. The closest thing they have to a star on their books is R. L. Burnside, and he has something like thirty-seven grandchildren to support and will consequently be lured out of his Mississippi countryside ranch only by the promise of money.* When I saw them Fat Possum were pinning all their hopes on two acts: The Black Keys, the goofy duo from Akron, Ohio who had come by the house a few months earlier to explain their own vision of the blues, and an eighty-something former logger and chain gang inmate from Greenville, Mississippi called T. Model Ford.

I met the founders of Fat Possum in a restaurant on the main square at Oxford. Bruce Watson wore prescription shades and looked a little like Elvis Presley in the early seventies, and Matthew Johnson would have been deeply nondescript were it not for the fact that his dark, probing eyes suggested both a fierce intelligence and a malevolent criminality. They didn't seem to understand why I wanted to talk to them. 'My social skills are, shall we say, limited,' said Matthew, the more forceful of the two. 'But I promise to do my best.'

I asked them what their aim was with Fat Possum, and what made for a good blues player. 'It seems that the best music isn't always made by the nicest people,' offered Matthew. 'Anyone who meets R. L. Burnside would be able to tell you that. And if you look at someone like Junior Kimbrough, who has a totally unique style, you realize that he developed his music by not wanting to please anyone. When I met him he had been working as a truck driver for years, and he had accepted that life wasn't going to get any better. He decided that he wasn't going to try and help anyone. I think he developed his own style because he really lost interest in pretty much everyone else; not just other musicians but people in general.'

Bruce had a simple explanation as to why all the best blues came out of Mississippi. 'It's a shit-hole. I suppose that's why we

* R.L. Burnside died on 1 September 2005.

feel comfortable here. Personally, I couldn't stand the blues when I was growing up because my image of it was Eric Clapton in his Armani suit. It's only when I discovered this raw blues that it made sense to me.'

After lunch ('That was horrible,' concluded Matthew of his plate of pumpkin, cornbread and beef stew), I followed Bruce and Matthew in their jeep to Water Valley, a quiet residential town that is home to Fat Possum's offices. Inside a typical suburban bungalow, with a lawn outside that was markedly more dishevelled than the rest of the lawns on the street, was one of the most chaotic offices I have ever seen in my life. Piles of papers and CDs covered the floor. It was hard to tell if the dustbin was being used as an extension of the Fat Possum filing system or not (I suspected it was). There were two younger men inside staring at computers. 'Did anything important happen while we were out?' asked Matthew.

'Not a thing, important or otherwise,' replied one of the young men, not bothering to look up from his screen.

'Good.'

Matthew took me into his office – he was the worst offender when it came to disorder – and gave me a stack of CDs that he thought I might like. I told him I needed to get some practical advice on playing dirty blues guitar. He said T. Model Ford would be the best man to talk to. 'T. Model will talk to anyone,' he said. 'He loves having visitors but I've got to warn you to watch your back down there in Greenville.'

T. Model Ford deserves his own special category. He thought he was eighty-five, but he wasn't sure and neither was anyone else. He picked up his first guitar at the age of fifty-eight after his fifth wife left him. He has spent most of his life in Greenville, and according to Matthew and Bruce, T. Model seemed unconcerned about the crack trade that had pulled his city apart, although he had been upset that the eighty-eight-year-old white woman who was teaching him to read and write had recently been raped and beaten to death. Greenville was one of the poorest places in the Delta and drugs had hit its mostly black population hard. It was home to Nelson Street, once a strip of bars and juke joints that jumped with the toughest rawest blues in the US: now the crack trade had given Greenville the highest per capita murder rate in the country and scared off audiences and performers alike. T. Model rocked up to what was left of this drug-ravaged wasteland once a week with his simple-minded drummer Spam to play five-hour sets, either too much in his own strange world or too mean to care about the danger. He never learned to read or write, and his grip of geography is not good. When Fat Possum booked him to leave America for the first time to play a few concerts in Canada, he greeted his audience with the words: 'Hello Germany!'

T. Model is tough. When he was in his twenties he killed a man with a knife at a logging camp, following a gambling argument. He was sent to a chain gang, but the owner of the camp valued T. Model so much as a worker that he arranged for him to be set free after a few months. Since then he has been back to jail so many times he has lost count – 'I reckon every Saturday night back there for a while' – and I discovered that, being an essentially cheerful and strong-willed soul, he didn't fit into the stereotype of the mournful blues man sitting on his porch and accepting his lot. His music was brutal, too: I had an album of his called *Bad Man* on which T. Model boasts of his anarchic attitude and his less than pure lifestyle. And he was living the life he sang about in his songs – Bruce Watson told me that T. Model had contracted gonorrhoea for the first time at the age of seventy-nine.

Bruce telephoned T. Model's girlfriend Sylvia and told her

that I would be coming to meet them the following morning. He gave orders for T. Model to come and pick me up in his '71 Blue Lincoln from the McDonald's on the main street that runs through Greenville, and he told me to stay put if T. Model was late. 'Greenville's not a place you want to go wandering around in,' said Bruce. 'There are a lot of crack addicts who would like to grab hold of some money to get enough hits for the next week, and if they don't like you they'll take your car too.' Having thoroughly scared me, he realized that perhaps he had gone too far. 'Hey, you'll be fine. You'll be with T. Model. Nobody would mess with him. On second thoughts, he did recently have a brick thrown through his window and get robbed for $2,000 . . .'

When a place has been built up in your mind as a hotbed of terror and violence, it is quite a surprise to arrive there and find a dull town that looks much like any other in America. It was certainly poor, but there were the same uniform McDonald's golden arches and Sonic Drive-In neon signs as everywhere else. The main feeling one got from driving through Greenville was of boredom. In the daytime, Nelson Street was drab and lifeless, and the city wasn't a place filled with knife-wielding gangs hanging out on every street corner, but of old men with baseball caps and cigarettes who sat in cafés hardly saying a word, and young mothers in tracksuits and complicated hairstyles busy trying to keep their children under control. I waited in the McDonald's and did my best to get through a cinnamon roll caked in a sugary goo-like icing and a bucket of weak but scalding hot coffee. The manager lent me her cell phone to call T. Model's girlfriend Sylvia. Within five minutes the sight of a huge, multi-dented, powder-blue Lincoln with a grinning old man with a face like beaten leather inside shattered the mundanity.

T. Model introduced himself and told me to follow him to a

quiet street a few blocks away, where tall trees shadowed broken paving stones and rows of wooden bungalows. T. Model's house was more chaotic than most. An old pram and various car parts heralded the steps leading up to the front door, where a screen hung from its bottom hinge. He limped into the house with his stick – over the course of the morning he told me that he got his limp when a tree fell on him *and* when a man attacked him with a chair for no reason – and requested I sit down on the old sunken sofa. The living room had a television, baby toys and clothes, T. Model's special armchair and the sofa I sat in. A hazardous mass of wires grew out of a wall at one corner and there was the dense, cloying odour of nappies and baby food. On the walls were a few curling photographs of smiling children.

People passed through the room. There was T. Model's girlfriend Sylvia, a large woman who looked as if she might be in her fifties, and various younger women with their babies and children who I assumed were his daughters. A woman sat on the sofa breastfeeding a tiny baby. She mumbled a hello. 'They say I've got thirty-eight grands,' said T. Model in his thick southern growl. A little girl was jumping around between the two of us, showing me her doll and trying to get her grandfather's attention without talking. 'I've got four grands in this house here. That little bitty grand right there is Renee.'

T. Model asked if I wanted a coffee, then called out a name. Five minutes later a man who looked about thirty appeared with a mug and carefully bent down to hand it to T. Model. 'Ooh!' said T. Model in a high, singing voice, crunching up his face. 'That's too much coffee for me. Ooh! Give me half of that!' The man took it off him and reappeared with a smaller cup, which T. Model looked at before nodding and accepting it. One of the women appeared to offer him a bowl of nuts, but he waved her away. I asked how he came to learn the guitar.

'I was working in the woods,' he began in a voice that fell between a growl and a mumble, settling into a storytelling position. 'I was married at the time, and man, this woman, we had three little ones and she were pregnant with another of mine. I was working and bringing my money home and she done the shopping. One day I parked my truck and come into the house and see the chillun, and every time I hit the door they call at me, saying "Daddy, Daddy, Daddy," and laughing at me. They say sit down there. My wife, Nodie was her name, say "Hey!" And I say "Hey there baby!" She say "You see your present?" I say "What present?" "Look behind the bed." "What is that?" She say "I bought you a guitar." I say "Hell baby, why you spend my money on something like that? I can't play no guitar. Don't know nothing about no guitar." She say "You can learn." I didn't say I could and didn't say I would.'

T. Model took a sip from his coffee and sighed with the memory. Bruce had already told me that it was T. Model's fifth wife who bought him the electric guitar, when he was fifty-eight. 'Later that night I come in, I see a strange car sitting in my driveway. I go on in and see my mama-in-law and brother-in-law and sister-in-law, and they say "Hey James!" – that's my birth name – and I say "Hey Mama!" And she say "Ain't nobody goin' to hurt you, James," and I say "I know that," cause I wasn't crippled then. I had good legs. And my wife Nodie say, "I did got to telephone to say mama come and get me."

'I still didn't know what was going on. They had packed all her things in the car. I sat there. I had money in my pocket. "We are leaving" say my wife. I said "Do you want some of this money I got in my pocket I got for you and the chillun?" "No." I didn't know she was mad or nothin'. She say "I don't want nothin' you got." Mama-in-law say "James, we're going to go now." Whole of them got up and walked out.'

The woman breastfeeding the baby, who was now asleep, stood up with a yawn and went to sit outside on the steps of the house. She left the door open, giving light to the dark room.

'They say I'm the daddy of twenty-six chillun and I ain't going to say I ain't cause I got chillun all over the state. But now I was alone in that house. I heard Muddy Waters and Howlin' Wolf in my growin' up days. I liked that Muddy Waters sound and that Howlin' Wolf sound, and could nobody else play like they sound to me. And every time I'd be in the wood or in the trucks going to the wood I'd be humming that Muddy Waters song and that Howlin' Wolf song a little bit. And on Friday night I'd be in the house. I'd sit there by myself and look at that thing and I'd say, "I can't play no damn guitar."'

Eventually T. Model decided to make use of his wife's leaving present, if only to fill the void that now lay at the heart of his domestic life. He bought a small amplifier from a local man.

'I sit it down and I look at it. I took the plug and I stuck it in the wall, and no light come on. I turn on a button and nothing happen. Then I turn on another button and I say "Shoot, this thing ain't no count." Then I hit another button and the light jumped on and I say to myself: "Look at that." I went back there and got the guitar. I look at the guitar and say: "Hm." Then I saw a hole in the guitar and a hole in the amp, and I saw that coil and I know where it went. I stuck it in the guitar and I stuck it down that amp. Then I saw a switch on the guitar and I hear boom boom! And I say "Aw . . . haw . . ." I didn't know how to tune it and I didn't know shoot but it made a sound.

'I mess around with that thing and it got good to me. Then I remember my wife had bought me a gallon of moonshine whisky. I'd taste a little bit of that after I'd get in from work, then I started to play that guitar and went bam, bam. I was bamming on that and a man come and bump on my door. I say

"Come in, I'm playing the guitar." He say "Hey, you can't play no damn guitar." I say "Well, I can do something." I went on bammin' that guitar and then took a sip of that moonshine, and that was some of the best whisky I ever put in my mouth. Next thing another someone comes knocking on that door. Two women. They say, "T. Model, you sounding good! Give me a drink of that whisky you got! Your wife gone and left ya?" I say, "She gone. Which one of you want to be my woman?" One say, "I got a boyfriend, but we on bad terms." Both of them women stayed all night.'

T. Model's professional career took off after that night.

'Soon people are coming and saying, "You can play that guitar as good as anybody. Shoot man, come on down to our house and play it." They have a house full of women and men. So I went down there and I was bamming on that thing and before I knew it I was playing a guitar. I've been playing ever since and ain't nobody can beat me. I'm bad. I'm eighty-four . . . no, eighty-five years old and all of my peoples is dead and I'm the only one living and ain't nobody can play like me.'

Once T. Model had started on his self-esteem tip he found it difficult to stop. He recalled sitting on a local woman's porch, playing the blues, when the owner of a bar on Nelson Street asked him if he would be prepared to play in front of a proper paying audience. 'I tell him that I was OK playin' in front of those women who were drinking my moonshine and tempting me, but I was too shy to play on Nelson Street. He say "Just come down and play three songs and open up." So I go down there and play Howlin' Wolf and Muddy Waters and the place was silent. I was rockin' the house! Then all the men and women get wind of it, and they put up a poster saying T. Model Ford playing at some place I don't remember the name of. And man, that place was packed! I was bad. I'm still bad! I ain't afraid of going up to play in front of anybody. I play the guitar a way you'd swear I was playing two guitars, but it ain't but one.'

That was the way to do it. For my own debut gig I could open up for another band and just play a few songs, because that was the natural order of things: you had to start at the bottom of the bill. As I listened to T. Model explain the beginnings of his own new career, I took inspiration for my own.

T. Model described some of the joys and frustrations of making it as a professional musician. He had been having problems with his drummer Spam, who was 'breathalating' because he smoked too many cigarettes and sniffed too much snuff, and T. Model decided that he would have to talk to Bruce about Spam being out of breath all the time and not able to play the drums properly. He claimed that all kinds of people had ripped him off in the past, but Fat Possum had 'just about done right'. I asked him if he had any advice for a novice guitarist trying to find his way. 'You have to learn yourself something so that nobody can take your style. That's the way to play guitar.'

I needed some practical knowledge of T. Model's own techniques, so I asked if he could give me a demonstration and a guitar tutorial. 'Sure, we can set up and play,' he said, and told me to go to the boot of his Lincoln and lift out his equipment. He had a big old Fender Deluxe amplifier and a black Peavey Predator electric guitar. I put it in the living room next to his chair and he slowly plugged everything in, before taking off on a solid piece of guitar blues that lasted for about forty minutes without a break. He stared at me for the whole time, a Cheshire Cat grin on his face, as his head bobbed a little from side to side.

When he finally stopped I asked him to show me what he was doing. 'Most guitarists have corns on their fingers,' he said. 'They play like it has to hurt them. Feel my fingers.' The tips were soft, with no calluses. 'That's because I make all the strings loose and I strum them strings, and I don't hurt my fingers even though I don't even use a plectrum.'

He did his best to explain his techniques to me, but it was clear that he didn't really know what they were himself. As he was illiterate he had no way of learning a song from tablature as most guitarists do, and he simply worked out a way of playing that sounded like the guitarists he liked (there were only two: Muddy Waters and Howlin' Wolf). He wasn't playing any conventional chords. As far as I could tell he was knocking out a rhythm by moving his fingers on and off his weird chords. He certainly wasn't doing anything complicated, but he knocked out a grooving sound, and a unique one. It wasn't mournful blues and T. Model wasn't a mournful guy. He was like an eighty-six-year-old version of Doyle. Perhaps he had sold his soul to the devil to get that guitar style, using his family's welfare cheques to make up the deficit.

T. Model seemed like he was going to be happy for me to stay all day, even though he was performing at Nelson Street that night. The other members of his household paid no attention to his amped-up playing, although little Renee walked in and out of the room a few times with her hands over her ears. Sylvia shuffled around. I tried to get T. Model to divulge his secrets, but he simply couldn't articulate whatever it was he was doing. 'Don't you feel bad that you can't play like me,' he said. 'It might be easy like goin' up and eating a piece of bread is easy, but ain't nobody can play like this. Everybody wants my style and nobody can have it and that ain't my fault 'cause I just do it how I feel it. That's why the people like to hear me soon as I walk in the door.'

By midday I had to tell him that it was time for me to go. I was planning to get down to New Orleans by the evening to catch the garage festival and it would take me six or seven hours to drive there. T. Model nodded his head and said, a little hesitantly, 'Hey, did Bruce mention somethin' about money?'

At first I didn't understand him, and asked him to say it again. He spelled it out for me: he wanted cash for talking to me and giving me a guitar session/sort-of tutorial. It was fair enough. I dug into my pockets and pulled out what I had — forty bucks and a bit of loose change. He looked at it as if I had just handed over the keys to a brand-new Lincoln convertible. 'Oh yeah, that's good, that's good,' he said, jamming the money into the pockets of his old brown trousers before Sylvia could see. 'You can come back any time you like, any time you nearby you just come round here and we can do the same thing again.' Given his belief that Canada was Germany, I decided that there wasn't much point in explaining the distance between London, England and Greenville, USA. But in T. Model Ford I had found what I had been searching for: the blues.

Chapter Ten

Secrets from Two Old Masters

The observant reader may have noticed that I mentioned my desire to play an electric guitar a while back, and so far there is no evidence that I have done anything whatsoever about getting one. I can explain. It was bad enough dragging an acoustic guitar around America without being questioned by some humourless airport security guard on why I had two guitars with me if I wasn't a professional musician, and therefore without a work permit, and therefore in need of being ejected from the country at once with little chance of being allowed back ever again. Secondly, I still didn't feel I knew enough on an acoustic to reward myself by taking off on the jet plane of electricity. However much I tried to combine the double bass line with the A minor melody of 'Anji', for example, I still couldn't do it. I could play both parts – just not at the same time.

Most of the music I have loved since I was a teenager has been played on electric guitars. Best of all is garage-punk: the primitive but frequently witty and self-deprecating style of rock'n'roll made in the sixties by middle-class American dorks who wanted to be like The Rolling Stones and try and get a girlfriend in the process. Most of these bands saved up their lawn-mowing money for one recording session and released their sole original song on a 45 for a local label, with a cover version on the B-side to back it up. A few of the garage band members went on to become professional musicians, but the vast majority grew up, left home (and their parents' garages) to become car mechanics, teachers, computer programmers, garbage men and, in the case of John Kerry, presidential candidates. Garage-punk was a product of the affordability of the electric guitar. After one summer of Saturday jobs you could buy a Fender Jaguar and a Vox AC30 amplifier and make music.

The festival in New Orleans was a two-night event: garage bands on Friday, blues legends on Saturday. As far as I was concerned Friday night would belong to The Seeds, the LA outfit that had two big hits in the mid-sixties: 'Can't Seem To Make You Mine' and 'Pushing Too Hard'. Built around a tinny Wurlitzer piano, two or three chords and lead singer Sky Saxon's nasal, sneering whine, these songs are garage-punk personified: simplistic, brutal, downtrodden and defiantly arrogant. 'Can't Seem To Make You Mine' is about the standard garage problem of sexual frustration. 'Pushing Too Hard' is an expression of what it was like to be young and hassled by squares in mid-sixties America. Having created such a fine formula, The Seeds saw no point in messing with it. They rewrote those two songs for the rest of their career, throwing a bit of flower power into the stew when the times demanded it.

Sky Saxon is one of the great sixties loons. When The Seeds had their initial hits it was hoped that he could become an American Mick Jagger, but the record company didn't take in the fact that while Jagger is nothing if not a tough operator, Sky Saxon is completely crackers. In 1969 he got involved in the nature-worshipping Ya Ha Wa Cult, moved to Hawaii, and recorded the first of a series of albums in homage to dogs. Since then he has made sporadic attempts to claim his rightful place in the rock'n'roll pantheon, but his wayward character has meant that it has never really been possible. In 2003 I saw Sky play with a new line-up of The Seeds in London and they were great – tight and energetic – while Sky did his best to leap around the stage like the psychedelic granddad he was. The packed venue was digging it. Then the band went to Greece where two members met strippers, decided that life wasn't going to get much better, and stayed. Sky Saxon cancelled the rest of the tour.

I drove into New Orleans at about seven in the evening, going straight from T. Model Ford's house in Greenville on to Highway 82 and connecting back to Highway 61, past Baton Rouge and along the seemingly endless, heavily congested bridge that crosses over the murky Louisiana swampland and decomposing forests surrounding the city. I had an hour to drop off the white Chevrolet at the hire car depot, take a cab to the house in the Garden District where I was staying (with some retired lecturers who, in the infinite kindness that is easy to find in the southern states, had offered me a room in their house purely on the strength of being a friend of one of their former students), say hello, have a shower and leave for the New Orleans Rock'n'Bowl, a bowling alley/concert venue beneath a flyover where the shows were being held. Rosan, the woman I was staying with, drove me there.

'Jesus, look at this nut!' she said as a stick-thin old freak with long silver hair, purple hipster trousers, an Indian-style cotton shirt and all manner of brightly coloured bangles and necklaces hanging off his skeletal frame wandered around the parking lot of the Rock'n'Bowl in a state of confusion.

'That's Sky Saxon!' I told her. I called out his name and he tottered over to the car.

'Hey man, could you help me out?' he said, sticking his white beard and long yellowing teeth in through the passenger window. 'I gotta find some sunglasses badly.'

Rosan muttered something about having some in her handbag and produced a pair of half-moon reading glasses on a cord, but Sky didn't seem to think they were suitable. 'Listen man, I'll see you in there. I really need to find some shades before I do anything because right now I'm feeling pretty spaced out,' he said, and skipped off like an ancient satyr picking up the scent of a lissom maiden. I said goodbye to Rosan and followed Sky in search of some garage-punk.

The bowling alley setting was right for this kind of music. Garage was born from American leisure time, and it remains party music for the kind of people who don't get invited to too many parties. Unfortunately the decades that have passed since have created a bit of a fantasy about it. Thirty years on, all we hear from garage bands are the one classic track they recorded that has ended up on a compilation album. But the bands did of course play entire sets in their time, and they were chiefly made up of boring cover versions of standards like 'Shout' and 'Stand By Me'. I had always fantasized about garage bands being four or five cool cats in bowl cuts and Cuban-heeled boots, brimming with black-rimmed spectacles and attitude, who knocked out brutal rants while caged go-go dancers shook a tail feather on either side of the Neanderthal drummer. Within minutes of my walking into The Rock'n'Bowl that illusion was shattered for ever. A group of middle-aged men and one woman were on stage in Hawaiian shirts, smiling their way through R&B standards that everyone had heard thousands of times before. 'This is so much fun,' said the lead singer, which meant that at least one person was enjoying themselves.

But The Seeds, who were always on a different level of

primitive ambition to most of their peers, did not disappoint. They had a darker edge that took them out of suburbia and into a more glamorous and urban world. 'I don't write these songs, I'm a channel for them,' said Sky Saxon, before singing 'Pushing Too Hard' for the 17,756th time. His young band – he was the only original member left – grooved with conviction and Sky managed to entice some good-looking girls from the audience to dance with him. In his bobbing fez, giant fly-like sunglasses (I wonder where he found them) and skinny trousers he looked a world away from the overgrown frat boys in shorts and T-shirts who made up the audience. I heard a woman next to me say: 'Marsha, you've got to check out this guy,' in a tone of provincial disbelief. Sky didn't play guitar, but I decided that he would be the man who would best reveal to me the secrets of garage-punk, which I wanted for my own guitar style.

I caught Sky as he was telling a girl how much he loved her groovy hat while staring at her breasts. First he filled me in on his current mission. 'When Bush built 3,000 warplanes I decided to write 3,000 new songs to counteract that,' he said, pulling at his grey beard in contemplation. 'And as I can sell a billion records, what's the problem? But then, Bush doesn't want me to sell a billion records. I would be *too powerful*.'

I found it hard to believe that George W. would be losing that much sleep over Sky's prolific songwriting prowess, but it was good to see that he was back in the saddle after years in the wilderness. Sky – known to his parents as Richard Marsh – wanted to tell me about the importance of vegetarianism, which tied in with his belief that dogs are divine animals. 'I believe that if the people could just worship the dog and stop eating meat, they could live for ever because God is in the dog,' he said. 'I've been put here on the planet as a medium for whatever God might want me to say about helping the dogs and stopping madmen like Bush from bombing the earth. My one real regret is that I didn't get Jim Morrison of The Doors to embrace the flower spirit until it was too late. If I had managed to get Jim to stop eating bacon, he would still be with us today.'

As bowling balls clattered down the alleys and beery cheers followed the sound of pins being struck, I told this essence of sixties freedom about what I was doing with the guitar: what I had learned ('I Can't Seem To Make You Mine' was in my repertoire after all), what I had stumbled over, and what I was still trying to do. He didn't appear to notice anything I had said, returning to his favourite subjects of dogs, bacon and bombs. It seemed like my quest was not to be furthered. But then he said: 'Hey Will, this has been really cool. Why don't you play guitar for The Seeds when I'm next in London?'

'But I've only been playing guitar for a few months,' I told him. 'It's very nice of you to offer, but I don't think I'm good enough.'

'There are only three or four chords that you use all the time,' said Sky, scratching his head. 'What's the problem?'

It was a mind blower of a proposition. To actually play with The Seeds would turn an oft-imagined fantasy into a reality, and for a moment I pictured an album photograph featuring Sky, myself and a few other garage-punk cats looking mean in our matching bowl cuts, Cuban-heeled boots and psychedelic paisley shirts. But then I looked into Sky's glazed eyes and wondered if I was really ready for that kind of trip right now – or, more importantly, whether he would remember who the hell I was if I did approach him in London. I had a feeling that being in The Seeds would remain a beautiful daydream, at least within the timeframe of my first gig. But Sky had defined the adolescent, primitive joy of garage-punk. In his world there really were only three or four chords and that was all you needed as your passport to another dimension. Now I could go to New York.

I had harboured a crazy dream of finishing my American adventure by sharing a bottle of Jack Daniel's with Keith Richards at his Connecticut mansion, the two of us sitting opposite one another in battered wicker chairs with guitars on our laps. I would strum through 'Wild Horses', and Keith would crunch up his eyes and give a wicked laugh at a beginner's enthusiasm.

'You're gonna knock 'em dead, kid,' he would say. 'Hey! I've just realized. I'm going to be in London in time for the show. Maybe we can do a duet together.'

Then a po-faced New York airport customs officer started asking me questions about drugs, guns and terrorist threats to America – maybe it was the black curly hair – and Keith disappeared into the ether.

But meeting Les Paul was going to be a reality. The father of the electric guitar, a jazz player who became popular in the 1950s for his duets with his then-wife Mary Ford, did more than anyone to create the sound that rock bands now use. As soon as you amplify a guitar there is no reason why you cannot play around with its sound in other ways, too, and Les Paul pioneered such effects-pedal standards as echo delay and phase shifting, as well as pretty much inventing modern recording techniques such as overdubbing and multitracking.

Les Paul was born in 1916. He was thirteen when he first amplified his guitar using a phonograph needle, having picked up the instrument at the age of nine. He was playing professionally in dance bands a year later, and, in 1941, he built the first solid-body guitar when he took a four-by-four board, nailed the neck of an Epiphone guitar on to it and added some electric pick-ups. Electric guitars existed before Les Paul, but they worked on the same principle as acoustic guitars, which create a sound by being hollow and responding to the vibrations of the strings. The early electric guitars were simply acoustics with pick-ups, but Les Paul created what has become the solid-body standard, something that was thought of as impossible at the time. When a serious car crash shattered his right arm in 1948, he asked the doctors to rebuild it at an angle so it was positioned perfectly to play guitar. Les Paul was the world's first bionic guitarist.

After various failed attempts Les Paul managed to convince Gibson to manufacture a solid-body electric model, so in 1952 the Gibson Les Paul began its career as one of the most iconic guitars of all time. (Their arch rivals Fender had in fact beaten them to it with the introduction of the solid-body Broadcaster, later to become the Telecaster, in 1948.) If anyone was going to help me to understand the electric guitar, it was Les Paul. He was the man who practically invented it.

The Chelsea Hotel is undoubtedly selling itself on its name, but it has somehow managed to resist any of the vulgarities of the modern age that might cramp its style. The tiny lift creaks up to battered rooms that use an old-style key, not the electronic card that is ubiquitous everywhere else in American hotels, and the lobby does not appear to have a computer in it. The staff are refreshingly rude, although everyone is in New York. My room on the seventh floor had an ancient porcelain bath, a huge old television, rickety windows that did not shut properly, a great view of West 23rd Street and two buzzing flies. It was ideal. The Chelsea still had its resident freaks, including a camp man on my floor whose job it was to make bitchy comments to whoever he shared a lift with, and every time I passed the lobby the manager was shouting down the phone at some poor soul who had dared to complain about the fact that hardly anything worked and the entire hotel was falling apart. It is the only place to stay in New York.

When one is away from home, one has the freedom to indulge in clichés. The first thing I did upon settling down in the room was get out my guitar, sit on the old radiator by the window, and play 'Pale Blue Eyes' by The Velvet Underground. Here was the spiritual home of the band that had captured the tawdry glamour of sixties New York better than anyone, and over the last few years that glamour had gone. The bars were empty since smoking was banned, rents were so high that Manhattan had become a playground for the rich, and the underbelly of homeless people, thieves, drug addicts and muggers had been magicked away, making the city safe but sanitized. The New York of Max's Kansas City and CBGB's, of The Velvet Underground, The Ramones and The New York Dolls, was a memory now. The Chelsea Hotel is the last link to that old rude, dirty and endlessly exciting world, although how the resident freaks afford the rates is anyone's guess.

That night I went to see Les Paul. The Iridium is a proper jazz supper-club with table service, high prices and a clientele of tourists and middle-aged couples out on dates. A man with grey hair and a face carved out of stone who clearly did not take to English people who had managed to get themselves on to the guest list met me at the entrance. He put me at the very back of the room where I could not frighten the paying guests. I told him I was here to interview Les Paul. What should I do? 'Nothing,' he said, staring at me as if I had just challenged him to a fight. 'Sit over there and wait until it's over.'

It may be sacrilegious to criticize anything that Les Paul does – and everyone in the guitar-playing universe has been down to the Iridium on a Monday night to pay their respects to the master – but I thought his set stank. He sat on a high stool and looked like a tiny, ancient and withered sacred bird surrounded by acolytes prepared to marvel at anything he did. Judging by the way he was shouting he was fairly deaf, and I had heard that he was suffering from severe arthritis, but his fingers still moved with enough agility to hit the right notes. The problem was that he had been so proficient for so long that any imagination he might have once had was long gone. As he ran through old supper club classics like 'Misty' and 'These Foolish Things', and filed his way down his list of well-worn banter with his five-piece band ('You've changed a lot since I last saw you.' 'Well, I've got a different tie on.' 'Do you remember being nineteen?' 'I was never nineteen,' etc.) I felt a profound sense of despair. Here was the father of the electric guitar, a man who had achieved so much, performing against all odds in New York, the most cosmopolitan city in the world. It should have been great, but all of those elements were what made it awful. I liked the cliché of the Chelsea Hotel. This cliché was lifeless.

The set felt like a practical demonstration of the versatility of the electric guitar, rather like a high-end audio salesman demonstrating the remarkable qualities of a quadraphonic home entertainment system back in the seventies. Les Paul picked a note, gave it reverb, and bent it until it made a funny sound that made the audience laugh. It was smooth but it was not interesting. Audience participation – something that Americans do very well but which we English find as enjoyable as root canal treatment – came in the form of a sing-along of 'Got My Mojo Working' at the end of the set. I asked the silver-haired Mafioso manager/maitre d' character about interviewing Les Paul, and he said that he still had another set to get through. I told him I would stay. 'Well you can if you want, but they'll charge you for it. Go away and come back in an hour and a half.'

I wandered around Times Square and returned in time to catch the end of the second set. It sounded familiar ('Do you remember being nineteen?' and so on). When it came to an end there was an announcement that anyone who wanted to meet Les Paul could hang around and he would come out. CDs and photographs were on sale and Les would be happy to sign them. I told the manager that I had flown over from England specially to meet Les Paul. 'So what?' he said. Would it not be possible to talk to him properly, one-on-one? 'Sure,' he replied, his face remaining as impassive as ever. 'Get in line with everyone else.'

For another hour I stood in a queue with about twenty other people, and I was the only one not clutching a just-purchased photograph or CD. My so-called interview – forget the guitar lesson I had been hoping for – was part of a process designed to make a bit of extra cash. But then everyone in New York is on the make, from the endless demand for tips to the overcharging at the hotels to the total consumerist abandon that the city is gripped with. There is no reason why Les Paul and the Iridium Jazz Club should be the exception. In front of me in the queue was a grumpy family from upstate New York who had decided to come and see Les Paul instead of taking in a Broadway show as it worked out at about the same price. They were calculating if they got their money's worth by comparing the length of his set to that of the average musical.

Finally he came out, and sat down at a little chair at the front of the line. I saw the same smile a dozen times as he posed for the camera with another person who bent down so that their head was on a level with his, usually holding up the CD they had just bought. When it was my turn I told him about my mission to learn the guitar and understand its significance in time to play it in front of an audience in two months' time. He nodded in a way that announced he had heard it all before. I asked him to reveal the secret of playing guitar.

'Practice.'

He stared at me as if I was simple. I looked into his eyes for clues and saw only contempt. I asked if there was anything more I should know.

'Learn from a good teacher. Listen to a good record and find out what the guitarist is doing. The toughest part is to develop your own style and not sound like everybody else, but that comes to you in time. Come on! Let's keep this line moving!' And with a wave of another photograph from another middle-aged couple, my interview was over. I was half-expecting the manager in the camel coat to pick me up by my shirt and throw me out on the street with a shout of 'Got your goddam interview, ya limey punk?' before crunching my guitar-playing fingertips into the sidewalk with his black Gucci loafers. But he had gone home.

Chapter Eleven

Going Electric

One of the most significant moments in the history of the twentieth century was when Bob Dylan went electric. Having established himself as the voice of liberal-thinking young America in the early sixties after he emerged from Greenwich Village folk clubs armed only with his voice, an acoustic guitar and a false biography, Dylan became the symbol of a kind of purity and commitment to honesty that stood against gaudy, consumerist American culture. He was, of course, a product of that culture, but he was smart enough to comment on it while, ultimately, representing nobody but himself.

The big moment in Dylan's electric journey came when he arrived in England in May 1966. He had become an almost mythical figure by then, the elected leader of a new generation of the dispossessed and idealistic. Then he toured the country with the Canadian rock'n'roll singer Ronnie Hawkins's former backing band. It seems likely now that nobody in the Dylan camp had thought of playing electric guitars as a particularly groundbreaking gesture – they had been used constantly in popular music for the last ten years, after all – but when he played London's Royal Albert Hall the audience came with the angry knowledge that Dylan had betrayed his acoustic roots. He brought out his rock'n'roll rhythm section for the second half of the set and a mass shuffling of duffle coats followed.

There can't be too many people who would admit to being against Dylan's electric revolution these days, but the reactions he received from audiences at the time say more about the symbolism of the acoustic and electric guitar than they do about Bob Dylan's new purchase. He had unintentionally made the acoustic guitar the prop for a generation in search of authenticity. He moved on and Joan Baez stuck to her acoustic guns, and history has not proved her to be the more significant of the two.

The electric guitar brought liberation. The jazz guitarist Charlie Christian was one of its early exponents, seeing it as a chance for the guitarist to escape imprisonment in the rhythm section of big bands in the thirties and forties. Les Paul started playing the electric guitar as far back as 1928, figuring that if he could be heard properly he would make more in tips, and in 1935 Eddie Durham laid the first amplified guitar down on record with his solo for The Jimmie Lunceford Big Band's 1945 record 'Hitting The Bottle'. It's remarkable to think that Dylan was met with so much hostility for electrifying his guitar when jazz and country musicians had been doing it for decades. Charlie Christian taught the blues player T-Bone Walker a thing or two about the electric, who went on to turn B. B. King and Chuck Berry on to its egalitarian charms. Had women and weed not killed Charlie Christian in 1941 at the ripe old age of twenty-three he would be far more widely acknowledged as the father of the electric guitar.

My own purchase of an electric guitar was perhaps a little less significant for the world at large than Dylan's, but it meant a lot to me. It invited me into a club that is generally joined by boys at around the age of thirteen who are looking for a way to buy a bit of rebellion, express themselves, and annoy their parents. The domestic honeymoon period that followed my return to England, when NJ, Otto and Pearl were still happy to see me and not yet irritated by my endless bludgeoning of 'Anji' on the Godin Seagull, seemed like a good time to part with a wad of cash for a decent electric and an amplifier. For that period running up to my debut gig, I let guitars take over my life as much as practicality would allow.

'So what is the point of you buying an electric guitar, apart from being a way to indulge your ego and fantasize about being a rock star?' asked one friend who had recently had a baby, as we pushed prams through the woods of Hampstead Heath on a cold midwinter Sunday morning. 'I'm sure the family are overjoyed at you spending your money on an electric guitar instead of making sure the rent is paid, or even taking them on a holiday for once. Good God, as if NJ hasn't got enough to cope with . . .'

'The road is my mother, the highway is my brother, and I was born to wander,' I told her, before Pearl started screaming from the pram and demanded to be allowed to roll down Parliament Hill on her own. I was determined to venture into a world that turned out to be far more complicated than the one in which I had so far trodden. It's easy to get a handle on an acoustic guitar: it needs tuning up every now and then, but apart from that there is nothing to worry about beyond practising and learning the chords and scales. An electric guitar has so many more variables. Will you go for a Gibson ES 325 with a centre-weighted humbucking configuration, or the elegant simplicity of a Fender Telecaster with its single-coil pick-ups? It may not sound like much but bands have split up over less. Then you have the choice of amplifier, effects pedals, colour of finish . . . the list is endless.

The other element to remember about the world of the electric guitar is that it is just as elitist, image-conscious and authenticity-obsessed as that of the acoustic. The wrong model could bring shame on you and even hamper your chances of making it as a professional. Denmark Street in London seemed like the best place to start exploring this confusing world, and I only realized how much I had come on when it dawned on me that I was no longer intimidated by the idea of going into one of the shops and road-testing a potential purchase with a riff. As luck would have it I knew one of the greatest guitar snobs of them all. Andy Hackett runs a shop called Angel Music on the first floor of a building on Denmark Street that you have to ring a bell to gain entry to. With his long hair, cowboy shirt and faded Levi's, Hackett looks very much the vintage guitar man, and he's only too happy to admit to having a less than egalitarian worldview. 'Oh, I'm a total elitist, and there's certain guitars I wouldn't go near however nice they sound,' he told me when I went up to his shop, a week after returning from New York. 'I like guitars that are old. I would find it hard to play a brand-new one. Especially on stage . . .' He looked into the distance for a moment. 'Actually, that would be unthinkable.'

Hackett played in various bands, but he seemed content at the centre of his own guitar universe, surrounded by vintage models that were bought and sold by rock superstars and normal people alike. I knew that a Fender Stratocaster was one of the most popular guitars, and it had been the model of choice for no lesser player than Jimi Hendrix. I asked Hackett if he thought I should start on one.

'That's the guitar that divides more people than any other – it's loved or hated,' he said, leaning against his counter. 'The alternative music crowd really hate the Strat, mainly because of its association with people like Mark Knopfler of Dire Straits

and Eric Clapton. I was speaking to a guy from an independent
record company recently who said that he wouldn't sign a band
if their guitarist played a Stratocaster. I personally think that's
going a bit far, but it gives you some idea of how seriously
people take it.'

I tried playing a few chords on a Strat that Hackett had in the
shop. I couldn't say that it instantly transformed me into a
balding man with a headband knocking out neatly chiselled
riffs and singing about playing 'gee-tar on the MTV', so I don't
really know what the fuss was about. But it seems that the
classic status of the Stratocaster is the reason why alternative
musicians don't like it. It is seen as the guitar of the muso.
Instead, they go for cheaper Fender models like Jazzmasters,
Jaguars and Mustangs. 'They want these because their heroes
played them, in particular Tom Verlaine from Television,
Talking Heads, and J. Mascis from Dinosaur Jr,' explained
Hackett. 'But if you ask any of those people why they played a
Jazzmaster they will tell you it's because they couldn't afford a
good old Strat. Serious musicians bought Jazzmasters and
Mustangs because they're cheap, and all these indie kids
who come into my shop buy them because of the image.
You can try and explain to them why a Jaguar is a bad guitar
– the bridge set-up leaves a lot to be desired, for example – but
they won't be put off. Without a doubt, image sells the guitar.'

The great heavy rock guitar is the Gibson Les Paul. As played
by golden gods from Jimmy Page to Slash from Guns 'N' Roses,
the Les Paul has been subjected to more guitar pornography
than any other model. There are books that feature page after
page of nothing but Les Paul Standards in a sunburst finish
dating from 1958 to 1960. 'It does have a very fat sound,' said
Hackett, when I asked him why it has such rock appeal. 'But in
all honesty Les Pauls don't sound great when they're played

clean through an amp. They're best when they're distorted and overdriven, which is how most heavy rock is made.'

I pointed to a beautiful Gretsch Country Gentleman. These are big guitars with a tremolo arm to pull notes out for longer, and they are semi-acoustic: although electric, they are hollow-bodied and pick up sound through the vibrations. The Country Gentleman hanging from the wall of Angel Music did look fantastic, although it was going for over £2,000. 'I wouldn't recommend that for a beginner,' said Hackett. 'It's a lovely guitar, and you can get a great rockabilly sound from it, but they're notorious for going out of tune. I had a really nice Country Gentleman that I had to sell to Gem from Oasis because my wife wanted to go on holiday. To Strasbourg.' After a quiet moment of reflection from Hackett, we moved on.

For a brief period in my youth, I found myself enjoying the heaviest form of heavy metal, or grindcore as it was then known. The music, which was made by emaciated vegans with ex-tremely long hair in bands with names like Napalm Death and Carcass, sounds like asteroids colliding with each other at the speed of light. I wondered how I could get that kind of noise on a guitar. 'You would need something like this,' said Hackett, picking up a jet-black guitar with a simple, classic rock design, 'A Gibson SG. And you would need to put as much overdrive as possible on to it. But if you were heading towards straight heavy metal you might also consider a guitar with strange pointy bits on it, like a Jackson Warrior. And for endless solos the Paul Reed Smith is a good bet.'

He took two guitars down from the wall. One was a futuristic-looking object with thrusting, pointed edges. It looked very masculine, like a phallic lightning bolt. The other was more traditional. 'This plays great and it's perfect for a real rock sound,' said Hackett, handing the member-like Jackson

Warrior over to me. I got a firm grip on it and strummed it hard, and through a Marshall amp it sounded heavy. But I could never pull off playing an instrument like that. I didn't have the right hairstyle.

The Paul Reed Smith was more elegant. I asked Hackett if he has ever used one. 'Good God, no,' he replied. 'I wouldn't be caught dead near it. I'm not saying that it isn't a great guitar, but there's quite a cultural hang-up about it. I would never play one on stage. Come to think of it I wouldn't even play one in the studio, even if no one else were there. It would be too shaming. It's the Carlos Santana connection, I suppose.'

There was no doubt that I was in the presence of a prime guitar snob. So when I asked him about the guitars that he played, it came as no surprise to see him get rather excited. 'I've been around every make of guitar you can think of, and in my time I've owned a lot, but I sold them all off because I wanted to buy a boat. Now I have the three classics: a Fender Telecaster, a Stratocaster, and a Martin D-28 acoustic. You could call them workhorses. You can get a pig of a guitar in any make, but those three will be your safest bet.'

From under the counter he ceremonially revealed to me his pride and joy: an extremely rare Telecaster from 1965 with an original black finish. I asked him what made this guitar so fantastic. 'To be honest with you, it's not any better than your average bog-standard Telecaster. It's just really, really rare.'

The Telecaster did look like a nice, simple guitar, and I liked its twangy sound. 'A Telecaster is liked by just about everyone,' he said. 'People who are really good at the guitar like the fact that it is so basic: it has two pick-ups and it hasn't got a tremolo arm so it stays in tune, and beginners like it because it's easy to play. A lot of country musicians use them because they have a clean sound, and it was popular with R&B guitarists like Steve

Cropper from Booker T. & The MG's for the same reason. It's just a well-engineered, well-designed, classic piece of equipment.'

Hackett explained how when Oasis were at their height, the sale of Epiphones went through the roof because Noel Gallagher had one, but he currently had a signed Noel Gallagher Epiphone on the wall and it didn't look like it was going anywhere, which said more about the then-stock value of Oasis than it did about the quality of the Epiphone. But I didn't want to buy a guitar that was sold on its connection to some big rock star. I needed one that I could learn to play on. Hackett told me about a customer who was in his late fifties and had bought twelve very expensive guitars from the shop in the last few years. He said that the man was an absolutely awful player, but he was convinced that when he found the right guitar the notes would magically fly into his fingers. Four-and-a-half months on the acoustic had told me that this was not going to happen. The guitars in Angel Music were out of my league, and I really needed to start on something cheaper and less authentic. Hackett realized this too.

'What you can buy now for £150 is such a good instrument compared to what you could get in the 1970s for £150, when I was starting out,' he told me. 'In real terms guitars have come down in price massively. When Strats first came over in the early sixties you could buy a new one for 170 guineas. That was about the price of a new car. Now you can get a good Squier Strat for £140.'

Squier are Fender's own 'copy' brand. Dismayed at the fact that Stratocasters and Telecasters were being copied by so many other companies, Fender decided to do it themselves, manufacturing guitars that are the same as the classic models but made on cheap production-line factories in China where the

employees are paid around a bowl of rice a day. I had seen Strat
starter kits that came complete with guitar, lead and amplifier
for well under £200.

The notion of authenticity and image plagued me. Having
started taking guitar lessons in the hope of brushing up in time
for the debut gig (and if I kept to schedule it would be around
six weeks' time), I asked my new guitar teacher, an eminently
sensible sort, what I should do about an electric guitar. He
pointed to his own, a classic shape in rock black. 'A Squier
Telecaster,' he said. 'They do the job fine.'

'For God's sake, don't get a Squier,' said a friend who didn't
actually play the guitar at all, although during his college years
about ten years previously he had briefly played bass in a funk
band. He had given up after suffering a devastating blow. For
the band's big gig in front of a thousand students at Glasgow
School of Art he had been working up to his bass solo. When
the time arrived he stepped to the centre of the stage, closed his
eyes, jerked his head backwards and forwards like a chicken, and
slapped his bass for all it was worth. It was only afterwards that
he discovered he wasn't plugged in and nobody could hear a
thing. 'You can't get a guitar that has just fallen off a production line somewhere in the Far East. You have to buy a guitar
with a bit of soul. It has to be second-hand – at least twenty
years old. You want to get it from some old hippy who's down
on his luck and needs the money to buy a camper van and
relocate to the South of France.'

This was, of course, nonsense. A guitar provides a function
and it is the person who brings the soul to it and makes good
music or bad music, not the instrument. In the wrong hands,
authenticity is another way of separating fools from their
money. On the other hand that 1962 Gretsch Chet Atkins
in the window of Andy's Guitar Centre did look pretty cool . . .

Meanwhile, I was no longer spending my precious free time practising, but flicking through the back pages of *Guitar* magazine and comparing prices in endless lists of all the many different models on offer. It was time to take stock of the situation.

I remembered an incident that would forever serve as a warning about the folly of obsessing over guitar makes and models. A year prior to picking up the guitar I had travelled to Brazil where I had met the former members of a sixties rock group called Os Mutantes. A teenage trio from São Paulo, they had made up the psychedelic wing of the country's sixties revolution. The brothers Arnaldo and Sérgio Dias Baptista and Arnaldo's girlfriend Rita Lee dressed up as witches and con-quistadors, built their own instruments, and made endlessly inventive, inspired music. Good-quality electric guitars were not available in Brazil at that time, so Arnaldo and Sérgio got third brother Claudio to do some clever things with electronics and build them their own.

Claudio studied the techniques of the master luthier Stra-divarius for the basic guitar bodies, and then used a series of Heath Robinson-like contraptions to copy the sounds of dis-tortion, fuzz, phasing and tape delay that Sérgio heard on records by The Rolling Stones and The Beatles. For one classic song by Os Mutantes, 'Batmacumba', Claudio connected Sér-gio's guitar to the motor of a sewing machine in order to control the vibrations going into the pick-up, thereby creating a bizarre warbling sound. He would put a pick-up on every string (pick-ups usually cover all the strings) to create controlled and multi-variable distortion. Os Mutantes were forced to be inventive because of practical limitations, and they made wonderful music as a result.

Os Mutantes's wild imagination and adventurousness came

at a price however. The band discovered free love and LSD in a big way in the late sixties and early seventies. Rita Lee left in 1972 and Arnaldo went on to blow his mind on acid, and for the rest of the decade he launched a wayward solo career that was interspersed with stays in various mental institutions. In 1982 he attempted to escape from a psychiatric institute by jumping out of a fifth-floor window. He survived, but was left in a coma for two months. When I met him in 2003 he had made vast improvements in his mental health, but he was still quite shaky. He did seem to spend disproportionate amounts of time staring out of the window with a mysterious grin on his face, as if laughing at an inner joke that only he would ever get.

I grew fond of Arnaldo and his brother Sérgio, so it shocked me to find out about the bizarre feud that all three members of Os Mutantes have been locked in since the early seventies. Rita Lee and Arnaldo Baptista's problems stem from the fact that they were childhood sweethearts, deeply in love with each other, who went through the madness of sixties Brazil's military dictatorship and counterculture lifestyle together. But Arnaldo and Sérgio's problems stem from their choice of guitars.

'I am totally against Sérgio,' said Arnaldo, when I asked him why he hadn't spoken to his brother in years, 'because he does not use the guitar that Led Zeppelin used: the Gibson Les Paul. Instead he uses Fender guitars and I cannot believe that he would do such a thing. The Les Pauls have three or four times more volume than Gibsons so for this reason I am against him and the way he plays. That was why I left Os Mutantes.'

Arnaldo really did believe that his brother's brand loyalty to Fender was a reason not to talk to him for thirty years. Kurt Cobain attempted to get the band to reform to support Nirvana on a tour of Brazil in the mid-nineties, but they refused because of the guitar problem. In 2000 the brothers almost made their peace. Arnaldo went to Sérgio's house in São Paulo fully prepared to forgive and forget, but he walked in to see a Fender guitar lying around and left immediately. They have not talked since. It was such a shame. They were wonderful, inspiring, hugely likeable and creative people. Yet Arnaldo, in his confusion, put a Gibson Les Paul before his own brother.

The electric guitar has become too iconic, with many people believing that having the same model as your hero will somehow rub off some of their magic on to you. Jimi Hendrix made the sale of Fender Stratocasters go through the roof in the late sixties, and as Jeff Beck said in 1968: 'This instrument thing is out of hand. If Eric Clapton sold his guitar and bought a ten-dollar one, the kids would do the same.' Still, I had my reputation to think of. If I went on stage with, for example, a Carlos Santana-endorsed masturbatory tool of a guitar, I might never be able to hold my head up in polite society again.

Pete Millson recommended a large guitar shop in Crouch End, North London called Rock Around The Clock. He suggested I would be better off avoiding the high prices and attitude of Denmark Street for somewhere that catered to its neighbourhood musician's needs, so while NJ attempted to stop Otto from climbing on to every drum kit and crashing every cymbal in the joint, I went into the 'try-out room' at the back of the shop to be handed a steady stream of guitars by the cheerful heavy metal fan who worked there. First up was a Fender Stratocaster.

If most people picture an electric guitar in their minds they will probably be thinking of a Strat. It is the bestselling guitar ever, and it has remained in production since first coming on to the market in 1954. It is the world's most copied design, with its three pick-ups and double cutaway body being found on cheaper

models everywhere. In Britain, the sixties started in earnest when
Hank Marvin of The Shadows ordered a Strat after having a
Fender brochure sent over from America. The Shadows had made
money as an early beat group, but American guitars were hard to
find and until then Marvin had been using a cheap Japanese
model. It was decided that the band would buy the most
expensive Stratocaster available because that's what the American
rock'n'roll idol Ricky Nelson's guitarist James Burton used. The
sight of Hank and his Strat went on to inspire a generation of
British guitar heroes. It was only after the guitar arrived that they
discovered that Burton actually played a cheap old Telecaster.

By the mid-sixties the Stratocaster was unfashionable, chiefly
because of its association with Marvin. Then Jimi Hendrix came
along and pushed the instrument into new dimensions, making
sounds through a Strat and a Marshall amp that had no relation
whatsoever to the traditional guitar. I first heard Jimi Hendrix
at the age of twelve when 'Foxy Lady' came on the radio, and I
was confused, intrigued and gripped. This was the eighties,
when pop music was generally devoid of raw passion, and
Hendrix knocked me for a loop. Albums like *Are You Experienced*
and *Electric Ladyland* were played to death so much in my teens
that I hadn't gone near them for years, but since learning guitar
I was having something of a Hendrix renaissance. Of course
there was 'Hey Joe', but more recently my guitar teacher had
taught me how to play 'Little Wing', always one of my favourite
songs off the second Hendrix album *Axis: Bold As Love*, and
Doyle had demonstrated the riff to 'Remember'. You can't play
like Hendrix, but it isn't so hard to play one of his songs. Like
all the best guitarists, he kept it simple in essence.

A top of the range Strat was great, but it was also far too
expensive and my limited skills would have made me feel like a
spoilt rich kid valuing the object over the process. Rock Around

The Clock had some Squier Strats for as little as £99 but they were awful. They went out of tune in an instant and had a tinny, thin twang. Even Pete, with his years spent practising his Bryan Adams and Dire Straits guitar licks in his bedroom, couldn't get a decent sound out of them.

I tried five or six Stratocasters, some at the same price, and they all sounded different. None of them were working for me. Next came a Gibson Les Paul Standard, which at £400 was more than I could afford, but the sales assistant thought he would try his luck and seduce me with this classic guitar's solid sound and weight of history. The British blues boom owed a lot to the Les Paul: when Eric Clapton put his one into overdrive through a Marshall amp to create distortion, tremolo and feedback for the 1966 Bluesbreakers album, he helped launch the Les Paul as a cult object. When Clapton left the Bluesbreakers he was replaced by Peter Green, the best slide guitarist in Britain at the time, who used a 1959 Les Paul with a unique sound that came from the fact that he had taken the guitar apart to clean it and refitted one of the pick-ups the wrong way round. It was a Les Paul standard through a heavily distorted amp and a microphone on the other side of the recording studio that Jimmy Page used for Led Zeppelin's 'Whole Lotta Love', and David Bowie's guitarist Mick Ronson had one. Steve Jones from The Sex Pistols introduced the world to punk-rock on a Les Paul. Variously credited as bringing an end to the Vietnam War and destroying civilized society, it is the guitar of the guitar god.

Put through a Marshall practice amp it sounded crisp and clear, but it was too good for me. I didn't deserve it, especially as buying an electric guitar in the first place was something of a folly: I didn't have a real band and was unlikely to get one unless I wanted to throw in my lot with a bunch of fifteen-year-old heavy metal fans in need of a 'mature' member with an enlightened attitude towards shelling out for rehearsal space. 'You'd be mad to buy this,' said Pete, a man who has been known to complain when supermarkets raise the price of their value baked beans from 9p to 10p. 'You'd be paying for the name.' He was right, and I remembered hearing the tale of when the eighties biker band Zodiac Mindwarp And The Love Reaction signed a record deal. They went to Andy's Guitar Centre in Denmark Street and asked for the most expensive guitars in the house. They were told that surely they wanted the best guitars. 'No we don't,' they replied. 'We want the most expensive.'

But I don't even like guitar gods. Eric Clapton's neat, clipped, freshly-pressed-denims style of playing has never done it for me, and my least favourite kind of music is eighties rock, when technology and technique were seen as more important than songwriting. What did I need a Les Paul for? One of my favourite guitarists is the late Johnny Ramone and he played a Mosrite, which in the seventies was considered one of the worst brands available. Come to think of it, how about a Mosrite? Did Rock Around The Clock have one in stock? (No.)

The Rickenbacker 360 12-string that was hanging on the wall brought happy memories of Roger McGuinn's jingle-jangle sound, and although, once again, it was too expensive, I had to give it a try. Used by The Beatles, The Byrds and The Beach Boys, it comes with an impeccable pedigree and great curves. John Lennon first bought a Rickenbacker 325 in Hamburg in 1960, and by the time The Beatles visited America in 1964 the company's owner F. C. Hall presented George Harrison with a brand-new 360-12. Just strumming the thing created that sixties vibe that I had always loved: peaceful, enquiring, innocent and melancholic. But my big clumsy fingers kept hitting the wrong strings – all twelve of them – on the narrow neck. Roger McGuinn's jingle-jangle sounded more jumble-bumble in my hands. Another one returned to the racks.

The multi-pierced and tattooed sales assistant was doing his best not to show any signs of irritation at having half his stock used and then returned, while Pete was muttering about getting back home for his four o'clock pot of tea (one teabag would be enough for all of us), but I still hadn't found the right electric guitar. The sales assistant brought three at once to save time. Two were Fender Stratocasters and variously too expensive and too awful, and the third was a Squier Fender Telecaster. This looked like an electric guitar reduced to its absolute essentials: one volume control, one tone control, six strings and a big, heavy chunk of wood around them. I tried it. I liked its brittle twang.

The Telecaster, originally known as the Broadcaster, is the Model T Ford of the guitar world. Before Leo Fender brought it out at the end of the forties, electric guitars were elaborate, finely carved works of art, with F-holes modelled on violins and perfectly executed paint finishes. Fender had the idea of turning the guitar into a production-line object, affordable to all. The Telecaster is a solid piece of ash with an all-maple neck that is attached to the body with four screws. The bridge is a Neanderthal piece of stamped steel. Any factory-line worker could turn out a Telecaster, so it marked the arrival of the guitar as a mass-market product. Keith Richards, the ultimate rhythm guitarist, has one.

It was easy to play, too. I liked its timeless lack of finesse. I played 'You Ain't Going Nowhere' on it, followed by a lead accompaniment for the song in E minor that Michael Tyack had taught me. It sounded perfect on the Telecaster. I was sold on it.

Then there was the question of the amp. Seeing that he was finally getting somewhere, the sales assistant brought one out by a company called Line 6. It came with built-in effects like phasing, tape delay and reverb, and although having a digital button to recreate the sound that, back in the sixties, people like Brian Wilson and Phil Spector had spent years perfecting through incredibly convoluted processes felt like cheating, you could get all kinds of psychedelic guitar sounds instantly. Why had I been bothering with the fingertip-tormenting process of learning an acoustic guitar for the last five months? All you had to do with an electric was plug in and rock!

In terms of authenticity, the Line 6 amp was on a par with a cowboy town in Disneyland. It had four buttons that you could press to get the sound you wanted. There was 'clean', which, with a bit of delay, could recreate U2's 'Where The Streets Have No Name' (according to the instruction booklet). Then there was 'crunch', which got you the dense sixties distortion of Jimmy Page's guitar on 'Whole Lotta Love'. If you dared, you could press the self-explanatory 'metal', which would give you instant access to the kind of squealing monster riffs Metallica have inflicted on so many suburban homes the world over. And finally – although this was not recommended for those of a nervous disposition, sufferers of heart conditions or pregnant women – there was 'insane'. I didn't dare press it.

They knew I was hooked. With a few crazy effects going through it, even my rendition of 'You Can't Always Get What You Want' was a mind-expanding journey into weird. One could only imagine what it would be like to play a Telecaster with heavy reverb on the 'insane' setting backed by a full electric rock band. If I could convince Pete to stay out beyond nine o'clock for just one wild night, and if I could get Doyle to remember not to collapse into a gutter, we could just make it happen.

Chapter Twelve

Double Fantasy

There is a reason why the young make rock'n'roll. They have the time and the energy for it. The guitar is an instrument best learned after school and at weekends, and there is no better era for being in a band than when you are either a student or on the dole. Put time into playing the guitar in early adulthood and it can save you from working for a living. You discover that you can pass hours and hours sitting and doing practically nothing by playing the guitar: you can slouch on the sofa, and as long as you always have a guitar on your lap to strum you can convince yourself that you are doing something vaguely useful and productive. If you are sufficiently lazy you can get good enough to be in a band that makes it big, especially if you team up with a driven, career-minded lead singer. Look at Mick Jagger and Keith Richards.

The problem is that being in a band is a logistical nightmare even when your fellow members are doing nothing else with their lives, so when you find that your friends are all working hard to make ends meet and spending their free time with the families they are supporting, it's almost impossible. The first time I realized this was when I gave Pete Millson a call to convince him to back me up on the debut gig.

'I'm out with the boy right now,' he said, referring to his two-year-old son. 'I'm playing in the sand with all the fit mums in the park. Perhaps we could work out an afternoon when we're both free as the evenings are generally taken up looking after him while Rachel studies for her psychology exams.'

'What? You've got to have an evening off from looking after that kid! If you carry on being such a perfect new dad you're going to sprout breasts. Then where would you be?'

Sadly, Pete really did put fatherly duties over playing guitar and getting wasted with a bunch of losers, but we managed to find an hour in the middle of a Saturday when his son was having his nap, his wife wanted to be left in peace, and Pete was prepared to emerge from the womb-like security of his flat. I knew what I wanted to do. I showed him the lead part to 'You Ain't Going Nowhere' and he played rhythm and sang. Lead guitar is, in theory, easy: you simply have to stick to notes that are in the same key as the chords being played and you can make it up as you go along within those boundaries. Some things work and some things don't and that is the nature of im-provisation.

While NJ took Otto and Pearl to the library, Pete and I worked out a great version of the song. With Pete being skilful enough to hold down a tight rhythm and make it clear about when I should change to a new pattern of notes, it worked. In that brief hour during his son's nap, we learned to play an entire song on two guitars, and Pete introduced me to the concept of forming lead patterns for an introduction, a verse and a chorus. Playing the finished version, which came together through a rapid process of trial and error, remains one of my life's achievements. We played it to NJ when she returned with Otto and Pearl. The children were more than unimpressed — they were irritated — but NJ, in her calm and generous way, listened carefully, nodded when we came to the end, and said: 'It's good.' That's effusive for her.

Pete was a fine guitarist and imaginative in his self-effacing way, but I knew that I would never get the spirit of rock'n'roll from him. In terms of pure rock malevolence there is one guitarist who has always been head and shoulders above everyone else, and ever since I spoke to Johnny Marr I had been wondering how I might find him and ask about life in the greatest, most filthy garage band of all. James Williamson, the lead guitarist on The Stooges's third and final album, *Raw Power*, was something of a shady figure. A troubled youth from the Detroit area, he joined the band after the original line-up collapsed under the weight of drugs, poverty and madness, and after The Stooges's singer Iggy Pop's idea of taking the building blocks of the blues and applying them to life as a delinquent product of post-war suburban America had proved too incendiary for mainstream audiences. By 1971, the band had forsaken music for taking heroin and committing robberies. That's when James Williamson came in.

Williamson knew the band already. The Stooges were from nearby Ann Arbor in Michigan and the Motor City was where they played most of their concerts. During a visit to New York in 1970 Williamson bumped into Iggy Pop – at the Chelsea Hotel (where else?) – who suggested that he join the band. Having nothing better to do, Williamson moved from Detroit to Ann Arbor and entered into the band's twilight world of drugs and alienation.

A *deus ex machina* came in the form of David Bowie, who managed to convince CBS Records to fly Pop and Williamson to London in 1972 and put them up in the Kensington Gardens Hotel to record *Raw Power*. The eponymous debut album by The Stooges is charged and brutal garage-rock; the second, *Funhouse*, is lurid chaos. But *Raw Power* has sophistication in its debauchery. One song, 'Gimme Danger', features the best opening guitar riff of all time. It sounds sleazy but enquiring. Another track, 'Search And Destroy' ('I'm a street-walking cheetah with a heart full of napalm'), is the musical equivalent of having a gang of hell's angels break down your door, gangbang your wife (who would openly enjoy it), squeeze the toothpaste from the top and leave the cap off. Rock guitar doesn't get any better.

I didn't know too much about James Williamson, though. The most complete story on The Stooges is in *Please Kill Me*, New Yorker Legs McNeill's history of punk, and James Williamson is the only former member who did not agree to be interviewed. He is painted as a dark cloud on the band; a negative force that sucked the life out of an already fragile entity. In the pictures I had seen of him he was certainly intimidating: with his thigh-high boots, long hair and permanent snarl, he looked like the toughest degenerate on the block. So it was all the more surprising when I tracked him down to discover that he was a married father of two working as an executive in the electronics industry.

Williamson lives in Silicon Valley, California, undertakes regular corporate business trips to Tokyo, and, in his own words, has 'rode the wave of the PC boom for the last twenty years'. At first it seemed like he might be as mean as his image suggested. 'What makes you qualified to write about guitarists?' came back the reply to my letter. It took a while, but eventually he agreed to talk.

It is tempting to imagine James Williamson slouching out of the womb with a cigarette hanging from his spitting newborn mouth, but it turned out that he was a reasonably normal boy from Oklahoma who picked up his first guitar at the age of eleven when he and his mother went to visit his uncle in Texas. 'I bought an old F-hole guitar from Sears on that trip, took it back to Oklahoma, and talked my mother into letting me take lessons from a guy by the name of Rusty Sparks,' he told me over the phone from California, in a voice that belonged more to a bank manager than a maniac junkie rocker. 'It turned out that Rusty Sparks hosted a local television show that featured country and western music, and once I had mastered a few chords Rusty had me come on his show and sing and play the song "Good Ole Mountain Dew". I guess I got my first taste of show business from that experience.'

By the time he moved to Detroit with his mother at the age of twelve, Williamson was listening to the folk bands of the early sixties like Peter, Paul And Mary and The Kingston Trio, before moving on to Bob Dylan, The Beach Boys, The Beatles and The Rolling Stones a few years later – 'You know, the usual stuff. I liked the Stones because they were on the dark side. But then, how dark can a fifteen-year-old be? It was innocent back then.' In 1966 he formed a garage band called The Chosen Few with Ron Asheton, the original guitarist of The Stooges, who moved to bass after Williamson joined the band. 'The Chosen Few were my first real band. We were pretty cool – at least we thought we were. That was when I first met Ron Asheton, who had already been in a blues band called The Prime Movers, for which Iggy played drums.' Then Williamson got sent to juvenile hall for refusing to have his hair cut – the official line was that he was 'incorrigible' – and his career as a rock'n'roll outlaw started in earnest.

The Stooges's sound and presence – primal rock'n'roll, with Iggy stripping off on stage, cutting himself, jumping into the audience, starting fights and, in a brief nod to nutritional awareness, smearing his body with peanut butter – was unlike anything anyone had seen before. 'I knew those guys so I had a different perspective on it, but nobody was doing anything that came close,' said Williamson. 'The nearest – and this happened later – was Alice Cooper, and he got a lot of his ideas from Iggy.'

Williamson wouldn't open up on the debauched period when he lived with other members of The Stooges in Ann Arbor at the beginning of the seventies, but there is no doubt that heavy drugs dominated life back then. He contracted hepatitis and moved away to stay with his sister in Detroit for six months, clean up, and recover. By the time Iggy Pop got the call from David Bowie to make a record in London, Williamson was fit and healthy and ready for a new adventure. And when The Stooges arrived they worked hard and stayed straight. Initially, only Williamson and Iggy Pop went over, but after finding that English musicians couldn't play the tough style they wanted ('They were a bunch of foppish dandies'), the pair put in a call to the Asheton brothers. 'We weren't doing anything more than practising every night until four or five in the morning and drinking beer,' said Williamson. 'I had a blast in London: it was my first real album and I was delighted just to be given the chance to do it.'

I asked him how he came up with his guitar style. He said it was because he never tried to be anything other than what he was – a disaffected working-class guy from a city going down the pan – and the fact that The Stooges never did cover versions. 'The Doors and The Rolling Stones were our big influences, but we never had any pretence of being as good as them,' he said. 'Our main goal was always to express ourselves. I remember one night we were playing at Max's Kansas City in New York. Lou Reed came up to me and said that we should do some of his songs. I told him that we wouldn't. He seemed annoyed.'

The rock monster that is 'Gimme Danger' was created by James Williamson in his hotel room at Kensington Gardens on a Gibson B25 acoustic, and it was recorded on a Martin D-18, a classic folkie guitar. Williamson used a Gibson Les Paul through a Vox AC30 amp for most of the rhythm tracks and a Marshall amp for most of the solos, and there are no effects used at all on the album, although David Bowie, in his role as producer, threw on a couple during the final mix.

The album bombed. 'We knew it was a terrific record,' said Williamson. 'But in hindsight its dismal failure in the market-place isn't surprising. It was so ahead of its time.'

It's a vicarious thrill to imagine how great it must have been to be the guitarist in the meanest rock band in the world, but The Stooges split for a reason. If playing guitar for a living was really so good, then presumably Williamson would still be doing it. These days he's completely housebroken, with a job and a family to keep him in check and the wild days long behind him, and it didn't sound like he missed them at all. 'After London we went to LA and we didn't have a deal. So we started touring constantly and fell back into drugs, and Iggy's self-destructive tendencies began to take over again. He's a great guy but it was hard work being with him, partly because his social skills are really quite pathetic. I can't imagine still being out there with him on the road at my age.'

When I tracked him down in 2004, Williamson had not played for years and wasn't in any position to teach me how to get that Stooges sound – he couldn't remember how he did it. 'As my son wrote in a school essay, my guitars are the "coffins in the corner",' he said, when I asked him how often he still liked to kick up some raw power riffage . 'They belong to a side of me that I left behind a long time ago.'

I was sure that Williamson was much happier as a corporate electronics family man than a mascara-clad deviant. But it still made me feel sad to think about those coffins in the corner.

Then I heard something cheering. A few weeks after I first talked to him, Williamson wrote to say that my interest in his playing, and my constant hassling to force him to talk, had got him playing again. He had been doing some of the old Stooges guitar parts for the first time in thirty years. I imagined him returning from a hard day at the cutting edge of corporate electronics to blast into, say, 'Your Pretty Face Is Going To Hell', before his wife called him for supper and reminded him to wash his hands before sitting down at the table.

There was one thing left to do: ask him how I could blow up the world with my electric rock madness.

'Have fun with it,' said James. 'In the end, that's all there is.'

It was time to understand how I might be able to get a band happening, even if I was doing it fifteen years too late, and in my limited way, play guitar in front of an audience. For that it seemed to make sense to meet the man behind the first band I ever saw, an experience that hit me with the seedy glamour and excitement of rock'n'roll the likes of which has not been matched since. It was 1984 and I was fourteen. Thee Milk- shakes were playing in a tiny basement bar in Hammersmith, West London called The Clarendon. I arrived to see a group of fearsome beauties with ponytails and bad skin and skinny men with quiffs and leather jackets standing around outside. I joined the queue going down the stairs into a low-ceilinged room with black walls where the toilet door was hanging off its hinges and a large man with long grey greasy hair and a nose like a red onion was acting as some form of security. A middle-aged woman with a red perm, nicotine-stained fingers and a pout was behind the bar. The carpet was covered in a beer-saturated adhesive. Can you imagine a cooler scene?

Just getting past the longhaired doorman by doing my best

impersonation of an older person was enough to make my year. Then Thee Milkshakes came on: four men with short, waxed hair and leather jackets who looked a little like The Beatles in their early days at The Star Club in Hamburg. Their music was the most basic form of rock'n'roll: every song was about a girl and rarely deviated from a Chuck Berry riff and a couple of chords. In-between songs they were grumpy and cynical; like old men. Their lead singer was, I later discovered, called Billy Childish and he also painted, wrote books, and was something of a one-man cottage industry. Thee Milkshakes made albums in a day, released them on Childish's Hangman label, and sold about a hundred copies. There was a suggestion that anyone could get up and do what they were doing, but they had an arrogance that proclaimed nobody could do it as well as them. They were certainly lording it over the room.

Twenty-one years later Billy Childish was doing the same thing he had always done, although now he had over a hundred albums, four novels and countless paintings to his credit. He had become an underground hero to rock stars who liked the idea of someone doing everything on their own terms: Jack White of The White Stripes, Beck and even Kylie Minogue had been a few of his more celebrated fans. He still lived in Chatham, the dreary town in Kent where he grew up, and he was still making a name for himself by celebrating all things provincial and unsophisticated. His entire life appeared to be based on the old punk ethic of doing it for yourself and doing it quickly, without worrying too much about levels of talent or skill or polish. He formed one band after another that all sounded the same: the only thing that changed was the personnel he managed to convince to buy into his version of the world. I was interested in the thrill I had felt when I had seen Thee Milkshakes back in my burgeoning youth and how I could, with my new knowledge of the guitar, take that thrill somewhere new.

I drove down to Childish's little terraced house in Chatham where modern technology has been eradicated, his own paintings fill the walls, and everything is raw, unfinished and old, from the bare floorboards to the tarnished whistling kettle he makes his herbal teas with. With a giant handlebar moustache, short-back-and-sides haircut and military trousers, Billy looked like he had just crawled out of the trenches of the Somme in 1916. His pretty American girlfriend Julie, who had been learning to play herself and had glued the names of all the notes on to the neck of her guitar, made us fresh vegetable juice while Billy expounded on his philosophy of life.

'Most things are mystified by professional guitarists because they want to keep the scum out,' he said with simmering vitriol. 'I don't believe that there is any mystery to playing the guitar and there shouldn't be. An example of this is a programme I once saw about Eric Clapton. I would naturally think of him as someone who embodies nothing of the blues – we call it "wristing off the blues" – but this programme had him sitting down with an acoustic guitar in front of his record player, banging along to a Robert Johnson record. And I felt that I misjudged this man: he really does like this music and he can do it. But then he goes and does his own music on a demo for a new album and it's just bad rock. The documentary-makers ask Eric how he's getting on and he says that he really likes the demos, and it's a shame that he can't just release that and not the more polished version of it that the record company want him to release. So here is a man who likes blues music, and he likes the raw version of his own music, but he's forced, in his view, to take it to the studio and re-do it and re-do it until the spirit has gone. Eric Clapton is at the top of his tree and he's wealthy, and there's no reason why he can't do what he believes in and not be a monkey for anyone. So why do it? He must feel compelled to show off and keep guitar playing mystified.'

I asked Billy to show me how he learned to play. He told me that friends had demonstrated how to hold down an E chord when he was nineteen, and he worked out how to get a rhythm from hitting a single chord from there. He learned to play barré chords and a few riffs and didn't bother with anything else for the next ten years, which covered his period in Thee Milkshakes and a few other bands besides. He had based everything he played on his two favourite guitarists: Link Wray and Bo Diddley. Link Wray was a rockabilly instrumentalist from fifties America who made classic gang fight-style guitar songs like 'Rumble' and 'Brandy', and Bo Diddley took the blues and speeded it up to make the rolling stock sound of early R&B. Billy showed me how to play Link Wray's 'Rumble'. It only has three chords, but it is the feeling of menace that Link puts into it that gives the song its magic.

'If you're learning to play guitar and you're interested in rock'n'roll then you should just do the blues and Link Wray and not bother with anything else,' said Billy as he showed me how to drag the plectrum over the strings to get the evil twang of 'Rumble'. 'Link Wray was the greatest guitarist bar none. He had nasty-sounding chords before anyone else and he's the most spirited player. I can't even go near what he does.'

Billy ordered me to play slowly – just behind the beat – for extra power, and he said that I should tap my foot to keep a rhythm. (I find swaying works better.) I kept trying to make him show me more licks, but he wanted to throw in more opinions on how the world should be. 'People want to feel good about themselves by thinking they're great guitarists, when in fact you should feel bad about yourself,' he said as I tried to get him to tell me what his fingers were doing as he played a Bo Diddley riff. 'Most people would rather buy a new pair of shoes every six months that have been made by children who aren't allowed piss breaks than get their old ones re-soled,' he announced while I wondered if it was necessary to dampen the strings to play 'Rumble' correctly. 'Hardly anyone cares about how things are done, but I think caring matters because what we do and being alive matters,' he proclaimed as I finally cracked the timing of the D to G change in Link Wray's 'Brandy'.

It became apparent that there was a discrepancy between Billy's professed total lack of any formal knowledge of the guitar whatsoever and the reality of what he could do. He kept telling me that he didn't know where a G or a D chord was, and then he would give himself away by telling me to play a B major 7. But he did seem quite surprised when I played the claw hammer style that Bert Jansch had taught me. 'You're already highly accomplished,' he said, and I don't think it was intended as a compliment. I told him I was taking lessons. 'I'd knock those on the head right now. Remember that too much noodling is bad for the soul, even if it is good for the bank balance. You're already a neater player than I am. You seem to be doing fine – just keep it simple and learn to play a few nice songs the whole way through.'

As for forming a band, Billy had plenty of advice on that too. 'Stick to a three-piece. That way you've got nothing to hide behind. All the best bands were three-pieces, like The Jimi Hendrix Experience. When someone presses a key on a synthesizer it will sound the same whoever does it, but with a guitar no two people play the same way. It expresses the character of the person playing it. Also, guitars sound better when they're slightly out of tune.'

After myriad complaints about the state of live music and the impossibility of making a living from being in a band and staying true to yourself, Billy did show me a few more moves. And I did feel that he was encouraging to anyone prepared to make an effort and take their life into their own hands, which is what playing the guitar is all about. 'You're not meant to be learning to play guitar,' he said. 'You're meant to be watching the professionals do it on MTV and spending your money on other people who play guitar. So you should stick with it.'

By the end of the afternoon I had enjoyed the healthful benefits of a glass of vegetable juice, listened to various rants, and learned how to play some hellfire rockabilly that sounded like it had just emerged from the primordial ooze of creation. It seemed strange that Billy did not have the curiosity to look beyond what he first learned as a teenager, but he was all about setting rigid boundaries for himself and his art. His paintings were always in the same heavy-handed style, his writing was autobiographical and used his dyslexia as a badge of honour, and his records were made on the cheap in a matter of days and never varied from a basic template. He didn't allow himself to go into situations where he wasn't in control. The self-imposed limitations were at the heart of the creative process.

Billy had inspired me to think that this crazy plan to play guitar in front of an audience within six months wasn't so crazy after all – as he pointed out, Steve Marriot of the sixties mods The Small Faces had only been playing that long when the band had their first hit. Billy knocked out a new song every couple of days. What was I waiting for?

The next day I called up Pete to arrange another rehearsal. He came over that afternoon. Already the guitar was destroying my working life. On a Wednesday, when I should have been out earning bread, I practised in the morning and knocked out a bona fide pop smash with Pete in the afternoon. He arrived at one. At ten to one I realized it might be good to work out a new song together rather than just play numbers written by other people. As the children fought over a broken plastic ruler I sat down at the table with a pen and a notebook and resolved to write something immediately. I always liked the way Marc Bolan made nonsense poetry sparkle – surely it couldn't be too hard to combine earthly imagery with cosmic allusions in the way that Bolan did so well. So I thought of two words that I liked together: mystery fox. It took about a minute to come up with:

> Mystery fox
> Come out of your box
> It's time for me to chase you up that tree
> O mystery fox.

I needed another animal. How about a cat?

> My domestic cat
> Get out of your flat
> It may be warm but then, so is my lawn
> When we lie on it flat.

And another:

> O slippery newt
> You were caught in my boot
> Then something took root
> And now you're bearing fruit
> You slippery newt.

The doorbell rang and I hadn't come up with a chorus. As the children charged towards the door, as they always do at the

prospect of anyone arriving at our flat, I knocked it out in the
time it took for me to write it on the paper.

> My moonlight time
> In the forest is fine
> Give me a push
> And I'll come out of a bush
> In the moonlight time.

Once I had met Pete's demand for payment – a cup of tea – I
showed him what I had written. He took the Telecaster and
knocked out a riff that sounded urgent and powerful, but
slightly mysterious: exactly the right kind of sound for the
lyrics. Then he worked out a time structure to crowbar the verse
and chorus into. He played the rhythm while I played the lead,
which simply consisted of picking a few notes that would have
sounded barren by themselves but were great against the other
guitar. We had a song within half an hour. Pete, with an army
of chords at his fingertips and a natural ability to bash out tunes,
had made 'Mystery Fox' a living, breathing entity.

'Do you know the number of a good psychiatrist?' I asked him.

'Why?'

'Because you have just blown my mind.'

'We need a couple more verses to fill it out.'

'Well that's easy enough,' I told him, and wrote the following lines:

> Hefty graceful bear
> With your curtain of hair
> You broke my arm
> With your gallons of charm
> Hefty graceful bear.

O tapir of old
Let me see your gold
It would only be right
On this silvery night
O tapir of old.

It was instant rock with a touch of psychedelic folk and slightly suggestive woodland wizardry. 'That's a hit!' I said to Pete. We ran through 'Mystery Fox', and reacquainted ourselves with 'You Ain't Going Nowhere'. We had the A-side and the B-side of our first single. NJ returned in a rush to get Otto to nursery on time, but I forced her to listen to 'Mystery Fox' before she left. She conceded that it was a winner and dragged a screaming child off round the corner.

I had always known that if Pete was going to represent the safe and gentle side of my musical project, I needed the forces of chaos within it, too. I wondered if it was too early to call Doyle. With the new Telecaster and wisdom gleaned from top rockers James Williamson and Billy Childish, I wanted to play some electric rock'n'roll, so that the big gig would consist of a few garage-rock numbers as well as the delicate finger-picking ones. Doyle had just returned from a trip to India with his girlfriend, who had gone back to Japan. Consequently, he would presumably have more time on his hands. This quiet, polite girl who I hardly knew had caused me no end of problems in the past when I tried to entice Doyle out of his lair on the Holloway Road. She viewed it as her mission to ensure he did not fritter his money away on drunken escapades and as a result she saw his friends, myself in particular it seemed, as a bad influence. He had not been as available for guitar sessions as I would have liked. Now he would be alone, miserable, and a little more financially solvent. It was one o'clock in the afternoon; that seemed like a good time to catch him.

After muttering something unintelligible about not wanting to go to school, Doyle demanded to know who was waking him up in the middle of the night. I explained that we had to get rehearsing, and quickly.

'I just did a twelve-hour shift, and I've discovered something even more important than rehearsing,' he croaked, the timbre changing with his rising consciousness. 'It's called sleeping.'

I had told a friend about my plans to form a band with Doyle. She had met him twice: the first time had been the night of the ankle-biting incident (see Chapter One), when he misguidedly attempted to chat her up by saying that she looked like a pig; the second had been on his return from India when, lonely and maudlin, he had become equally drunken at Tapestry, the social club of which the festival we went to in the summer was connected. On that night his winning line was: 'Are you gay?' My friend felt that someone had to look after Doyle, although she didn't put herself forward for the job. 'My God, the thought of you and Doyle on the same stage is quite terrifying,' she said. 'Perhaps you could call yourself Double Fantasy.'

The name worked on different levels. There was a double fantasy going on in the heads of Doyle and myself, and of course we might be a Double Fantasy for some rather short-sighted girls out there. Never mind that Pete would be with us: Triple Fantasy didn't have the same ring to it. I could see it now: Pete with his tank top and pot of tea sitting on top of the amplifier, Doyle in an animal hide and Viking belt buckle, spitting fragments of tooth at the audience, and me in a cravat and denim waistcoat like some seventies rock star gone to seed. And I had asked the attractive French girl from Circulus to be our singer as it was inconceivable that anyone would pay good money to look at three ugly gits in their thirties playing guitars (mind you that never stopped Crosby, Stills And Nash). When I mentioned the name to Doyle he muttered something about refusing to wear spandex or a cut-off T-shirt. Then he managed to tear himself away from the railway tracks for one Friday night so that we could have our first proper writing and rehearsal session.

Doyle is the perfect delinquent uncle to our children. They recognize that he has no natural authority and treat him with the utmost disrespect, but they love him dearly and, given the amount of time he has ended up sleeping in our basement, assume that he lives in a hole underneath our flat, emerging only when the smell of frying bacon draws him out of his lair. Doyle had spent that afternoon in Hamleys, the famous toy-shop on Regent Street in London, and arrived laden with two carrier bags of presents including an Etch A Sketch for Otto and a talking backpack for Pearl. In-between Hamleys and our house he had stumbled into a pub and downed a couple of pints. The rehearsal session did not start in earnest until after ten o'clock, when we had finally managed to get two extremely excited children to sleep.

Even then, Doyle was more interested in talking about girl trouble than he was in working out our set list. From what he told us, this poor girlfriend of his must have had saintly patience to put up with his paranoia and possessiveness. After explaining how he discovered in India that she had been lying to him for the past year about old boyfriends that she swore she was no longer in touch with, and after he told us that he had spent thousands of pounds on trying to keep her happy whether she wanted the money or not, he asked us if he thought it would be a good idea to hire a private detective to discover if she had been unfaithful, despite the fact that he had no reason to believe that this was the case.

'Do you really need me to tell you?' I replied.

'Maybe she does love me.'

Poor Doyle. From what I had seen of her this girl wasn't exactly the tactile sort, and she certainly knew how to survive with or without Doyle, but I was sure that she did care for him none the less. Unfortunately, Doyle's insecurity meant that whatever she said and did would never be enough. I suggested that he try and write a song about his experience.

'She's like a diamond,' he said. 'Expensive and hard enough to tear you to pieces.'

He started strumming in the key of A minor. It sounded melancholic and brooding; perfect for a tune about a woman who graciously destroys you. Over several beers we tried to write words for the tune he came up with.

'How about "A diamond sparkles with a brilliance that deceives, the shifting sands of best intent will give you no reprieve"?' I offered, imagining Doyle's girl in the unlikely role of femme fatale.

'It's too poetic,' said Doyle.

'What do you mean? It's meant to be poetic.'

'It's too sophisticated. You have to speak to the people on their own level. Our audience won't understand that sort of thing.'

'What audience? We haven't got an audience. For God's sake, we don't even exist yet!'

'Ah, you see, you're giving up already,' said Doyle, nodding his head, as if he had anticipated as much. 'You've got to have stamina to do this sort of thing. I always knew that you lily-livered office-worker types weren't cut out for the rock'n'roll life. There aren't enough soft cushions in it for you.'

'What's your lyrical contribution, then?'

Doyle stared at his beer. 'She's a goddam bitch but I love her.'

'Is that it?'

'No, there's more. "She's a goddam bitch but I love her, but she can fuck off if she thinks she's getting any more of my money. Then again, if she just says sorry for lying to me for the last year and promises she'll always tell the truth from now on I'll forgive her and come out to Japan and marry her." '

'Does that scan?'

Doyle stared hopelessly at his guitar.

We gave up trying to come up with our own material after that and settled into an extended version of 'The House Of The Rising Sun'.

'Jimmy Page is the best guitarist of all,' said Doyle, picking out the over-familiar notes as I strummed the chords. 'Jimmy Page and Brian May, because he built his own guitar.'

'Why does that make you great? I suppose you think that Emerson, Lake And Palmer were the best rock band of all time because they each had their own personalized tour vans. Davey Graham is the real deal. He was Jimmy Page's hero and the hero of every other guitarist worth his salt in the sixties.'

'Who?'

My ongoing efforts to play Davey Graham's, 'Anji' were getting really frustrating. It felt like I had all the parts to a jigsaw puzzle that I couldn't piece together: however much I tried I could not get the bass line to run in parallel with the melody. It is said that people spend years mastering it so I didn't feel too defeated. Mr David Viner claimed it was the first song he ever learned and I was beginning to wonder whether I should believe him. I had noticed that quite a few guitarists had a shaky relationship with the truth, Doyle among them. I played him the original version of 'Anji' that evening in our basement. He lit a Marlboro and shook his head.

'It's nowhere near as good as Jimmy Page,' he said. 'It's the kind of thing you hear a wasted old hippie play on a beach in Goa. I could do better than that.'

'Go on then. You play it.'

He couldn't even get the opening line. He muttered something about being able to if he wanted, but he couldn't waste his time on rubbish. I felt like writing a press release to announce that Double Fantasy had split due to musical differences, but decided to ignore Doyle's philistinism.

As more beers were drunk, listening to music took over from any attempt to play it. By two in the morning we were marvelling at the incredible eleven-minute guitar solo that is 'Maggot Brain' by Funkadelic; apparently Funkadelic's leader George Clinton told his guitarist Eddie Hazel to 'play as if your mother has just died', and he certainly did: with an electric guitar and some controlled use of a wah-wah pedal Hazel produced one of the most mournful psychedelic guitar workouts of all time. I tried writing more lyrics to 'The Diamond' and Doyle inevitably rejected them as being too depressing. So I played him 'Mystery Fox'. 'That's genius,' he said. 'That's the sort of song that Double Fantasy should be playing.'

Pete and I had bashed out a song in five minutes and it had worked. I had been labouring endlessly over clever metaphors to explain Doyle's situation with 'The Diamond' and it was all too forced. This was my first lesson in writing songs: trying to be clever rarely makes good popular art.

Double Fantasy had its first full rehearsal a week later, on a Friday afternoon when neither Doyle nor Pete had any work on. I had written the lyrics to two new songs in preparation. 'I Found Out' was an angry rant from the perspective of a woman who has discovered that the man she loves has been cheating on her – with another man. 'Until Daylight' was a melancholic but romantic enticement to share a night of passion with a friend:

the narrator describes a cosy scene of a bottle of whisky, a log fire and a warm bed, but it becomes obvious that both people have partners. Doyle was the first person to arrive that afternoon, so I showed him the songs.

'It's a bit twee, isn't it?' he said of 'I Found Out'.

'It's not twee at all, you bloody idiot!' I snapped. 'The girl's just discovered that her boyfriend's sleeping with another man.'

'I'm not doing that,' said Doyle, shaking his head resolutely. 'I'm not singing a pro-gay song. Next you'll be making me wear a leather jock strap.'

'It's not pro-gay,' I said with a sigh, deflated at the realization that my good friend and band member was a moron. 'It's not anti-gay either. It's just the story. The girl's angry.'

'Angry? She should chop his bloody head off. The bleeding pervert.'

There seemed little point in attempting to describe the subtle nuances of my creation any further to Doyle, so I moved on to 'Until Daylight'. Again, it took a great deal of explaining for him to realize what the song was about. The lines 'I've built the fire, I've chopped the wood, I think you're looking pretty good' seemed self-explanatory to me, but apparently not to Doyle. Even after the verse 'Let's forget the others awhile, you've got my whisky, I've got your smile. They won't know about tonight until daylight', he didn't have any inkling of the subject matter.

'Ah, I get it,' he said, looking pleased with himself. 'They're going to have a shag.'

'That is, without a doubt, correct. But the point is that they're old friends who are now with other people, and they're going to sleep together for the first time.'

'So it's another song about perverts,' he said. 'Why can't you write a nice song called something like: "Our parents introduced us, and now we are very happy together"?'

'Perhaps it's better if you don't worry about the meaning of the songs. Just play the bass and don't think about it too much.'

He seemed content with this arrangement. I had got hold of a bass from an old friend – the one who had not gone near the instrument since his funky solo moment of glory had gone disastrously wrong at Glasgow School of Art – and I had also borrowed a second amplifier from a seventeen-year-old girl who had been playing guitar for the last few years, as had, I discovered with surprise, many of her girlfriends. All the new equipment was now in the basement. By the time Pete arrived Double Fantasy's own private rehearsal space was ready and waiting.

Pete and Doyle treated each other with wary courtesy. Perhaps unconsciously I had set up Double Fantasy as a bizarre social experiment in which you take three wildly different people, confine them to a small space, give them things to play with and see what happens, as sociobiologists like to do with monkeys. Our basement is a cosy little room to spend the evenings in, but it's not so great in the daytime. The ceilings are so low that tall men cannot stand up straight – Pete is six foot four, I'm six foot two, Doyle has no problems even on tiptoe – and there is no natural light. The long, thin shape of the room means that it is difficult, with all the amplifiers and equipment taking up space, for two people to pass without rubbing against each other. The air gets stale. Pete has never had so much as a puff on a cigarette and Doyle chain-smokes. Doyle is not afraid of making constant demands for food, cups of coffee and trips to the pub for pints of beer, while Pete will show touching levels of gratitude if you throw him so much as a cream cracker.

I thought that Doyle's demands might be kept in check that afternoon as he had been making much of the new diet he was on. In his ongoing attempt to woo his girlfriend back to

England, of which working suicidally long nightshifts to make huge amounts of money was a part, he had decided on a regime of going to the gym and following a strict weight-loss plan. Over the next few hours, however, he got through a bar of marzipan, five beers, an entire box of chocolates, a large bag of peanuts and two cheese and bacon sandwiches. When he wasn't eating he did manage to play the bass a little bit. We started by working out 'I Never Loved Her' by The Starfires, the 1965 garage classic that Doyle had shown me a few weeks earlier. It was elected that I should sing it. I can't sing at all, but neither can the guy in The Starfires. He growls.

Doyle started off the song with a rumbling bass, I played the simple chord progression on the acoustic and Pete played the trickier lead riff. It was sounding good until I started singing. Every time I said a line, my guitar playing went out of time.

'What are you doing?' said Doyle as the song petered out. 'Why can't you follow the beats?'

'Oh, go jump in a hole, you turd,' I replied. 'I'm doing the best I can.'

We tried again, and again, and it kept happening. I couldn't seem to combine the two skills of singing and playing. Apparently I'm not the first to suffer this problem: Dee Dee Ramone, the bass player in The Ramones, had to stop playing entirely every time it was his turn to sing something. I pointed this out to Doyle.

'He was a junkie,' he replied. 'You're not. Now do it!'

'It's actually a very hard thing to do because of the speed of the chord changes,' said Pete, diplomatically. 'I've got an idea. Just try and strum along in the chord of E and I can do all the changes. Then you can keep the beat on the guitar and you'll probably find it a lot easier to sing at the same time.'

My role had been marginalized in my own band, but it

worked. Playing the guitar now actually helped me keep time in singing this song about a guy who is acting tough and pretending that he doesn't care about the girl who broke his heart. Our version of the song came together after half-an-hour's practice. Even Doyle didn't have anything to complain about.

It was only a matter of time before tensions rose between my band members. I was the weakest link in the band – the other two had been playing for years – but one's taste in music is as important as one's ability to play. Pete's reaction to the lyrics for 'I Found Out' had been much more positive than Doyle's. 'It's great,' he said. 'The words scan really well and there are some good lines in there. I've got a great chord sequence and melody for it.'

He played a pleasant, breezy tune and sang in a way that was reminiscent of all those wry singer-songwriters of the early eighties beloved of students. Doyle listened with his mouth slightly open, his eyelids drooping. Pete began to sway from side to side as he sang the chorus: 'I used to think you had it, I was never in any doubt, that you and I were the perfect fit but darling, I found out.' I had intended the song as a nasty, sarcastic riposte to a scoundrel's philandering – it does contain the line 'Get out of my life', after all – but Pete's version was devoid of all menace. I don't know why I should have been surprised. He was the kind of man who felt guilty if he left the toilet seat up.

He gave us a big, hopeful smile when he finished the song, and said: 'What do you think?'

'It sounds like "The Beautiful South",' said Doyle, lighting up another cigarette.

'OK . . .'

'It's too flowery for the words, which are meant to be angry and bitter,' I added. 'Can't you make it have more bite?'

'Right then,' said Pete, whose huge body moved awkwardly on the little stool it was perched on. 'I'll find the chords with more bite. I know where the minors are, or the suspended fourths, or the dominant sevenths, but I can't remember my chord book telling me where the "bites" are.'

Doyle turned up his amplifier and knocked out a low, threatening rhythm. 'This is more like it,' he said. 'Listen to this and you can imagine some chick ready to rip the fucker's eyes out.'

Pete shook his head and joined in on the Telecaster, and I found a few notes to put down on top on the acoustic, and it sounded good. Doyle sang the words with lascivious menace. The song was working perfectly.

'Let's go with that, then,' I said. 'It's coming together.'

'Yeah, it's great,' sniffed Pete, 'except for the fact that it's got no tune, no melody, anyone with half a brain could come up with a riff like that, and it sounds like a thousand other bad punk songs that are already out there. But it's your gig so if that's what you want, fine.'

The room was silent except for the occasional bass note. Then I said: 'Pete, what's wrong?'

'I don't see the point in doing this when I'm not contributing anything,' he replied. 'And if you're going to reject my songs outright then I'm not allowed to contribute, am I?'

'But you've contributed loads,' I told him.

'What? Remember I'm doing this as a favour to you, and frankly I've got plenty of things I'd rather be doing on a Friday afternoon. So maybe you should keep that in mind before taking the piss out of anything that I come up with.'

If he hadn't been holding a guitar and sitting on a stool, I'm sure Pete would have crossed his arms and stamped his foot. I certainly had not been witness to this side of his character before.

Doyle looked up and said: 'Don't you like "The Beautiful South", then?'

I suggested we give 'You Ain't Going Nowhere' a try instead, just as we had done before and had enjoyed so much. Pete sang and played rhythm, I did a few lead notes and Doyle worked out a bass line. I could feel the harmony returning. Then Doyle said: 'It's a bit boring, isn't it? Are we going to advertise our gig to people who have trouble sleeping?'

Pete muttered something about needing to get back in time for his son's bath. I asked him if he was prepared to do another rehearsal the following week, as I didn't feel we were quite ready to throw ourselves at the mercy of the world just yet. 'There's no point in doing it if I haven't been enjoying myself and so far I haven't enjoyed it at all. Why would I when I've been treated like an amateur and an idiot?'

'Don't you want to do the gig, then?'

'Hang on, I didn't say that.'

'See you next Friday, then.'

'OK.'

When Doyle – who slept in the basement, after we stayed up drinking until five in the morning – finally left the following day, I told NJ about my fears of the band collapsing before it had even begun because of the inevitable problem of musical (character) differences that make these arguments happen. 'Well, Pete is doing you a favour, honey, and you should try and remember that,' she told me. 'And you do push Doyle around.'

'What are you talking about? Doyle was causing all the trouble, not me. I was as good as gold. Anyway, you have to tell Doyle what to do. Responsibility confuses him.'

'I know what you can be like. If you want this to work you're going to have to consider their feelings too. Especially Pete, who knows that he's a bit gentler than you and Doyle. You can take the piss out of each other but Pete's not like that. You shouldn't make him feel like the odd one out. He's been good to you.'

I grudgingly accepted that, as ever, NJ was right. And as the fights had started on our very first rehearsal, even before our singer had joined and brought with her another set of potential problems, it was clear that I had to be magnanimous if Double Fantasy were ever to be a reality.

But my search for a true understanding of the guitar, and what I could do with it in a band, was not yet over. I knew that it wasn't my destiny to deny the expressiveness of the guitar by sticking to a few rock'n'roll chords and never deviating from them for fear of what Billy Childish called 'wristing off'. James Williamson had made fantastic rock'n'roll music that didn't stick to well-worn clichés, and illustrated that the best kind of playing isn't merely simple: it has mystery, too. There was one guitarist left that I had to find: that obscure and elusive figure that had fascinated me ever since I first picked up the guitar. If I was really going to understand the reason for this quest I had undertaken, and most importantly, if I was going to play 'Anji' at the gig, I had to find Davey Graham.

Chapter Thirteen

Guitar Total

Six months is not a long time to master the guitar and understand the world it has created. It is so short, in fact, that you can only hope to be absorbed by a few tributaries that diverge from the river of knowledge concerning the instrument. To this day I know very little about classical guitar, and I'm unlikely ever to understand it properly as I cannot read music and somehow doubt I'll ever bother to learn. For the same reason jazz guitar remains a mystery to me beyond what Django Reinhardt did, and he simply captured my ear and my imagination for whatever reasons anyone does. I hadn't gone near flamenco, or even the guitar with nylon strings upon which flamenco is always played.

Despite these missing patches – continents – in my musical education, I was still interested in the idea of the total guitarist; the figure that is so absorbed in his or her instrument that they will it to take over their emotional and intellectual life. After all, I had surprised myself at how fixated by the guitar I had become, despite coming to it so late, and as a result I wasn't, despite the lack of confidence I began with, too bad at the thing now, although playing guitar could only ever fit in around everything else that makes up the reality of existence. On the one hand there was someone like Elizabeth

Cotton, the inventor of the claw-hammer technique, talking of playing the guitar as her reward after dealing with the everyday process of living, and then there was the person who has sacrificed him or herself to the guitar to such an extent that normality is not possible.

The two guitarists I knew of that fit into this category were João Gilberto and Davey Graham. João Gilberto was the man who, along with the pianist and composer Tom Jobim, invented bossa nova. Alongside getting his wife Astrud to sing the world's most famous bossa nova song 'The Girl From Ipanema', Gilberto raised the guitar into a high art form in South America and developed a way of playing it that would need no accompaniment. Because bossa nova is so hard to master it requires total dedication, which Gilberto was prepared to give it to the exclusion of everything else: his family, his friends and his sanity.

Davey Graham has, according to legend, become equally eccentric through his total dedication to the guitar. In his late teens, while his friends were doing their best to make the day trip to Brighton Beach, he was hanging out with master musicians in Tangiers and hitchhiking to Beirut, learning about the world's many approaches to making music on stringed instruments along the way. He was seventeen in 1958, when he had the idea of combining the styles of jazz bassist Charles Mingus and blues guitarist Big Bill Broonzy. By the early sixties he was so far ahead of everyone else that he could never be anything more than the musician's musician; the source that others used and diluted to present to a wider audience. He was a heroin addict too. I knew from Bert Jansch that he was alive, and there had been sightings of an intoxicated Graham in pubs in the Camden area of North London. So I contacted Topic Records, a small but long-established English folk label that Graham was once signed to. The woman I spoke to had never met him, but she had friends who had friends who could ask around. It was worth a try.

João Gilberto was also alive, although aloof. Even his daughter Bebel wasn't allowed to see him: the closest she got was when he stayed in a hotel and gave her instructions to pass him notes under the door of his room. Despite his impenetrability he did perform concerts occasionally, by himself in huge halls, without his acoustic guitar being given even as much as a microphone, and if anyone talked during the performance he was likely to storm out in a huff. He had not granted an interview in decades.

There was a jobbing, touring, interview-giving bossa nova guitarist, however, who was following in João Gilberto's musical tradition. His name was Vinicius Cantuaria and he was a Brazilian living in New York who was coming to do a show at Ronnie Scott's jazz club in London. So at around seven o'clock on a frosty Sunday evening in December I went down to the Soho club to find a polite, courteous, extremely cold Brazilian who was only too happy to talk about what bossa nova meant to him and his country.

Cantuaria is a gaunt but handsome middle-aged man who, with his woolly hat and goatee, looks like the bohemian jazz musician that he is. He was sitting in the shabby little bar in the basement of Ronnie Scott's where the musicians go before and after their gigs. 'It's not easy to play bossa nova because it uses a lot of strange chords, like in jazz,' he said, when I asked how to master it. 'But it comes from samba, which is the traditional Brazilian music and that is easy to play as long as you can get the rhythm. João Gilberto and Tom Jobim grew up with samba, like all of us, and they took a good listen to the American music made by Gil Evans and Gerschwin. So bossa nova is jazz, but in a Brazilian way. With samba the chords are simple and you can make an involvement with the rhythm. Bossa nova is a mix of harmony and rhythm and if you try to play both, probably you can't do it. João Gilberto is a one-orchestra man because he plays the bass and the melody at the same time, and he worked out how to play piano melodies on the guitar. This is something that takes a long time to learn.' This was the same as the process on 'Anji'.

The frustrating thing about bossa nova is that it looks and sounds so easy. It is melodic, gentle music filled with catchy harmonies, but this is a smokescreen for the fact that it is damn near impossible to get your fingers round – so hard, in fact, that most guitarists outside Brazil simply don't bother. 'It's like soccer,' said Cantuaria. 'When you watch the great soccer players they make it look so easy and this is what bossa nova should do. But you have to remember that we have grown up with this. We have been listening to it and playing it every day for so many years. You have to have the music inside you to really understand it.'

When I gave Cantuaria and his band a quick demonstration of my guitar-playing abilities, they politely suggested that there was no point in giving a primer lesson in bossa nova an hour before they were going on stage to play it perfectly themselves. So they consoled me by explaining how the philosophy of bossa nova – no noise, no vibrato, and no notes that do not contribute to the song as a whole – came about. The guitarist Roberto Menascal was with the singer Nara Leão in her flat in Ipanema, one of the upmarket beachfront areas in Rio. Leão was a twelve-year-old girl at the time living with her parents, and she did not want to incite the wrath of her neighbours by making loud music. So she and Menascal worked out a way of making the quietest music that would still contain a full gamut of expression.

At the same time Gilberto and Tom Jobim were hanging out at a tiny club in Copacabana in an alley called Du Vivier. All the famous Brazilian musicians played there — the pianist and composer Sérgio Mendes, the diva Elis Regina — and the neighbours found the noise hard to take, especially as it went on until four in the morning. One night a particularly sleep-deprived man started throwing bottles out of his window and down at the people hanging out in the alleyway outside the club. So Gilberto and Jobim worked out a way to play music quietly to defuse the problem. Bossa nova was born.

As if to make sure that I wasn't about to include a bossa nova number in Double Fantasy's forthcoming set, Cantuaria told me about his process of learning a song. He would play it for about a year. When he was completely comfortable, he might start making a little chord change that suited him. That took another year. A year after that he would be happy about playing it in front of an audience.

That night Cantuaria performed bossa nova songs that the predominantly Brazilian audience knew, and he played them with the kind of languid insouciance they demand. Judging by the fact that he had spent around three years learning each one, to learn his set of fifteen songs would take forty-five years. I didn't have that much time. I would have to be content to be a passive consumer of bossa nova and its difficult charms.

It was winter and England was barren. For the brief few hours of daylight the sky was a slate grey and the bare trees that line London's streets were skeletal and apologetic. Against this spartan backdrop the barrage of consumer cheer that is the run-up to Christmas felt forced and unwelcome. While NJ, who had been given a boost of confidence after starting to teach at a London fashion institute, stayed healthy and got ever more stylish, Otto, Pearl and myself fell prey to a lingering flu for the first half of December. 'I'm not feeling very well,' said Pearl as she lay on the sofa night after night, refusing to get into her own bed and asking for a blanket. 'Daddy, we're ill, aren't we?' croaked Otto, pleased that I was no longer capable of much more than assisting him with his drawings of cars and men with large heads.

At first I imagined that being sick would mean I could gently strum the guitar in bed for hours on end, but I lost enthusiasm even for that as my fingers ached from the flu and my cotton wool mind could not keep a rhythm. Besides, the children recovered quickly and found the strength to object to my guitar playing. For four days I didn't touch the guitar. I would get up and go to the office, come back at about two in the afternoon and climb into bed to do virtually nothing until the next morning. NJ brought hot lemon and honey tea and the children made me laugh. Pearl insisted on telephoning her imaginary friend Dia (she is four, she goes to work, she has long hair and she is very pretty), and Otto showed remarkable kindness to his poor ill father. 'I'm going to buy you a guitar for Christmas, Dad,' he told me. I replied that this was extremely generous, and he shouldn't think of spending his nonexistent pocket money on such an extravagant gift. 'Actually, I won't buy you a guitar. I'll buy you a pick.' You can never have enough picks. They're always going missing.

It was during this bedridden period that I received a call from the woman at Topic Records. She had found Davey Graham. There was a friend of her boyfriend who knew him, and if I could make my way to the friend's flat in Camden by five that evening, Davey had promised to turn up. Of course I would be there – in an hour's time. It was Friday.

The flat belonged to a jovial man called Tim. He was at the

flat with friends of his called Bob and Len, and they were cracking open beers and celebrating the end of the working week. All three played guitar and were friends with Davey Graham. 'Or at least as much as it's possible for anyone to be friends with him,' said Tim.

I asked them what he was like. 'He's very eccentric, and how he acts completely depends on his mood at that moment,' said Tim, who went on to tell me of a recent night when Davey had left his front door keys in a taxi, so he called up the emergency services and convinced them to deal with the problem for him. 'He can be absolutely charming and lucid about any subject you like – and he's very well read and knowledgeable – but if you catch him at the wrong moment he might make no sense at all. It depends on a lot of factors: when he last went to sleep, what he's been thinking about, the medication he's been taking . . .'

'He can be hard to understand,' offered Bob.

'Do you mean in what he says or how he speaks?' I asked.

'Both. Mind you, it's got a lot better since he had his new teeth put in.'

Remarkably, this legend of the guitar world was poverty stricken. Tim told me how Davey was signing on – claiming welfare – and living on his own in a tiny flat. His back catalogue of albums was in disarray, and even though he had written 'Anji' and invented the DADGAD tuning system he received no royalties from past recordings, which were now either very rare or only available as bootlegs. He hardly ever played live, and the rare occasions that he did were hit and miss affairs, most often in some tiny pub backroom, where he could either be dazzling or a painful mess. Michael Tyack from Circulus, who considers Davey Graham to be the grand master of the guitar, had seen him perform at the 12-Bar Club in Denmark Street two years back. 'It was agonizing,' said Michael. 'He had just lost it. It's as if his fingers could no longer do these amazing things that they did when he was sixteen.' Drugs and alcohol probably had a lot to do with that.

Bert Jansch had already warned me that it was difficult to have a normal conversation with Graham. He was just too otherworldly. With this in mind, I watched the clock on the wall approach five o'clock and pass it. 'It's possible he got scared and changed his mind,' said Tim. 'I talked to him this afternoon and he was up for it, but you never know what he's going to be like from one moment to the next.' He put on one of Davey Graham's most celebrated recordings, an album called *After Hours*. It was made in a student's bedroom on a cheap tape recorder in 1967 after a concert at Hull University. There are incidental noises in the background as Davey does things one would have not thought possible on a guitar, creating an entire world of sounds that glide, swoop and drop and evoke everything from the flat fields of Mississippi to the sun-shimmering Ganges. One track, a reworking of the old Irish folk tune 'She Moved Through The Fair' that segues into an eastern-style piece called 'Blue Raga', is the most beautiful piece of guitar playing I have ever heard. The only thing I can compare it to would be Ravi Shankar's sitar at its most spiritually charged. It doesn't sound like any kind of guitar style I had ever heard before. Davey looked cool on the album cover, too, with his slightly wicked grin, short caramel afro, single earring and sailor's cap. John Renbourn, another great British guitarist, said of him: 'Back in the sixties he was so far ahead of any would-be picker that it was practically miraculous. We all owe him a huge debt.'

It was half-past five. I had read more about Davey, about how he was always a bohemian outsider to the traditionalist British folk circles, with their vision of a jug of warm ale, a socialist worldview, an Aran sweater and a musical style preserved in aspic and untainted by imagination; of how he was found asleep under the counter of a London folk club called The Gyre And Gimble in 1961 with his girlfriend Angie by his side, a little before he wrote the song dedicated to her that became so famous; of how his debut EP, *3/4 AD*, transformed British popular music through its innovation and influence. 'Anji' changed everything: it is played with the picking technique of classical guitar; it has the bass line of blues, the elegance of baroque early music and a grounding in folk. You would need to be occupying another dimension to come up with such an idea in the first place.

'I have to say, I'm not entirely surprised,' sighed Tim as the clock hit 5.45. 'He's not the kind of person who you can imagine sitting down and doing an interview like a normal musician. He's so far removed from that kind of world that it would really mean nothing to him.'

'He hates being eulogized,' added Len. 'He has all these famous people coming up and telling him how important he's been for them and it makes him feel awkward. He doesn't respond well to compliments. Anyway you shouldn't give up. He always emerges sooner or later and we can try and arrange for you to meet him on another day.'

Perhaps, but I didn't have long until the gig now. I tried not to be too disappointed. After all, Davey Graham had not been turning up to his own concerts as far back as 1965. Perhaps it was just as well. My throat was swollen and it was painful to talk. I really should have been in bed rather than drinking beer with Camden musicians, waiting for a legend who would never show. In fact I started to become nervous at the prospect that he *would* turn up.

What could I say to him, with my limited understanding of the instrument he revolutionized? Born in Leicester in 1940 to a

Guyanan mother and a Scottish father, he grew up in Notting Hill in London at the height of the area's racial tensions. Even when he was hanging out with the New York Jewish doctor's son and slumming beatnik 'Rambling' Jack Elliot at Elliot's London bedsit in 1959, he was an elusive figure: when others arrived he would leave, but they might catch a moment of Graham playing Ravel's *Bolero* – and be able to tell where each orchestral instrument came in – unaccompanied on his guitar. It was no accident that Graham became a heroin addict in the mid-sixties: he planned it. All his heroes – jazz greats like Sonny Rollins and Charlie Parker – had been junkies. It was part of the life he sacrificed himself to.

Suddenly a tall man with a regal bearing and a broad smile appeared at the door. He was wearing a wide-brimmed hat, smart grey trousers, a shirt with buttoned-down collars and a pinstriped three-button jacket. One eye looked like it might have been made of glass. 'Hello, hello!' he said in the grand voice of a kindly old English public school boy. His face bore the scars of yesterday's caresses. He looked like a man whom women would find attractive, if entirely impossible to deal with. This was, of course, Davey Graham.

He sat down next to me on the sofa and asked for something 'to oil the throat. A beer?' Then he pulled out a huge lump of hash and a ready-made joint, lit the joint, gave the hash to Tim, and told him to get rolling. He took off the hat to reveal a strange little ponytail sticking out of the back of his head that compromised his otherwise perfect elegance. 'So you're writing your book from the point of view of brands of guitar, eh? Good angle, that,' he said, nodding his head. I had no idea where he had got this from but I didn't contradict him.

'I started on a ten-pound Spanish guitar in my teens and tried most of the guitars around at the time,' he began. 'Not the expensive ones – I never went in for collecting them or anything – but there was a company called Tatay that made a Spanish guitar with the name burnt into the back of the machine head. Then you had Barnes & Mullins, very good and very cheap. Going on to steel string, there was Flyde, Hondo . . . Emil Grimshaw used to make guitars with mahogany sides, and of course you know about Gibsons and Martins. There was a Balkan blues player called Tony Zemaitis – nobody could play the blues like him and I'm very much in his court – and he used to make guitars for all the pop musicians.'

He went on to list various other guitars that I had never heard of, concluding that the best guitar in the world is made by Brian E. Lowden, and that he used to have one but he had to give it back (to its owner, presumably). He explained that he had owned twenty-eight guitars over the course of his life, that he started on nylon string guitars, moved to steel string, and has now returned to nylon, playing a guitar that was once his sister's and has been in the family for fifty years. He talked about the relative merits of both, before stating: 'People say you cannot play the blues on a nylon string guitar. This is not true; the difference is that when you bend a note, you bend it up a semi-tone or a tone. You can bend nylon strings although they don't have the same bite. But from the angle of playing guitar total you can go backwards and forwards. My friend's teacher says that you can't play nylon string fingerstyle and steel string fingerstyle because the styles are inimical and quite separate, which is true, but I'm a maverick so I think you can.'

He took a deep draw on the joint, which glowed fiercely and dropped its ash on to Tim's carpet, before passing it to me. It scratched my throat like sandpaper. 'I had a lesson to get started with Oliver Hunt, who was professor of guitar at the London College of Music and wrote a musical called *The Barber Of*

Baghdad. After that I went on to teach myself, chiefly by listening to Segovia, Big Bill Broonzy, Blind Lemon Jefferson and Josh White, and I never got much homework done because I was always in the West End watching people like Admiral Benbo and Diz Disney. My sister at that time was married to Roy Guest who was a half-Welsh, half-Greek impresario. He brought over the American blues and gospel players in the fifties and Josh White was one of them. Josh was a big inspiration, chiefly because he would play standing with his shirt open to his navel. A long time later John Mayall used to say that all guitarists should sit, and Peter Green used to play with his back to the audience so that nobody could see what he was doing. He didn't like anybody photographing his fingers while he was playing.'

Sometimes I tried to steer the conversation in a single direction, but it was impossible: Davey would throw in a comment that was diverse to what he was talking about and then chase after it. He told me that in southeast Asia there are tiny flags that hang over the musician's fingers because you are not allowed to see what their fingers are doing. Then he told me that his sister taught Bert Jansch how to play guitar in Scotland, and just as I asked him about this he told me that he joined various bands before going solo because there was more money in it, which he needed at the time because he was 'following strange gods'. He opened his eyes wide, flattened his mouth, and made a noise like 'rah, rah, rah!'

I knew that he had spent time in Paris as a teenager, busking on the metro and playing for Elizabeth Taylor at her parties – she even paid him to perform at a party in St Tropez. I asked him when he first went to Paris. 'Oh, it's only a hundred miles as the crow flies, so I do recommend it for a visit. I was living with a sculptress, and then a ballet dancer, and at that time I

was a librarian at my grammar school where I would read five
books a week. Then I hitchhiked to St Tropez about a dozen
times and for the last thirty-five miles or so there is a road that is
nothing but bends with a cliff on one side and a precipice on the
other. Take the Nice route if I were you, that mountain road's
far too treacherous. It's in the pig-hunting region where you
might find the occasional scorpion and a lot of insects that are a
cross between a crawdad and a grasshopper. I've never seen a
snake down there but they do say you can get them . . . terribly
sauvage . . . cork trees and so on . . .'

The joint was affecting my mind. Davey offered a treatise on
the wonderful green copper colours of the Paris Metro stations
and a eulogy on the charms of the American girls who used to
sell copies of the *International Herald Tribune* on the streets and
who he would co-opt to collect money when he was busking his
way through renditions of jazz pieces by Horace Silver and
Miles Davis on his steel-string guitar. He explained the genius
of Hausmann's street designs for Paris and ran through the five
dynasties of Moroccan kings, an entry point for a brief story of
his hitchhiking trip to Beirut, where he learned to play the oud
and worked out a way of transplanting the playing style of the
oud on to the guitar (the basis of the DADGAD tuning). Then
he ran through the history of the development of western music,
all of which he had transposed on to the guitar. He took my
notebook and in a heavy scrawl that almost ripped the paper,
wrote:

Cantus Firmus
Secular Monody
Divisions on a ground
Greensleeves
Renaissance

Baroque
  (i) theme
 (ii) development
(iii) variations
(iv) reiteration of

He told me that I needed to understand this – in particular 'Greensleeves', which was the cornerstone of western music, if I wanted to play guitar. Then he drew a profile of a face with an enormous chin and a pointed nose. He muttered about how easy it was to transpose the music of Bach on to the guitar: all you had to do was understand counterpoint, know where to put the bass, treble and middle voices, and realize the importance of the descending melody. Then he announced that we were going to the pub.

I had forgotten that I was ill. I was more concerned about the fact that, three joints in, I was feeling decidedly strange. As soon as we walked out of the door Davey started howling at the moon, and shouted 'Cuckoo! Cuckoo!' over and over again. He stopped to show me his two fingernails. 'You see, the left one is the same as the moon as it waxes,' he said, turning serious. 'The right one is the moon as it wanes. Oh yes, I put varnish on my nails to make them harder. Cuckoo!'

Tim, Len and Bob were making stoned giggles behind us while Davey led the way to the nearest pub, a womb-like room of soft furnishings and swirling patterns, where there were ten old Irish men drinking pints and smoking cigarettes. They turned to stare at us. One of them said: 'Would you look at that. The band's arrived!' which gave rise to a few chuckles. Davey tipped his hat and a few smiled back. I ordered a round from the angry-looking overweight teenage barmaid in a white vest and tracksuit trousers and the rest of the party found a quiet table at the back of the pub where we were least likely to cause offence by our presence. The barmaid's big white arms rumbled with fleshy threat as they pulled down the arm of the draughts, before her palm flapped out in front of me with a demand for 'Ten pahnd ah-ee'.

The good-natured chaos of Davey's genius, confusion and elegance back at the flat was replaced by tension at the pub. As anyone who has had a joint knows, you often don't really feel stoned until you leave the environment you smoked it in and unwisely go to engage with the outside world, at which point you realize that you are out of harmony with everything around you. After we sat down at the table I turned the tape recorder on, but for about a minute Davey just took gulps of his beer and said nothing. Then he started to mutter about some of the people who had been around when he first emerged on the underground folk scene in London, such as John Peel, Bert Jansch, the American guitarist and singer Jackson C. Frank, John Renbourn and Paul Simon. He was politely dismissive of most of them, although he did hold great admiration for Jackson C. Frank. Bob asked Davey if he realized that Bob Dylan got a lot of ideas from him. 'I am not familiar with his work,' he said, politely.

Then I discovered how he did not like compliments. I mentioned his invention of the DADGAD tuning system. 'I did not invent it,' he countered. 'I merely transposed the tunings used on an oud to guitar; tunings that had been used for about a thousand years.' Failing to realize I was barking up the wrong tree, I suggested that he was the first person to play Indian sitar music on the guitar, as he had done on his track 'Blue Raga' before The Beatles and The Rolling Stones met the Maharishi and the sixties went eastern. 'Quite wrong,' he said. 'The classical maestro Julian Bream played a duet with Ali

Akbar Khan at the beginning of the sixties, and then when you look at Elizabethan court music and lute music . . .'

The grumpy barmaid had put the song 'Roll With It' by Oasis so loudly on the pub stereo that normal conversation was impossible. The crass, brawling sing-along was entirely wrong for the moment. Davey stopped mid-sentence and began to mutter 'Relax, relax' under his breath. 'Turn that thing off!' he snapped, shooting a glance at the tape recorder. 'You've got enough there. I don't want to say anything else.' He downed half a pint of beer in one continuous gulp. 'I fear . . .' he looked less panicked and more reflective. 'I fear I'm breaking off.'

It was easy to see why, despite his genius and innovation, Davey Graham was not more famous than he was. While Bert Jansch worked the clubs in the mid-sixties and became the man associated with 'Anji' by playing it beautifully, Davey disappeared to the Middle East for months on end and was too wayward to do such mundane things as release records and embark on tours – although he did both sporadically. He made it clear that he considered Bert Jansch, the big hero of so many guitar players, something of a pedestrian. He had much more admiration for Jackson C. Frank, who died in 1999 after a tragic life and whose name has become significantly more obscure than Graham's.

'I *did* like Jackson Frank,' said Davey, perking up at the mention of his name. '*Blues Run The Game* is very sweet. I remember listening to it with John Martyn in the restaurant upstairs from Les Cousins, which had been a music venue two hundred years previously.' Then he closed his eyes tight and said: 'I think we should go.'

He stood up and, with a military air, marched out of the pub. We followed him. Outside he instructed me to hold my stomach in if I wanted to be able to cope with the icy weather. He led the way to his flat two streets away, pulling at car exhaust-fertilized herbs in scraggy, detritus-strewn front gardens and instructing us on the beneficial qualities of what he had found. He inhaled a sprig of rosemary as if it was supplying him with the world's last reserve of oxygen. His flat was in one of the large Georgian houses that Camden is filled with: once smart, they fell into decline after the war to be divided up into cramped flats with a family in every room, then turning into squats and welfare bedsits in the seventies and eighties before the gentrification of the area in the nineties made prices skyrocket. Davey's flat was dark and cold but ordered in its own monastic way: between the yellow walls of the living room there was a metal fold-up bed with a flattened duvet and a nylon-stringed guitar lying on it, and a dented oriental shade covered the light bulb hanging down in the middle of the room. There was a wheelchair in the corner of the room, an old wooden desk, and another guitar leaning against a wall, a mantelpiece with two-dozen books and a portable CD player on a shelf.

There was a joint sitting on the bed that Davey lit, and he passed the big lump of hash over to Bob to make another. He stood up in the middle of the room with a tiny mandolin that I hadn't noticed before and, holding it high against his chest, strummed it with a look of beatific concentration, his eyes clenched shut and his mouth stretched flat.

It was hard to tell if he was playing brilliantly or terribly. It was jagged and atonal, but he was using strange techniques and employing complex ideas that perhaps called for awkward playing. I tried to convince myself that his playing was better than it was. Every now and then Davey would get into a groove and the music would flow, but mostly it sounded like he was in the process of searching for something he was never going to find again.

The joints went round and round; there always seemed to be one being handed to me. I had forgotten about my sandpaper throat; now it felt like a leather tube. 'I'm currently attempting to play in two keys at once,' said Davey. 'It puts you in danger of splitting your head in two.' He held his palm up to the middle of his face and his one good eye stared at it with comical concentration. Then he stopped to play a CD. It was by an Iranian outfit called Saz-e-no and it was some of the strangest music I had ever heard: hypnotic, cyclical and deeply serious. As the joints passed and Davey sat down in his wheelchair (stolen on his last hospital visit), I began to feel like I was being transported to another dimension. Bob sat on a chair, nodding with his eyes closed, while Tim strummed Davey's guitar on the bed and Len stared at the ceiling, looking somewhat distracted and childlike. After twenty minutes of the eerie sounds of the eastern instruments, a woman started wailing over the top of them.

'My God,' I said. 'That's the longest intro to a song I've ever heard.'

Davey grinned and waved one arm in the air in time with the music. He seemed ecstatically happy. I saw the rest of the flat on numerous visits to the toilet over the next hour, and it was simplicity itself: a bare minimum of what a man needs to live. The bathroom contained a toothbrush, toothpaste, soap and shaving equipment. The kitchen had a few pots and pans in it. The other bedroom had a bed and a clothes cupboard. In my time I had met rock stars with mansions that had their own pub in the basement, a full-size pool table in the dining room and a multitrack recording studio in the barn. In his dark little flat, Davey Graham was occupying an infinitely more exotic world than the millionaire, middle-aged rockers in their gilded wombs.

Eventually – it turned out that we had been at the flat for about two hours – Bob, Len and Tim said they had to leave. Davey had mentioned that giving guitar lessons was a better way of making a living than playing gigs, and hardly believing that it could be a possibility, I asked if I could pay for some lessons from him. 'I'll tell you what you need to do,' he said, politely. He took my notebook and scribbled down an address, which turned out to belong to someone whose playing he admired. He didn't know whether the man at the address gave lessons or not, but said that it would be worth turning up outside his flat and asking him. The address was: 'opposite the pizza restaurant, Hampstead, London.' My head was spinning. Through the haze of hash smoke I could still tell that my general ill health lay unchecked. I needed to get out of there.

With perfect grace, Davey thanked us for the company and showed us to the door. He said how much he had enjoyed himself and suggested we do it again some time. 'Perhaps you could show me how to play "Anji" next time we meet,' I said to him as I left the flat. 'Oh, anyone can tell you how to do *that*!' he replied. 'Far better to get the hang of "Greensleeves". Well, take care.'

NJ was furious. There had been six increasingly frantic messages on my phone – she had been expecting me back three hours ago. I tried to explain that I was stoned out of my gourd and had just met one of the strangest men in the world. 'I was worried!' she shouted. 'I thought something had happened to you.'

'Something did happen to me,' I replied. 'And I'm not sure what.'

'It's extremely selfish of you not to at least call,' she said, too angry to look at me. I wondered if Davey Graham contacted any of his wives or girlfriends as he headed eastwards for months on end to study secular monody in Indian ragas. It seemed unlikely, but then in his devotion to his art Davey Graham had chosen a life that, in excluding the concerns of other people, could be seen as the ultimate act of self-indulgence or the noblest pursuit of all.

The strangeness of the night was not over yet. When NJ calmed down I suggested we watch a film on our newly acquired DVD player. Our friend Liam Watson, who lived in the flat above us and who had introduced me to the incarcerated Memphis medievalist Teddy Paige, had plenty of films, although NJ had already vetoed many of the ones I was hoping to borrow such as *Cannibal Holocaust*, *Island Of Death* and *Dr Butcher, M.D. (Medical Deviate)*. We agreed on *The Servant*, a strange and extremely British little movie starring James Fox as a young London fop who falls into decadence at the hands of his sinister servant, played by Dirk Bogarde. Made in 1961, *The Servant* is one of those films that reveal a hidden history of England. There is a scene where Fox enters a beatnik coffee house. In the middle of a roomful of black polo necks and National Health glasses a young man with an intense stare, a head of tight, curly blond hair and a bold face carved from stone is playing guitar.

'That's him!' I said. 'My God, that's Davey Graham!'

'That's really weird,' said NJ.

Even then, Davey Graham looked otherworldly, the centre of and yet distanced from the scene around him. It made me realize that to be that much of an artist, to be so far ahead of everyone else in your field, necessarily means being alienated from the world too.

Somewhere in the space between cosmic freedom and a responsibility towards the people you love and who love you lies the answer to life. The guitar is a good place to go in search of it.

Chapter Fourteen

Impending Doom

A date and place was set for the gig. My first idea was to play at the 12 Bar Club, the acoustic venue in Denmark Street that has the advantage of being very small; I then discovered that it is not possible to call up these places and announce the night you are playing on when you don't have so much as a tape of one of your songs to recommend you by. I told Michael Tyack about the problem and he suggested we support Circulus. 'No new band would launch their career with a headline slot,' he said. 'And this is your first ever gig. You can even borrow our amplifiers. After all, you've already borrowed our singer.' So the debut concert of Double Fantasy was to be at a basement bar called Colours in Camden Town, North London, at the end of January.

It was Boxing Day. We had gone down to stay with NJ's parents in Cornwall for Christmas and Michael Tyack had come over for the afternoon, to take a break from his own family who lived nearby. We were with NJ's younger brother Charles, who was one of the best guitarists I had ever heard, but whose schizophrenia ensured that he remained a prisoner of his own mind. On very rare occasions, when he had drunk a few beers, Charles played a song or two at a pub in nearby Falmouth, but usually even having strangers in the house was enough to confine him to his room, with the quality of the CDs he was playing being a signifier of how much he was suffering. Some great jazz or blues meant that things weren't too bad; unthreatening singer-songwriters like Cat Stevens or Donovan meant that he was coping under duress; shallow chart pop or, worse of all, saccharine modern Christian music was a sign that he was tormented.

I got on well with Charles. I was always pleased when he came downstairs, put on a pot of coffee, rolled the first of a flowing stream of cigarettes and picked up his steel-string acoustic. He wasn't so good at explaining the details of his technique but he could knock the hell out of a blues guitar and, the voices in his head permitting, he was happy to let me jam along with him despite the gulf in our playing abilities. That afternoon he had been explaining to me his search for the lost chord; a semi-mythical musical tone that he believed to be embedded somewhere on the frets of the neck, deep within a sequence of more conventional chords, but the search for it might well take your entire life. I understood what he was saying: whether you ever found the lost chord or not was irrelevant. It was the search for it, and the faith that it existed, that mattered. The lost chord was Nirvana. As Johnny Marr had said in so many words, you would have to live several lifetimes to find it.

While NJ's father flicked between channels in his armchair, her mother made drawings with Otto and Pearl, and in her bedroom NJ scanned the eighties fashion magazines she had bought as a teenager, Charles, Michael Tyack and myself worked out some guitar parts. I thought that the arrival of Michael would send Charles into seclusion, but for once he was happy for the company, the darkness around his eyes lifting just a little as his fingers pulled and bent the strings of his dented guitar with such force that it wasn't surprising to see his three other guitars sprouting messy tentacles he had not yet got around to fixing. About half an hour of this level of society was enough for Charles, though. He went back to his room and we didn't see him for the next eighteen hours.

I told Michael about my ongoing effort to crack 'Anji', of my failure to get Bert Jansch or Davey Graham to teach it to me, and of how I couldn't seem to play the bass line and the melody at once. 'With difficult pieces of music like that you have to break them down to their component parts and play them very, very slowly,' he explained. 'You can't look at the bass and the melody as two separate entities. The secret is to work out when you play two strings at once and when you play a single note by itself. It all fits together like a syncopated jigsaw puzzle.'

Despite the fact that Michael made a living (of sorts) by giving guitar lessons, he was perfectly happy to spend the next three hours showing me how to play 'Anji' for free – and incredibly, we cracked it. Having tried to get various world-renowned guitar overlords to show me how to do it, all that was needed was a good teacher with the patience to explain it clearly. Michael took the music apart note by note. There is a mathematical logic and structure that guides the song, and, although I won't say it's easy when you know how, because you could go on for the rest of your life refining your playing of 'Anji', to understand how it is done is a pure eureka moment. Everything fell into place. By the end of the afternoon I was playing it – slowly, but correctly.

'It's incredible,' said Michael. 'If you think that when I met you – what was it, six months ago – you couldn't play guitar at all and now you can play "Anji", that's quite an achievement.'

'I've surprised myself. I felt like I haven't been getting

anywhere for ages, and then it all seems to have fallen into place in the last week or so.'

It was true. Christmas was something of a breakthrough. I was still a beginner and an unsophisticated player, but now I was making music. If they can stick with the guitar long enough – and for the non-gifted it takes around three months or so to really start getting a proper tune – I believe that most people will keep on playing for the rest of their lives. And I was proof that it was possible to begin well into adulthood. I was no longer having nightmares about getting up in front of an audience, just a healthy amount of blind panic every now and then. An image came into my mind of doing 'Anji' in front of a crowd of people – Bert and Davey, Polly Harvey, Roger McGuinn, The Black Keys, Mr David Viner, Les 'Practise' Paul, NJ, Charles, Otto, Pearl and even Saint Jimi of Hendrix himself – and as Michael Tyack wheeled around with virtuosity, I daydreamed about being sixteen and playing guitar in our school gymnasium, in front of all those people I hadn't seen for the last twenty years. They would be cheering at my remarkable fretwork. Like that beautiful girl I had a crush on, Chloe Martell, who had gone off with the American kid in the year above who was so good at football . . . I wonder what happened to her . . .

I was fired up by performance vainglory by the time we got back to London, and with Double Fantasy's debut now set to happen in only three weeks we had our work cut out. I decided on the set list. 'You Ain't Going Nowhere' and the garage song 'I Never Loved Her' would of course be in there. Then there were the originals: 'Mystery Fox', 'Until Daylight' and 'I Found Out'. Over a long, cold evening in the kitchen of our next-door neighbour, when I had been there by myself to keep an eye on their children, I worked out an instrumental based on the claw-hammer fingerstyle that Bert Jansch had shown me. Through a process of trial and error I had strung together a bunch of chords that sounded good, and they may not have followed any conventional rules of music but they worked as far as I was concerned. It was only a minute long and the concert could start with that: Loren, the French lady of Circulus, could wail over the top of it in a sorceress-like fashion. Then a solo spot would finish the set: 'Anji'. Pete and Doyle could go off to the bar for that one.

'What about the encore?' said Doyle when I told him of my plans.

'Do you really think it's going to come to that?' I replied as I casually played the incredibly difficult opening sequence of 'Anji' (Doyle refused to acknowledge it, but I could see he was secretly impressed).

'Miracles can happen.'

I had asked Loren about doing the gig supporting Circulus and she was only too happy, particularly as it meant that she didn't have to go anywhere. She had requested that I send her all the lyrics of the songs and a tape of our next rehearsal; then she would practise them before coming along to a rehearsal herself so we could work it all out together. I told Doyle about her charisma; her remarkable way of singing that was reminiscent of a magical spirit filling the air of the wicked woodland of Wier; her unwavering professionalism.

'Does she have nice jugs?'

Hopes for a glorious build-up to our big night were dashed by the practical reality of forming a band with two clowns and a woman with better things to do. I tried to work on the songs that night with Doyle, but he insisted that there was no point in doing it if Pete weren't with us, as he was the only one who knew what he was doing. It would be far more constructive, claimed Doyle, to go to the pub and talk at length about whether he should fly out to Japan unannounced and give his girlfriend a pleasant surprise or, depending on whether or not she really was being unfaithful to him, a nasty shock. Loren, meanwhile, was a school music teacher, she played in three other bands, and she liked going away to classic car rallies with her boyfriend at weekends. That didn't leave too much time for Double Fantasy. Plus she was going to France for a week. She promised she would work out some melodies for the songs while she was over there.

January is a quiet time. We didn't have too much money after Christmas but I didn't feel that we needed so much. It was better to stay in over the evenings and live frugally for a while. It was nice to be a hermit with a guitar. NJ wasn't so sure. I couldn't really think of hustling for more work either, as all I wanted to do was practise for the gig. I called Doyle and Pete and arranged for our first rehearsal of the new year. Doyle was on one of his fourteen-hour shifts that stretched through the night and into the morning and he was complaining of being ill, but he promised he would be there.

The following day everything was ready: the lyrics were printed out, the guitars and the amplifiers were plugged in. I had asked the others to be there by midday so that we could keep going until the evening. I had tried calling Doyle a few times to check that he was coming but there had been no answer; he hadn't quite got the hang of recharging his mobile phone yet so this happened all the time. At around one Pete called. A job had come in and he couldn't turn it down.

By mid-afternoon it was obvious that Doyle wasn't going to turn up either. The whole thing was falling apart before it had even started. NJ had taken Otto and Pearl out of the house so that Double Fantasy could be left to work in peace, and now I was sitting by myself in the basement, wondering if there was really any point in running through 'Anji' for the twelfth time that day. No wonder bands split up if this is the kind of thing they have to deal with.

When NJ returned I told her of my frustrations with the group, and of my increasing desperation at knowing that we were going to be embarrassingly under-prepared for the gig, and talked at length about the various ways in which the songs were not going to work. She poured two whiskies and suggested we take advantage of the situation by getting a babysitter and going out on a date.

'What's the special occasion?' I asked her distractedly, concentrating on the mournful G to B minor change at the beginning of The Rolling Stones's 'Wild Horses'.

'Our wedding anniversary.'

We never did make it out that night.

Double Fantasy rescheduled for the following week. Doyle arrived on the strike of twelve ('See my punctuality? Put that in the log book') and we started on a version of 'I Never Loved Her'. Pete wasn't there again, but I was sure he would turn up sooner or later. He was a reliable sort. We tried playing 'I Found Out' and 'Mystery Fox' before realizing that because Pete had come up with the arrangements of the songs, we had been following him and had no idea of how to do them ourselves. This would cause problems if we ever wanted to chuck him out of the band.

By two o'clock I decided to call Pete. 'Oh, hi Will,' he said breezily, as if surprised to hear from me. 'Actually, Rachel's thrown a bit of a wobbly and it doesn't look like I'll be making it today.' I always suspected that it was Pete's wife who pulled the strings in that relationship, and I was beginning to sense a degree of antagonism from her at my enticing him away from the domestic unit and into the dangerous world of rock'n'roll, or at least breaking his 9pm curfew.

'So what are you doing? You're not coming?'

'Yeah, you'd better count me out for today.'

'Pete, we now have less than two weeks until the gig.'

'Right, OK then, I'll see you next week.'

And that was that. 'He's such a big bloke,' said Doyle. 'You'd never think he would be so under the thumb.'

'Size has nothing to do with it,' I said with a sigh, and waited for Doyle to make the excuse that Pete's absence meant we couldn't practise the songs. We were in the pub half an hour later.

Incredibly, all of the supposed members of Double Fantasy actually turned up a few days later. Pete was contrite; he promised that he would be there from now on. NJ bought me a capo, a metal clip that you put on one of the frets of the guitar neck in order to play in a higher key, and it made 'Anji' sound great. Doyle plugged in his bass, came up with a rumbling opening phrase for 'I Found Out', and then said: 'What do you have to do to get a coffee round here?' Loren was only too happy to sing along to the songs and go with what we had already come up with, but the fact that she could actually hold a tune – so far Pete had been doing the singing and he had an uncanny ability to make everything sound like the kind of bands that were popular with sociology students in the 1980s – brought them up to a whole new level. Before Loren arrived I was beginning to think that our set, which I had imagined to be a cross between garage-punk, hippy-folk and country-soul, was a ramshackle version of the music played on stations with names like Magic FM and Melody Radio. Loren saved us.

Pete even tried to wimpify 'I Never Loved Her', that brutal

snarling rant of a song that Doyle and I had got going so well. Instead of the aggressive barré chords that we had been playing, Pete introduced all these melodic strums that went against the angry spirit of the thing.

'What are you doing?' I said as he gave 'I Never Loved Her' the Elton John treatment. 'You're playing it too soft.'

'I like it like that,' he replied. 'It sounds much better now. Maybe I should strum some soft chords for the chorus.'

'Maybe you shouldn't.'

Loren kept singing and stayed out of it.

Our problems with Pete continued. He completely rearranged 'I Found Out', despite coming up with the original arrangement himself, which threw Doyle and me out of alignment: we didn't know where we were meant to come in for the verse and chorus any more. 'That's not how you played it before,' I told him. 'Just do it like you did before and we'll follow you.'

'Has it ever occurred to you that I might have forgotten how I played it before?'

Doyle was pissing me off, too. I got the timing wrong for 'I Never Loved Her' every time I started singing. 'Stop being so mechanical about it,' he said, flicking his cigarette ash on to the rug. 'You've got to *feel* it.'

'How would you like to *feel* a boot in your face?'

'He's gone mad,' he said to Pete. Pete nodded. They were all against me.

'Can I get a coffee?' asked Doyle. 'Or maybe I want a beer. Let's go to the pub. Christ, I'm starving.'

'Most rehearsals involve sitting around and drinking one cup of tea after another,' said Pete. 'Will makes the whole thing become hard work.'

'That is *just* like Michael,' said Loren, talking of Michael

Tyack, the unchallenged leader of Circulus. 'Michael is a dictator. 'E make sure that nobody is allowed to 'ave an opinion apart from him. And if you stand up to him 'e lose his temper and shout at you. At the last concert I did 'e made me cry just because I changed my vocals on one song.'

That was it. Circulus were a great band and it was because Michael Tyack ruled with an iron fist. Davey Graham and Bert Jansch didn't sit around and take this kind of shit either. Somebody had to lead the charge and tell the others what to do, and although it was obvious Pete considered himself the leader because he was the best player, he wasn't. I was. It was the only way, especially when faced with people like Doyle. I may have been the worst guitarist of the three of us, and I may have been completely incapable of singing, and I may have had absolutely no idea about how you were meant to put a song together, but that didn't mean to say I couldn't tell the others what to do. It looked like it was time to get tough.

My new reign of terror proved to be remarkably ineffective. With a little over a week to go I scheduled emergency rehearsals and told the band to turn up to them or else. Loren came back with the one time that she was prepared to come round to the house – Thursday at six o'clock – and Doyle couldn't make it then as he was doing overtime to get the money together to go to Japan and stay in five-star hotels. In fact I don't think his mind was on the debut performance by Double Fantasy at all. We were to do the gig on a Monday night. He had his driving test the next day. Then on Wednesday he was off to Japan for a month. And all he ever talked about was his girl troubles.

'If it doesn't work out this time I'm going to give up the futile pretence of ever being in a relationship again,' he said one night when he came over for supper and steadily made his way through a bar of Lindt extra creamy milk chocolate and the beers I had in the fridge. 'But I've decided that I'm going to buy a Rolex watch in order to impress her dad. Because if I have her parents telling her that I'm a good catch she might actually end up believing them. Are you sure this chocolate is low fat?'

'Why don't you just go down to Chinatown and buy a fake Rolex for twenty quid?' I suggested. 'Her family will never know the difference.'

Doyle looked at me as if I was an idiot. 'That's not going to work at all. *I'll* know it's fake and then I won't be able to look them in the eye and ask for their daughter's hand, will I?'

'Can't you rely on your own natural charm?' said NJ, who was cooking us homemade pizzas. 'You really don't need to buy her all these expensive things.'

That was the problem: Doyle didn't trust his natural charm at all. He believed that he had to rely on external gestures, like flying his girlfriend to New York for a weekend at the Gramercy Park Hotel or buying a Rolex to impress her parents, in order to state his worth in the world. That was why he was killing himself with all this overtime doing dangerous maintenance on the railways, and that was why I was getting increasingly worried about what he would do at the concert. On the rare occasions that he did turn up to rehearsals he was exhausted. Then he could only seem to concentrate for an hour at the most before his mind wandered back to its default setting: his bloody girlfriend.

I don't really know what he wanted from her. He didn't trust her, and rather like poking a tooth that aches, he tormented himself by trying to prove that his paranoia was not unfounded. It seemed that all these endless gifts and money handouts were part of an attempt to own her.

'Why don't you concentrate on the gig for the next week, just so you can stop fretting about her for a while?' I said to him.

'The gig will be a disaster,' he replied. 'We're going to get crucified. I mean, one of the songs is called "Mystery Fox".'

'What the hell are you talking about? "Mystery Fox" is our psychedelic number! If we get crucified the reason will be that you and Pete are incapable of turning up to a rehearsal and practising. I've done all I can to inspire you. But if you don't care about it then it's a hopeless situation.'

'That's not fair,' said NJ. 'Everyone's got their own lives to lead.'

'When we get through this I'm going to get myself a new band with people who actually have a commitment to what they're doing.'

'Good luck,' said Doyle, taking another beer from the fridge.

The arguments were getting ever more frequent. After dinner I forced Doyle into having an impromptu rehearsal session, and he had forgotten all of his bass parts for 'Mystery Fox' and 'I Found Out'. We gave up, and he played 'If I Were a Carpenter' by the sixties American country-folk singer Tim Hardin on the guitar instead. He executed it beautifully: when Doyle stopped thinking about getting it right and cleared his mind, he was the only guitarist in town. He wasn't such a good teacher, though. I asked him to show me how to play Tim Hardin's song.

'It's just D and then this sequence,' he said, hitting about eight notes in succession. 'Sing the song in your head. You just have to feel it.'

'Oh, don't start with your fucking feel again,' I snapped. 'Just show me what you're doing.'

'You never listen to me, do you?' he snapped back. 'You'll listen to Pete but not to me. And then when you finally come round to doing what I'm telling you, you won't even admit that I was right all along. You just can't face doing what I tell you because you refuse to accept that I might actually know what I'm talking about.'

'That's because you never explain to me how to play anything! "Just 'feel' it, man." That's all you ever say. Has it ever occurred to you that you have to work out where your fingers go for a song before you can "feel" it?'

'I'm going to bed,' he said, throwing the guitar down. 'It's pointless trying to even talk to you when you're like this.'

So it looked like Double Fantasy's debut was going to be an unmitigated catastrophe. It dawned on me that Doyle might well not even turn up to the gig, and Pete was having too much of an aversion to the non-domestic world to venture outside of his flat except when forced. Maybe if I arranged for a pot of tea to always be within his reach throughout our set he would be a bit happier. Loren was such a good singer that she could bring a touch of elegance to our worst efforts, but it didn't look like she was going to know how the songs went in time. The situation was extremely worrying. Frustratingly, I actually felt confident enough to go out there and perform. After six (OK, almost seven) months of playing the guitar with a heavy load of intensity, I could do a fair bit. Of course it was rudimentary, but I could knock out a tune, keep time as long as I didn't start singing, and work through a handful of blues, folk and country styles. 'Until Daylight' was based on a bluegrass, Maybelle Carter-style technique of alternating bass lines to make a melody while keeping the rhythm on the treble strings, and 'I Found Out' used a blues solo based on the pentatonic scale that my guitar teacher had shown me. 'Mystery Fox' had a few bends and slides in it and the sum total of everything I could possibly do was thrown into 'Anji'. But all of this would be lost if my infinitely more skilled fellow guitarists would not do so much as turn up to rehearsals.

I had never done any kind of live performance before. But I did know that a good show didn't simply rely on musicians playing the right notes, so between returning from Cornwall and the big night I undertook as much research into putting on a gig as I could. One evening NJ and I went to a cabaret night in a working men's club that featured comedians, a burlesque stripper, and two acoustic guitar-playing singer-songwriters. The first was a man who went into detail about how difficult it was to get a record deal but he had pressed up his own CDs and they were available for sale at the bar. His three songs, all very well played with no mistakes that I could notice, seemed to go on for ever. The second was a woman who started her set by telling everyone to be quiet. She sang a few wistful, pitch-perfect songs, again well played, and it was agonizing to sit through. All anyone wanted to do was drink beer and have a few laughs with their friends, and here was this young woman attempting to control the atmosphere with her unremarkable acoustic whimsy.

'That was awful,' said NJ as the woman's set eventually came to an end. 'I can't stand those earnest types who think they're Joni Mitchell.'

'But at least they knew what they were doing,' I said. 'What hope is there for Double Fantasy, who haven't got a clue?'

'Just don't tell the audience to shut up and you should be fine.'

The rehearsals continued to not happen. Once again, Pete had a job on and Doyle claimed to be ill after working all night (I later found out he had a raging hangover) and now it was only a week to the gig. I practised each night in the basement by myself and decided that if I couldn't control other people, I could at least make sure that my own part was up to scratch. I started to worry about Pete's insistence on singing all the songs, too. 'I Found Out' and 'Until Daylight' were written for a woman, as anyone who listened to the words would hopefully realize. When Pete sang them he sounded like a homosexual. As he didn't look like one, I felt that this was an artistic slant Double Fantasy could do without. Michael Tyack told me that he would turn off Pete's microphone if it got too bad.

Something I had not so far considered was the technical side of playing live and the problems that can bring. David Viner had complained of not being able to hear himself on stage and of how difficult it was to play when this happened, and the various members of Circulus always had reports of technical hitches after a concert. Of course you would have to be prepared for people talking in the audience – if, indeed, there was an audience – but you also had to be prepared for a situation where you were far less in control than when you practised at home. My next research project involved seeing a hip American rock band perform their first show in England in years, where the level of anticipation in the sold-out venue was high. They came on after far too long a wait, the female lead singer was out of her mind and stumbling all over the stage, and all you could hear was the squealing guitar. There were some serious sound problems but the band refused to rise to the occasion and make the most of it. A lot of people had paid to see her, but the lead singer hardly ever went near the microphone and when she did she merely let out a torrent of abuse to nobody in particular.

It was a lesson in what not to do in the face of problems outside of your control. The fact is that nine times out of ten the audience don't mind or even notice the inevitable mistakes and technical hitches that occur in the average concert. They would much rather the guitarist played out of tune, for example, than spend half an hour fiddling around with the tuning heads.

Every example of a bad concert that I thought of heightened

my sense of impending doom. Nerves were constant: my hands
were permanently clammy and I appeared to be developing a
body odour problem. If I carried on like this the guitar would be
slipping out of my hands every time I tried to play it. I was as
preoccupied about the gig as Doyle was about his girlfriend.
There were certain things that *really* worried me, like singing 'I
Never Loved Her' and keeping the beat at the same time, and it
was going through my head constantly. One morning I was in
the reading room of The British Library, a huge hall where
hundreds of people diligently sit over laptops and piles of books,
and I started to sing 'I Never Loved Her' with my eyes closed,
entirely unaware of what I was doing. A bird-like woman with
narrow lips and enormous glasses hissed 'Shut up!' and I made a
rapid return to my studies.

There were good performances to look to for inspiration.
Devendra Banhart had been excellent when we saw him at an
ornate old music hall that held a sold-out audience of five
hundred. He captivated everyone – without having to tell the
audience to be quiet – with a few simple acoustic guitar
patterns and songs with smart but throwaway lines that were
sung in a high voice. His band must have been making all kinds
of mistakes judging by the half-empty bottles of Maker's Mark
bourbon they were clutching, but it didn't matter. You warmed
to Banhart because you felt that he was as respectful of the
audience as they were of him. Communication was the key.

There was no point in attempting to emulate their brilliance,
but there were the top professionals to keep in mind, too. You
only have to see The Rolling Stones perform to understand why
they are still at it. Mick Jagger knows just how far to go: he
tantalizes you by suggesting you might be welcome at a club
that you will never actually be allowed to join. Keith Richards
and Ronnie Wood look like a couple of old crows still grateful

for the gig and you love them for it. David Bowie maintains a theatricality that's compelling, and James Brown and Little Richard perform with such verve and passion that you sense you are watching them in their essence.

Eventually we did manage to have another rehearsal with the whole band. Pete kept saying that if the worst came to the worst he could do backing vocals on a couple of numbers, and then proceeded to sing the lead on all of them. It was decided that I would stick to acoustic guitar – I hoped that this place we were performing at had some stools to sit on as I had still not learned how to play standing up – and Pete would use the Telecaster. We ran through 'Until Daylight'. Loren sounded great on this song about old friends finding romance around the log fire of an old cottage for just one night: warm and seductive. She looked striking, too, and gave us a sophistication we didn't otherwise have. She did tend to wear rather dowdy shoes, though. I wondered if I could somehow get her into heels, but Michael Tyack had warned me of his many efforts to force Loren to wear something other than her beloved Kickers, and of how each attempt invariably ended in tears (hers, not his). Maybe it was that boyfriend of hers that was always hanging around who was forcing her to layer up the whole time.

A few days before the gig I bumped into Len, one of the three friends of Davey Graham I had spent that crazy stoned night with. I told him about my nerves at the forthcoming performance.

'Valium,' he suggested. 'Don't take too much because you'll go to sleep, but the correct dosage really does help steady your nerves.'

'Is that such a good idea?' I asked him. 'Surely I'll just stop caring about the outcome altogether.'

'A quadruple scotch, then. You need to have something

otherwise you *will* fuck up. Actually, you're going to fuck up whatever happens. You're bound to – it's your first ever gig. But don't worry. If the audience realize that you're starting out they may not bottle you off too violently.'

I found somebody else to talk to at that point.

'Nerves are good,' said Michael Tyack, who I called in a panic. He was in the middle of a guitar lesson. 'Nerves mean that you care about what you're doing and they help to fire you up if you use them in the right way. Have you ever seen a band that is jaded and just running through the motions? It's awful. You *should* be nervous. But after the first song and a bit of applause you'll love it and you'll want to go and do it all over again. That's the reason why the world is full of musicians who get a tiny bit of acclaim and carry on running after that initial thrill for the rest of their lives.'

It is also why the music world is full of drug addicts. The kick of performing in front of an audience is said to be so great that you want to replicate it instantly, so you take drugs as the next best thing. The boredom of being on the road is a spur to take drugs, too, apparently. At the gig where the American rock singer did her worst, I talked to a guitarist friend who had spent the last year touring solidly with his band. He had never taken drugs of any kind but almost everyone else he knew did. He explained how the long bus journeys soon become a drag, and how you'd arrive at the concert hall in a new town in the afternoon and have no choice but to stay there until your performance that evening. It is, he said, incredibly dull. You can't even read a book because there's too much going on and you've said everything there is to say to your fellow band members. So you take drugs for want of anything better to do. He alleged that being on tour was like one long endurance test, and a huge number of bands split up after their first one because they simply cannot bear the thought of going through it all over again.

Double Fantasy's ambitions did not stretch to getting a tour bus and a string of dates from here to Mobile, Alabama, but should we make it as far as, say, the Tapestry Goes West festival in Cornwall, I don't think we would fall prey to the usual rock'n'roll vices. Doyle was banned from taking drugs because of his work and he was admirably strict with himself. Pete claimed that in his youth he used to go wild for the shandy but there was no proof of this, and I found out early on that intoxication and small children don't mix. At this point, however, I was seriously considering Len's suggestion of a dose of Valium.

On the Friday night before the Monday of the gig I bit into a particularly hard bar of chocolate. A sharp pain followed a cracking sound.

'Ouch! I think I've just broken one of my fillings.'

'Oh honey,' said NJ. 'You had better sort it out before the gig. In the meantime, have a painkiller and a whisky.' It didn't seem too serious. We listened to an album by Davey Graham, looked through an art book on the Pre-Raphaelites that NJ had just bought, and discussed ways in which we might convince Loren to dress up like Millais's *Ophelia* for the gig. The tooth problem was not serious. The dentist was open on Saturdays and it would be sorted the next day.

But it wasn't a filling that turned out to have been cracked by that winter-hardened bar of Toblerone. It was an entire molar. The dentist had to take out the half that had come loose and cut into the gums to do so, leaving a gaping hole in the side of my mouth and a hell of a lot of pain once the anaesthetic had worn off. The tooth would have to be replaced by a bridge, and because the crack was so deep the lower gum needed to be

surgically altered. None of this could be done in time for the
gig. In the meantime I would have to have a putty-coloured
temporary filling. 'Try to avoid eating with the right side of
your mouth for the next few weeks,' said the dentist, helpfully.

That was Saturday. Pete and Doyle had agreed to come to the
flat on Monday afternoon for one final rehearsal. In the meantime I was receiving messages from friends who were excited at
coming down to the gig, so it looked like we would have an
audience whether we wanted one or not. Double Fantasy
consisted of a pained and increasingly toothless acoustic guitarist, a chaotic love-struck bassist, an electric guitarist who
would rather be at home doing his tax return, and a singer who
didn't know the songs. And no drummer. Doyle was right. We
were going to be the worst band in history.

Chapter Fifteen

The Gig

They did turn up at four o'clock, as they had promised. Everyone was subdued. Doyle didn't make his usual demands for sustenance and Pete quietly plugged in the Telecaster and started playing 'Mystery Fox'. We ran through our set list without too many mistakes. It was a cold, sparse working day outside: from the street end of the basement you could hear the yelps of children returning from school and the barks of mothers ordering their toddlers not to run into the road. We put on the electric heater, drank cups of tea, sat on stools with our guitars and stoically, solemnly practised without arguing – for the first half hour, at least.

'The big problem now is Loren,' said Doyle. 'She doesn't know the songs.'

'It doesn't matter,' I told him. 'She can have the lyrics in front of her and we can lead her through the changes. It'll be all right.'

'I could always help her with the singing,' chimed Pete, and I reiterated that I was sure Loren would rise to the occasion.

'No she won't,' said Doyle, glumly. 'She's only been to one rehearsal. She's going to mess it up and the whole thing will fall apart.'

'Stop being so bloody negative!' I shouted, with such a

sudden burst of fury that Pete developed an instant need to give one hundred per cent concentration to a tricky solo. 'You're going to ruin this whole thing with your moaning and whining. For fuck's sake, why can't you just enjoy it, you bastard?'

'Because they're going to crucify us.'

'If you're so scared of getting up there and giving it a go, don't do it. We'll get by without you. It'll be better than having you put a curse on us by your constant undermining.' My toothache seemed to be getting worse the more agitated I got.

Otto appeared at the door with a plate of biscuits and a smile. It was time to mellow out, take stock of the situation, and look to the positive. After all, what really mattered was in place: our outfits. After returning in pain and misery from the dentist's chair on Saturday I received a call from a friend whose brother's wife was the cousin of John Entwistle, the late bass player of The Who, who had died the previous year following a massive cocaine binge. They were clearing out the possessions that had been left out of the will at his gothic country pile and came across two tailored suits from the late sixties. The brother had tried them on but they weren't his size, and they had been wondering which tall, skinny man might be interested in having them. I was in the car and inside my friend's flat on the other side of London twenty minutes later.

It was incredible. John 'The Ox' Entwistle and I appeared to have exactly the same body. They could have been tailored for me: they were a perfect fit and in the very style I would have ordered. My favourite of the two was a three-piece maroon tonic in the finest artificial fibre money could buy back in 1968, with trouser creases you could cut your fingers on and just enough flare to look the part over a pair of Cuban-heeled boots. On the tailor's label on the inside of the three-button jacket's inner pocket – Major of 11 Royal Drive, Dawes Road, Fulham, London SW6 – were the letters J. ENTWISTLE written in indelible marker. There was my stage outfit.

I would live up to the stereotype I had wanted of being the smartly-dressed man about town, while Pete arrived on Monday in his usual five-year-old Hush Puppies, £10 trousers from the Next catalogue and a blue cardigan that I imagined his mother had bought him, so he was in character too. As we took a break from rehearsals that afternoon to try on our outfits, Doyle revealed his own exterior expression of his inner spirit. He changed into a pair of old denim hipster flares with an oversized belt buckle, a Captain Caveman gilet with nothing underneath, and his *pièce de résistance*: a WW1-era German soldier's helmet. He looked like a particularly vicious sixties biker, the kind that stomped heads at The Rolling Stones's concert at Altamont, California in 1969. It was perfect, except for one thing: his new boots. They were almost great – brown leather with big heels and round toes – but they had a metal ring on their side that made them look like the kind of thing a politically conscious millionaire singer of an eighties rock band might have worn.

'Great outfit, man,' I said. 'You're a real primitive. What's up with the boots, though? They're a bit U2.'

'What are you talking about?' He looked like he might burst into tears. 'These are straight from the sixties.'

'Do you remember those black-and-white posters in the eighties of a bare-chested hunk holding a baby? You can imagine him wearing them.'

'Yeah, or a photograph of a muscle boy emerging from a garage carrying a tyre in each hand,' added Pete. 'They're like the boots merchant bankers spend £400 on when they head out on the highways of Surrey with their brand-new Harley Davidsons.'

'Yeah?' said Doyle, now shaking like one of those small dogs that have been so over-bred they cannot regulate their body temperature, 'Well what's your outfit, Pete? A librarian?' He turned to me. 'And you'd make a very good second-hand car salesman. Congratulations on meeting this month's target.'

'Jealousy is a horrible thing,' I replied casually, determined not to show that the seeds of doubt had been planted in my sartorial mind. 'You know that this suit is amazing.'

'I have no doubt that it will help in the sale of your next Ford Mondeo,' spat Doyle, lighting a Marlboro. 'Mind you, when being a guitarist doesn't work out you can always find a dazzling future in double glazing.'

I stood up, grabbed the Telecaster, and lurched forward to do a Pete Townshend over Doyle's head. Thankfully NJ came in just in time.

'He said I look like a double-glazing salesman!' I cried, lowering the guitar.

'He started it!' said Doyle, pointing at me and panting. 'He said my boots were eighties.'

'I think you're all getting a little too tense,' she said, calmly. 'Why don't you pack what you need to take, come upstairs, and sit down for a while?'

We had to be at Colours by 6.30pm for the soundcheck. Pete asked which buses went to Camden Town. I told him we would be getting a taxi; he looked worried until I assured him I would pay for it. Personally I was more concerned by the fact that he planned to do the soundcheck, go back home to pick up Rachel, and return to the venue in time, hopefully, for our on-stage appearance. The reason for this madly over-optimistic scheme was that he wanted to have his car after the gig in order to eliminate the prospect of having to get a taxi home should he miss the last bus. I told him that if he gave me a heart attack, he could pay for the funeral costs.

We put the three guitars into the boot, climbed in, and sat in silence as the silver people carrier with a smell of newness made the half-hour journey through rush-hour London. Doyle fretted about the route the driver took and wondered aloud, more than a few times, if anybody would actually turn up to see us. I had decided to take up smoking, and drew heavily on a roll-up to let the tobacco bring its essential nutrients into my nervous system as I stared out of the window and speculated on what the hell this thing was going to be like. We walked down the disinfectant-smelling narrow staircase of Colours to find Michael Tyack and Loren already there, and another man who I didn't recognize clutching a weathered Stratocaster.

'It seems that they've booked someone else to play without my knowledge,' said Michael. 'I promise I didn't know anything about it until tonight.'

'So what's happening? Don't tell me we've been bumped off the bill.'

'No, you've been moved up it. He's coming on first.'

This wasn't so bad, although it meant that we probably wouldn't be onstage until 10.30 – four hours away. I surveyed the dive. It was larger than I remembered – you could get a couple of hundred people in there easily – and there was no stage, but a space where the equipment was set up with the DJ booth on one side and the toilets on the other. There were black leather banquette seats at either end of the room, a long bar staffed by handsome Brazilians who were spinning cocktail shakers like they had overdosed on guarana and a handful of flashing lights. I liked Colours – it had a seedy charm in its vague attempts at sophistication. I commandeered the two high stools in front of the bar and placed them behind the drum kit to stop any punters nabbing them. Loren and I could sit on the stools with microphones before us while Pete and Doyle stood behind. An hour of waiting around passed remarkably slowly before it was time for the soundcheck. It was strange to hear 'Mystery Fox' through a microphone and a PA system, but in its odd, stop-start, drummerless way it didn't sound too bad. I began to feel a little excited at the prospect of the real thing.

We went to eat at a Spanish tapas bar a few doors down. Few words were spoken as we got through our meal with brisk efficiency. 'Great, I love quiche,' said Pete as he took a slice of tortilla. The patatas bravas scared him but he was pleased about the grilled sardines.

'Those boots aren't really eighties,' I muttered to Doyle, poking at a battered squid. 'They're quite sixties actually. I could imagine Peter Fonda wearing them.'

'I suppose you don't look like a used-car salesman,' he replied, somehow managing to smoke, eat and talk at the same time. 'John Entwistle was the coolest member of The Who. He was a geezer. He died snorting coke off a hooker's tits.'

'We've just got to have fun and make the most of this thing,' I said. 'A lot of people are coming and we can't let them down. We can make it work.'

'When you're actually up there you find a way to channel your energies in a way that you never did before,' said Pete. 'In a strange way it's easier playing on stage because you have no choice but to get on with it and give it your total concentration.'

'It's Loren I'm worried about,' repeated Doyle, as he tended to do when something was bothering him. 'She don't know the songs.'

'Just concentrate on getting your bass parts right,' I said, 'and forget about Loren. She wants to get it right too.'

We returned to Colours at nine o'clock – too late, thankfully, for Pete to think about nipping home – and the place was packed. Everyone I knew had made the effort to come out on the worst night of the week in the worst month of the year to support us. John Moore, who had been so instrumental in setting me off on my knowledge of the blues, was there with good advice on how to handle the gig. 'You look cool, so half the battle is won,' he said. 'Nobody really cares too much about what you play.' NJ appeared in a floaty floor-length dress from the early seventies, waving red hair reaching down to her waist, and looked exactly like the kind of timeless muse I needed right now. 'Are you nervous?' everyone kept asking. 'Of course I bloody am,' was the standard response. Rachel, Pete's wife, good-naturedly suggested that I must be *really* nervous.

'I suppose it's going to be very difficult at your age,' she began, breezily. 'If you were sixteen and it was your first gig you would have so much more bravado, you wouldn't really care about how it sounded, and nobody would expect you to come up with anything remarkable. But at your age you don't want to disgrace yourself in front of all these people because the humiliation will be so much greater. I mean, there's a good chance that it might all go wrong because you are such a beginner and then you'll just want to climb into a hole and bury yourself. Don't you think?'

I walked away from Rachel at that point.

The man with the Stratocaster took to the stage, backed by a drummer. There was a tragic inevitability to the fact that he was a former session guitarist who had been playing since the age of seven, and he was older than us. He was knocking out slides and heavy blues licks at the rate of ten a second. He was a total master.

'I think he missed a beat,' said Doyle, as we stood and watched the guitarist give Robert Johnson a run for his money.

'It's not about ability, it's not about ability,' I chanted quietly, rocking backwards and forwards.

The man, whose stage name was Catweazel, seemed to be playing for an eternity. We were waiting, and waiting, and waiting to get up there and get it over with, and it was agonizing. But I also noticed that the large crowd were finding Catweazel a little boring, despite or perhaps because of his remarkable abilities. At least there were plenty of people to talk to as the minutes crawled along and the tension grew. People asked if this was Double Fantasy's first ever gig. I replied that it looked like it would be their last. There were many offers of drinks but getting drunk was the last thing that was needed, and I thanked God for Doyle's driving test the following morning – if it weren't for that he would have been paralytic by now. Colours was almost sold out and most of the people in there had come to see us. I couldn't decide if this was a good thing or not, but one old friend, who had done many gigs herself, had the best response to my much-repeated confirmation that I was nervous. 'It's only a gig,' she said. 'What are you worried about?'

Finally, blues maestro Catweazel slid his last slide and it would soon be our turn. We had taken over a corner of the room far from the stage with our guitars and leads: we picked them up, walked calmly through the crowd to the other side of the venue, and prepared for our glorious arrival.

With the lack of any proper backstage area we used the tiny corridor leading to the toilets to get ready and for Doyle to get changed. I managed to knock my guitar against the wall and put it out of tune, resulting in a frantic, panicked attempt to sort it out with an electronic tuner. 'Where's a guitar tech when you need one?' I said as Doyle fussed over his caveman outfit and Pete twanged the Telecaster while a nervous young man attempted to push past and make it to the urinal. Loren joined us in a high-waisted Guinevere dress and confessed that she couldn't remember how the songs went.

'Excellent, it's our song,' said Doyle as 'The Harder They Come' by Jimmy Cliff came over the speakers. Then we took to the stage.

We got into position. There was a fair degree of knob-twiddling by the sound man as he tried to get the pick-up on my acoustic guitar to work, and for a moment I wondered what it would be like if it never worked; if the whole thing had to be cancelled. I looked out at the wash of faces before us, expectant, ready to be amused, and on our side, and prayed that the sound would come good soon. Then came the thumbs-up and the turning-down of the music on the stereo. A stocky man with black curly hair, the organizer of the night, stood before us and said: 'Down here we like to celebrate the strange and wonderful, and this next band are most certainly that. Please give a big hand for Double Fantasy!'

There was a roar from the crowd. 'This is . . .' only then did I realize that we hadn't bothered with a name for the opening claw-hammer instrumental, '. . . this is the first song.' My hands were sweating so much that trying to hit the strings with my right hand felt like manipulating an eel, and forming the chords with my left was like pinning down mercury, but somehow the music that I could hear coming out of the monitor speakers was as it should be: delicate and evocative and with the notes in the right place. Beyond the highway connecting my brain with the guitar were side roads of people talking; a few words including 'folk music', 'Double Fantasy' and 'Who are they?' caught in isolation. Loren picked up on the melody and gently lulled over the top of the guitar. It finished a minute later and there was a swell of applause. That had never happened in the basement.

'We're Double Fantasy,' I said, and even that got a round of handclaps. This was incredible. Imagine if the toilet whooped with joy once you flushed the chain, or the washing machine gave a standing ovation every time you loaded it up – that's what it felt like. 'And this is our psychedelic number. It's called "Mystery Fox". Let me just find my plectrum – got it. Take it away, Pete.'

Another cheer was followed by Pete's rocking A minor to D riff for the opener of 'Mystery Fox'. I began my sequence, based on the pentatonic scale of A and requiring me to hit a variety of notes in quick succession before ending by bending a high G, and it didn't go all over the place even though it felt like the plectrum was going to fly out of my hands at any minute. Together Pete and Loren sang: 'Mystery fox, get out of your box. It's time for me to chase you up that tree, O mystery fox . . .' as I did a slow bending of various notes to match the changes in the melody. Pete launched back into the riff, Doyle's bass rumbled into action and the song did indeed sound strange, but surprisingly dynamic.

It was halfway through 'Mystery Fox' that I had an out-of-body experience. The music playing in my head, I looked down on the scene of the four of us performing a song that I had written in a few minutes before Pete came round for a practice one afternoon, and the crowd of faces before us, many of whom I knew and who had all paid to get in, and wondered how this had happened. And marvelled at the fact that it was happening at all. For that brief moment I felt detached from myself, or rather from the person sitting on a tall stool in a dead rock star's suit playing guitar. It was great.

I climbed back into my body. None of us got anything wrong. We arrived at the chorus at the correct time, hit the right notes, and went back to the verse when we should. Pete

and Loren remembered the words – or were very good at reading
them without making that seem too obvious – and we even
managed to get the end section where the usual pattern of notes
was reversed. I turned round to see Doyle looking like a biker
statue, standing entirely motionless save for the interplay of his
fingers. When 'Mystery Fox' came to an end there was another
roar from the crowd. That's when I knew we were going to be
OK.

'I Found Out' came next. This was probably the least
successful of the songs I had written – Doyle's bass line was
powerful and the guitar parts were fine, but what had been
intended as an angry threat from a scorned woman had, for some
reason, become something of a whining, martyr-like lament.
And Pete still managed to get his vocals in on the chorus. But it
wasn't too bad. My short guitar solo at the end of the song,
which involved playing all the way up the neck and utilizing a
few slides and hammer-ons, didn't come off too badly – people
even cheered during it – although we all ended up finishing at
different times from one another and Loren quite clearly didn't
know how the song went. The way she sang it and the way the
rest of us had structured it were two separate entities. I don't
think anyone really cared.

'All right,' I said to the crowd, 'here's a little tearjerker for all
of you broken-hearted out there. It's called "I Never Loved
Her".'

'You bastard!' shouted a woman from the audience. Doyle's
killer bass kicked the song off and we joined in at the right
time.

'Why are you guys always picking on me?' I growled into
the microphone, and there were laughs from the audience.
'Come on, fellas, just let me be. You never give me a
moment's rest. You guys are bugging me to death! You

know that girl would have done me wrong. Just keep on, guys, and it won't be long.'

It didn't take long for the playing to go out of time with the singing, but I arrived at an instant solution to the problem: stop playing and come back in at the right time. This seemed to work on a level good enough for a live gig, and as I sang the tender and tormented chorus, which reveals the guy really *did* love her, I closed my eyes and gave it my best shot. It wouldn't have got too far with the choir of *Evita* but it was close enough for rock'n'roll and with Loren's spooky siren-like harmonies in the background, it worked fine. 'I Never Loved Her' got the biggest cheer so far. I could see NJ a few feet away, beaming radiantly, and a whole lot of other familiar faces besides. They were digging it!

Apart from the short opening instrumental, the four of us had played on all the songs so far, and any mistakes I might have made could easily be hidden. Now came the hard part of the show. 'Until Daylight' was my best song. It had lyrics that worked with the music and captured the right feeling of flirtatious romance, and the simple alternating bass line pattern I had come up with and Pete had developed had a good feeling to it: there was depth in its easy minimalism. The only problem was that, being finger-picked and without accompaniment save Loren's voice, it needed absolute precision to work and my fingers felt like they were coated in lubricant. There was nothing to do but start it. Somehow it kept going, Loren sang it beautifully, and it was a success. That was a wonderful feeling – to have a created entity get out there and be heard and, more importantly, enjoyed. For the outro Pete came up with a lead on the electric guitar as I kept the rhythm pattern going. It sounded relaxed and warm, as it should have done.

Then it was time for the number I was dreading: 'Anji'. Even while concentrating on the other songs I had been wondering how on earth I was going to play this song when my fingers were so drenched and my right foot was unhelpfully shaking. I was preparing myself for the beginning when the man with the curly hair appeared before us and grabbed Loren's microphone. 'Hang on, hang on. I'm sorry to interrupt,' he shouted, in a tone so strident that it negated his apology, 'but is that a Nazi helmet you're wearing?'

The room went silent as he pointed at Doyle. 'It's from World War One,' I said into the microphone, but the man didn't take any notice. Doyle stood there like a hell's angel caught in the headlights of a police truck.

'I do not find that helmet funny. Your wearing it is an insult to myself, my religion, my family, and I would appreciate it if you would take it off immediately.'

'Do you want to borrow it, then?' said Doyle. He casually removed the helmet and chucked it at the man, who stared at it like he was holding a defused bomb.

'That's just not the image we want to promote down here,' said the man, to a crowd that had already been won over by Doyle's ragged charms. Then the man raised his eyes for comic effect and said: 'I mean, you've got to have a dress code, haven't you?' He left and allowed us to get on with our set.

'I don't think I know anyone who is less of a Nazi than Doyle,' I said, digging the capo out of my jacket pocket to prepare to play 'Anji'. 'This one's for NJ.'

I went straight into it, feeling my fingers sliding over the notes and wondering if what I was playing bore any resemblance to one of the greatest songs ever written. I looked up to see Mr David Viner, the first person to help me on my quest to learn 'Anji', standing there with a big smile, holding his thumbs up. By the time I had got to the first change in the song, where a string is bent and played against the insistent low thump of an open A, I knew that it was going to be OK. Another change came, a breakdown that involves hitting a low series of notes that has no space for error, and I got it right. I knew there were times when I missed the rhythm notes that have to be played out on the bass strings, but it was working. The mistakes didn't seem to matter any more. The room was getting quieter and quieter as I played, and by the second half of 'Anji' I might as well have been back in the basement: I was aware of the crowd of people listening to my playing, but I didn't need to worry about their presence any more because the thing was working. The nerves had gone. The song came to an end and I looked at the crowd, taking a mental photograph of all the smiling faces I could see, and knew that all was right with the world.

The plan had been to march backstage before responding to the demands from the crowd for more, but there was no backstage – there was no stage – so when it was clear that we had made it into the audience's hearts we did one more song: Bob Dylan's 'You Ain't Going Nowhere'. This is easy to play, and even if you have never heard it, it's such a sing-along that you imagine you have anyway. By now the whole band was swinging and, as far as I could tell, enjoying it. Loren was more taciturn than I had imagined – she always seemed like she was trying to burst out of the shadows of Circulus but perhaps that is how she wanted it – yet she did the job of singing for Double Fantasy admirably. Pete, our hardy perennial, kept the whole thing together and Doyle's very presence was enough: the fact that he missed his cue on the bass more than once did not matter at all.

I felt strangely at home up there. It was the first time I had been on stage since being Second Shepherd in the school nativity play, and even then Third Shepherd had stolen the show by wetting himself. It was fun to talk to the audience, to do your best at playing this music that you have worked on so hard to get right. It became obvious after a while that the mistakes really don't matter: the key is to remember that there is an audience out there, that you are not doing this in your bedroom and if people have paid to see you then you should be conscious of them and treat them with the respect they are giving you by making the effort to be there. When I was a teenager I thought that bands that held their audience in contempt were quite cool. I don't think that any more.

It was only after the set had finished that I realized the reason why so many people are drawn to getting up on stage and risking a public shaming. A steady stream of people presented me with glasses of Jack Daniel's and ice. Women treated me differently: they were extremely affectionate. 'You were so relaxed, like it was the easiest thing in the world,' they kept telling me. David Viner was full of praise about daring to play 'Anji' in front of an audience and John Moore made a few comments about the necessity of sorting out good management before signing anything. NJ appeared with tears in her eyes and hugged me. 'How was "Anji"?' I asked her. 'Did it sound OK? I made so many mistakes.'

'It was beautiful.'

Pete disappeared with Rachel immediately after the set: we finished a little after eleven and they would still be able to catch a bus back to their flat. Loren prepared to go onstage with Circulus. Doyle hung around for a while to make use of the offers of beer before heading back home uncharacteristically early to prepare for his driving test the next day. I stayed, happy to see old friends, soak in the compliments, and come to terms with the fact that I had done something I would have never thought possible in the space of six months. I had become a guitar player.

Circulus arrived on stage in full medieval costume and Michael Tyack spouted all manner of cosmic repartee, but I couldn't engage with it: my mind was elsewhere. Catweazel congratulated us in a generous way – I had told him about the six-month project and my attendant fears during the sound-check – and he became excited when I told him I had met T. Model Ford, his favourite guitarist. 'You've got nothing to worry about by starting at thirty-four,' he said, cheerfully. 'T. Model Ford learned guitar in his fifties and now nobody can beat him.'

It was a good thing that Bert Jansch and Davey Graham didn't turn up. To have them listen to my less than perfect public performance of 'Anji' would have reduced me to rubble. But it was great to play to a full house, and to face your fears for a reason. And rather like the first hit of a drug I had a feeling that one might easily fall into the trap of attempting to recreate that high of coming off stage after a successful debut gig for ever more. It would be better to keep on enjoying the guitar without false ambition, to do the odd show every now and then when it arose, and to get on with life as it unfolded.

Drunk and happy, NJ and I stumbled into a cab around two o'clock laden with guitars, sank into the padded back seats and watched London pass by the windows like a rain-soaked film set. NJ walked from the door to the bed without passing through the bathroom, which I had never known her to do before, and I ordered a cab for the babysitter and apologized for being so late. It was impossible to go straight to sleep. I went downstairs to the kitchen, poured one final whisky, lit one final cigarette, and gave Davey Graham's 'Anji' another blast. One of these days, but not necessarily in this lifetime, I would play that damn song perfectly.

Epilogue

If the last six months had taught me anything, it was that Bert Jansch and Davey Graham are remarkable both as guitarists and as people. I would never get bored with James Williamson's rock action, or Johnny Marr's inventiveness, or T. Model Ford's instinctive style. But Bert and Davey's playing hit me hard. 'Anji' was the song that had soundtracked my adventure and they were the men that owned it.

Davey Graham's playing is transcendental, but he is so unreliable that you never know what you are going to get: inspiration or jagged confusion. In fact you can never be sure about getting Davey at all. He was booked for a major tour of Australia in the late sixties, when the plane made a stopover at Bombay. Davey forgot all about his commitments and wandered off through India in search of ancient knowledge of the sitar. Bert is a quieter, more reliable soul, and less of a pioneer than Davey, but his playing is like that of Jimi Hendrix: he takes the guitar into a different place through a combination of discipline and pure feeling. He discovered the instrument at a time when the notion of the Guitar God was yet to be invented and he explored it not through dreams of glory and adulation, but through curiosity and creativity.

I could hardly play when Bert Jansch first gave me a lesson.

Now I could – not brilliantly, but with enough enthusiasm and knowledge to get by. The success of the gig had filled me with hope and pride: it was hard to beat that thrill of playing 'Anji' to a full house lured towards silence by its delicate beauty. But before I launched my career as a world-renowned professional it was necessary to go back to Bert Jansch for further advice. I planned to play him 'Anji' – surely he would be amazed at my capturing of this complex masterpiece – and ask for direction towards the next step on the journey.

On the Friday afternoon following the gig I pressed the doorbell of Bert and Loren's basement flat in Kilburn, a bottle of wine in one hand and a guitar in the other. Bert was in the living room with the latest top-of-the-range Yamaha steel-string acoustic on his lap. It looked like an extension of his body. He was interested to hear about the strange night with Davey Graham, and confirmed that I would have been unlikely to get much of a musical education out of him – indeed I was lucky to leave his flat in one piece. Bert knew of someone that had gone to Davey for a lesson. Davey put the first side of a Ravi Shankar record on his turntable and went to the pub. Then he came back, flipped the record over, and went to the pub again. Then he came back and asked his student for five pounds.

Loren brought us a cup of tea and I got down to the business of playing 'Anji'. There were, as always, plenty of mistakes, but the rhythm was there and it sounded like the elements were in the right place. Bert had an inscrutable smile as he watched and listened patiently, without comment, until the song came to an end, when he gave a little chuckle.

'Ok,' he said. 'It sounds like we've got a lot of work to do.'

I was starting on the wrong string. The hammer-on was meant to be a pull-off. The flamenco-style interlude in the middle of the song, in which two strings are pulled simultaneously over a series of partial chords, was completely wrong. In a section where a B string is bent on a D note I was missing out the playing of a full A minor chord and the E minor and G chords that follow it. A breakdown made up of a series of low notes was from a different song altogether. 'Apart from that,' said Bert concluding this litany of errors, 'it's very good.'

'How can it be very good? I've got almost everything wrong.'

'Not quite. You've nailed the basis of it, which is great because you can vary it to your liking. That's what the whole game is about.'

Over the next two hours Bert patiently, diligently broke down the component parts of this complex song and showed me how to play them. His version, which made 'Anji' famous, is completely different from Davey Graham's. He explained how he had first heard it. As a fourteen-year-old in Edinburgh he visited a folk club where Davey's half-sister Jill Doyle gave guitar lessons. Jill brought a tape of Davey playing 'Anji' – this was before the song was released on record in 1961 – and everyone in the club made it their mission to learn how it was done. Bert was the first to succeed.

He told me about his frustrations with Davey's playing – that he was too academic, that he wouldn't relax into the blues – before concluding that Davey Graham and Andres Segovia are the finest guitarists the world has ever known. He told me that I should learn the techniques of classical guitar, of giving a finger to each string and of understanding how arpeggios worked, if I really wanted to make 'Anji' sound as it should, and he suggested that early music, blues, classical and folk styles have to be mastered before one can give the song its true value.

'It's only practice,' said Bert as he made sounds on the guitar that seemed to be coming from another world. 'Don't try and gloss over the notes with speed: play them slowly and get them right in the first place. Use the classical technique of playing two notes at once.'

We edged microscopically forward as the afternoon wore on. For a bit of light relief Bert taught me 'Blues Run The Game' by Jackson C. Frank. Then we returned to 'Anji'. I wondered how many times he must have played it over his lifetime.

It was dark when I emerged from Bert and Loren's flat, now fully aware that, as far as the guitar is concerned, I was still in the basement. The six months had come and gone and my goal of playing a gig had been reached. Double Fantasy's future was uncertain. Doyle was searching for love in Japan, Pete had returned to the domestic fold – I excitedly suggested that we should do another gig some time and he unexcitedly told me that he would rather throw his original copy of Elton John's *Tumbleweed Connection* in the dustbin – and Loren of Circulus was back with the professionals. Now it was time to learn to play the guitar, and there was nothing to do but practise. I had a feeling that it might take a while.

ACKNOWLEDGEMENTS

Thank you to Doyle, Michael Tyack and Pete Millson for making this adventure possible and to NJ Stevenson for her love and patience. Johnny Marr, Bert Jansch, Roger McGuinn, James Williamson, Roland Janes, Ronnie Drew, Richard Vine, David Viner, Davy Graham, Billy Childish, Davendra Banhart, Matthew Friedberger, John Moore, T. Model Ford, Charles Stevenson, Vinicius Cantuaria, Sérgio and Arnaldo Dias Baptista, Polly Harvey, The Black Keys, Phoenix, Teddy Paige, Fat Possum, Andy Hackett and Sky Saxon have all been generous with free lessons and guitar-related wisdom. Thanks to Les Paul for providing a one-word answer to a dilemma that has been troubling guitarists ever since their instrument was invented.

I wold also like to thank Simon Benham at Mayer Benham, Mike Jones, Colin Midson, William Webb and Victoria Millar at Bloomsbury, Lo Polidoro, Liz and Neville Hodgkinson, Nadja Coyne, Camilla McGuinn, Frank De Caro and Rosan Jordan.

I am indebted to the following books and their authors: *The Guitar Handbook* by Ralph Denyer (Pan, 1991); *Searching for Robert Johnson* by Peter Guralnick (Penguin, 1989); *Lost Highway* by Peter Guralnick (Mojo Books, 2002); *Guitars: Music, History, Construction* by Tom and Mary Anne Evans (Facts On File Inc., 1982); *The Country Blues* by Samuel Charters (Rinehart, 1959); *Zen Guitar* by Philip Toshio Sudo (Simon & Schuster, 1999); *The Gibson Guitar from 1950* by Ian C. Bishop (Bold Strummer Ltd, 1990); *Dazzling Stranger: Bert Jansch and the British Folk and Blues Revival* by Colin Harper (Bloomsbury, 2000); *The Guitar and its Music* by John Tyler and Paul Sparks (OUP, 1976); *The Lute in Britain* by Matthew Spring (OUP, 2001); *The Penguin Folk Guitar Manual* by John Pearse (Penguin, 1979); *The Guitar Book* by Thom Wheeler (Harper-Collins, 1978); *Timeless Flight* by Johnny Rogan (Omnibus, 1997); *Django Reinhardt* by Charles Delaunay (Ashley Mark, 1981).

A NOTE ON THE TYPE

Linotype Garamond Three – based on seventeenth century copies of Claude Garamond's types, cut by Jean Jannon. This version was designed for American Type Founders in 1917, by Morris Fuller Benton and Thomas Maitland Cleland and adapted for mechanical composition by Linotype in 1936.